FAVORITE BRAND NAME
MEAT, POULTRY & SEAFOOD

Publications International, Ltd.

Pictured on the front cover: Braised Chicken Thighs with Fruited
Rice and Lentils *(page 38)*.

ISBN: 0-7853-2472-0

Manufactured in U.S.A.

8 7 6 5 4 3 2 1

Nutritional Analysis: Nutritional information is given for some of
the recipes in this publication. Each analysis is based on the food
items in the ingredient list, except ingredients labeled as "optional"
or "for garnish." When more than one ingredient choice is given, the
nutritional analysis is based on the lowest amount. Foods offered as
"serve with" suggestions are not included in the analysis unless
otherwise stated.

Microwave Cooking: Microwave ovens vary in wattage. Use the
cooking times as guidelines and check for doneness before adding
more time.

FAVORITE BRAND NAME
MEAT, POULTRY & SEAFOOD

🍓 Pleasing 🍓

POULTRY

Parmesan Chicken Breasts

½ cup (2 ounces) KRAFT® 100% Grated
    Parmesan Cheese
¼ cup dry bread crumbs
1 teaspoon dried oregano leaves
1 teaspoon parsley flakes
¼ teaspoon paprika
¼ teaspoon salt
¼ teaspoon black pepper
6 boneless skinless chicken breast halves
    (about 2 pounds)
2 tablespoons butter or margarine,
    melted

• Heat oven to 400°F. Spray 15×10×1-inch baking pan with nonstick cooking spray.

• Mix cheese, crumbs and seasonings. Dip chicken in melted butter; coat with crumb mixture. Place in prepared pan.

• Bake 20 to 25 minutes or until cooked through.

Makes 6 servings

Spicy Parmesan Chicken Breasts: Substitute ⅛ to ¼ teaspoon ground red pepper for black pepper.

Double-Coated Chicken

- 7 cups KELLOGG'S CORN FLAKES® cereal, crushed to 1¾ cups
- 1 egg
- 1 cup skim milk
- 1 cup all-purpose flour
- ½ teaspoon salt
- ¼ teaspoon pepper
- 3 pounds broiler chicken pieces (without or with skin), rinsed and dried
- 3 tablespoons margarine, melted

1. Place *KELLOGG'S CORN FLAKES®* cereal in shallow dish or pan. Set aside.

2. In small mixing bowl, beat egg and milk slightly. Add flour, salt and pepper. Mix until smooth. Dip chicken in batter. Coat with cereal. Place in single layer, skin side up, in foil-lined shallow baking pan. Drizzle with margarine.

3. Bake at 350°F about 1 hour or until chicken is tender, no longer pink and juices run clear. Do not cover pan or turn chicken while baking.

Makes 6 servings

Spicy Fried Chicken

3   to 3½ pounds chicken pieces,
      (Best of Fryer)
⅓   cup all-purpose flour
2   tablespoons cornmeal
1   teaspoon baking powder
1   package (1.0 ounce) LAWRY'S® Taco
      Spices & Seasonings
1¼ teaspoons LAWRY'S® Seasoned Salt
1   teaspoon paprika
¾   teaspoon cayenne pepper
½   teaspoon LAWRY'S® Seasoned Pepper
¼   cup butter or shortening, melted
2   tablespoons lemon juice

Pierce chicken pieces several times with fork. In large
resealable plastic bag, combine flour, cornmeal, baking
powder, Taco Spices & Seasonings, Seasoned Salt,
paprika, cayenne pepper and Seasoned Pepper. Add
chicken, a few pieces at a time, to plastic bag; seal bag.
Shake until well coated. Place chicken in shallow
baking pan. Combine butter and lemon juice; drizzle
over chicken. Bake in 400°F oven 1 hour or until
chicken is no longer pink in center.

Makes 6 to 8 servings

Calorie-Wise Dill Chicken

    Nonstick cooking spray
 1 **cup plain yogurt**
1½ **cups natural wheat germ**
 ½ **cup chopped almonds***
 2 **teaspoons dried dill weed, crushed**
 ½ **teaspoon salt**
 ¼ **teaspoon pepper**
12 **chicken drumsticks**

1. Preheat oven to 350°F. Line baking sheet with foil; spray foil with nonstick cooking spray. Set aside.

2. Place yogurt in shallow bowl.

3. Combine wheat germ, almonds, dill weed, salt and pepper in separate shallow bowl.

4. Coat drumsticks, one at a time, in yogurt, shaking off excess. Coat drumsticks in wheat germ mixture, shaking off excess.

5. Arrange chicken in single layer on prepared baking sheet. Bake 50 minutes or until chicken is tender and juices run clear.   *Makes 4 servings*

*One-half cup slivered almonds chopped in a food processor with on/off pulses yields ½ cup chopped almonds.

Dijon Chicken Elegant

4 whole boneless chicken breasts, split
⅓ cup GREY POUPON® Dijon or Country
    Dijon Mustard
1 teaspoon dried dill weed or 1 tablespoon
    chopped fresh dill
¼ pound Swiss cheese slices
2 frozen puff pastry sheets, thawed
1 egg white
1 tablespoon cold water

Pound chicken breasts to ½-inch thickness. Blend
mustard and dill; spread on chicken breasts. Top each
breast with cheese slice; roll up.

Roll each pastry sheet to 12-inch square; cut each into
4 (6-inch) squares. Beat egg white and water; brush
edges of each square with egg mixture. Place 1 chicken
roll diagonally on each square. Join 4 points of pastry
over chicken; seal seams. Place on ungreased baking
sheets. Brush with remaining egg mixture. Bake at
375°F for 30 minutes or until chicken is done. Serve
immediately. *Makes 8 servings*

Baked Chicken with Red-Peppered Onions

1 **broiler-fryer chicken, quartered**
2 **teaspoons lemon pepper seasoning**
1 **teaspoon olive oil**
4 **cups thinly sliced sweet onions**
4 **tablespoons red hot pepper jelly**
1 **small sweet red pepper, cut into rings**
   Cilantro

On oiled rack of large broiler pan, place chicken; sprinkle with lemon pepper seasoning.

Bake in 400°F oven, skin side up, 50 minutes or until chicken is fork-tender.

Meanwhile, add olive oil to large nonstick skillet; heat to medium temperature. Add onions; cook until barely wilted, about 5 minutes. Add jelly and stir gently until melted. Spoon half of onion mixture onto large platter.

Arrange chicken over onions; top with remaining onions. Garnish with pepper rings and cilantro.

Makes 4 servings

Favorite recipe from **Delmarva Poultry Industry, Inc.**

Simple Lemonade Chicken

1 can (6 ounces) frozen lemonade
    concentrate, thawed
¼ cup white wine Worcestershire sauce
2 tablespoons red wine vinegar
2 teaspoons chopped fresh rosemary or
    ½ teaspoon dried rosemary leaves
2 cloves garlic, crushed
3 pounds chicken pieces, skinned
1 tablespoon cornstarch

COMBINE lemonade concentrate, Worcestershire sauce, 2 tablespoons water, vinegar, rosemary and garlic in large resealable plastic food storage bag; add chicken. Seal bag and shake until well coated. Marinate in refrigerator 1 hour or overnight, turning bag occasionally.

PREHEAT oven to 350°F. Remove chicken; reserve marinade. Place chicken on rack in roasting pan coated with nonstick cooking spray. Bake covered 50 to 55 minutes or until chicken is no longer pink in center and juices run clear.

Meanwhile, **BRING** reserved marinade to a boil in small saucepan over medium-high heat. Boil marinade, stirring occasionally, 10 minutes. Combine cornstarch and ¼ cup water in small bowl; stir until smooth. Gradually stir cornstarch mixture into marinade. Cook and stir 3 to 4 minutes or until sauce is thickened.

TRANSFER chicken to serving plate. Serve sauce on the side.   *Makes 6 servings*

Forty-Clove Chicken Filice

1 (3-pound) frying chicken, cut into
    serving pieces
40 cloves garlic (about 2 heads*)
1 lemon
½ cup dry white wine
¼ cup dry vermouth
¼ cup olive oil
4 ribs celery, thickly sliced
2 tablespoons finely chopped parsley
2 teaspoons dried basil leaves, crushed
1 teaspoon dried oregano leaves, crushed
    Pinch of crushed red pepper flakes
    Salt and black pepper to taste

*The whole garlic bulb is called a head.

1. Preheat oven to 375°F. Place chicken, skin side up, in single layer in shallow baking pan; set aside.

2. Peel whole heads of garlic; set aside.

3. To prepare lemon, hold lemon in one hand. With other hand, remove colored portion of peel with vegetable peeler or zester into small bowl. To juice lemon, cut lemon in half on cutting board; with tip of knife, remove visible seeds. Using citrus reamer or squeezing tightly with hand, squeeze juice from lemon into small glass or dish; remove any remaining seeds from juice.

4. Combine garlic, wine, vermouth, oil, celery, parsley, basil, oregano and red pepper flakes in medium bowl; mix thoroughly. Sprinkle garlic mixture over chicken. Place zest over and around chicken in pan; pour lemon juice over top of chicken. Season with salt and black pepper.

5. Cover pan with foil. Bake 40 minutes. Remove foil; bake 15 minutes or until chicken is tender and juices run clear. *Makes 4 to 6 servings*

Baked Chicken & Stuffing

   6   **chicken pieces**
   1   **package (6 ounes) STOVE TOP®**
         Stuffing Mix for Chicken

1. PLACE chicken in large baking dish; sprinkle with seasoned salt and pepper. Bake at 375°F for 30 minutes.

2. STIR stuffing crumbs, seasoning packet, 1½ cups *hot* water and ¼ cup margarine, cut-up, just until moistened.

3. ADD to baking dish; bake an additional 30 minutes or until chicken is cooked through.

Makes 6 servings

Baked Barbecue Chicken

1 (3-pound) broiler-fryer, cut up
1 small onion, cut into slices
1½ cups ketchup
½ cup packed brown sugar
¼ cup Worcestershire sauce
2 tablespoons lemon juice
1 tablespoon liquid smoke

PREHEAT oven to 375°F. Place chicken in 13×9-inch baking dish coated with nonstick cooking spray. Arrange onion slices over top.

COMBINE ketchup, brown sugar, Worcestershire sauce, lemon juice and liquid smoke in small saucepan. Heat over medium heat 2 to 3 minutes or until sugar dissolves. Pour over chicken.

BAKE chicken 1 hour or until chicken is no longer pink in center. Discard onion slices. Let stand 10 minutes before serving.   *Makes 6 servings*

Italian Chicken Breasts

1 pound BOB EVANS FARMS® Italian
   Roll Sausage
1 cup sliced fresh mushrooms
1 clove garlic, minced
3 (8-ounce) cans tomato sauce
1 (6-ounce) can tomato paste
1½ teaspoons Italian seasoning
4 boneless, skinless chicken breast halves
1 cup (4 ounces) shredded mozzarella
   cheese
   Hot cooked pasta

Preheat oven to 350°F. Crumble sausage into large
skillet. Cook over medium heat until browned, stirring
occasionally. Remove sausage; set aside. Add
mushrooms and garlic to drippings; cook and stir until
tender. Stir in reserved sausage, tomato sauce, tomato
paste and seasoning. Bring to a boil. Reduce heat to
low; simmer 15 minutes to blend flavors. Meanwhile,
arrange chicken in greased 11×7-inch baking dish.
Pour tomato sauce mixture over chicken; cover with
foil. Bake 40 minutes; uncover. Sprinkle with cheese;
bake 5 minutes more. Serve over pasta. Refrigerate
leftovers.   *Makes 4 servings*

Chicken Divan

¾ **pound fresh or frozen asparagus spears, cooked**

1 **pound sliced cooked boneless skinless chicken breast**

2 **tablespoons margarine**

2 **tablespoons all-purpose flour**

1¾ **cups skim milk**

½ **cup EGG BEATERS® Healthy Real Egg Product**

2 **tablespoons sherry cooking wine**

¼ **teaspoon ground black pepper**
Paprika

Arrange asparagus in bottom of greased 2-quart shallow baking dish. Place chicken slices over asparagus; cover with foil. Bake at 325°F for 20 minutes or until heated through.

In medium saucepan, over low heat, melt margarine; blend in flour. Cook, stirring until smooth and bubbly; remove from heat. Gradually blend in milk; return to heat. Heat to a boil, stirring constantly until thickened. Gradually blend half the hot milk mixture into Egg Beaters®. Return mixture to saucepan; blend well. Stir in sherry and pepper. Spoon sauce over chicken and asparagus; sprinkle lightly with paprika.

Makes 4 servings

Chicken Parmesan

- ½ cup Italian-seasoned dried bread crumbs
- 1 teaspoon dried basil leaves
- 1 teaspoon dried oregano leaves
- 6 boneless skinless chicken breast halves
- ½ cup 2% milk
- 1 tablespoon olive oil
- ½ cup (2 ounces) grated Parmesan cheese
- 1 jar (26 ounces) marinara sauce
- 1½ cups (6 ounces) shredded part-skim mozzarella cheese

PREHEAT oven to 350°F. Combine bread crumbs, basil and oregano in small bowl. Dip chicken in milk. Dredge coated chicken in bread crumb mixture.

HEAT oil in large skillet over medium-high heat until hot. Add chicken and cook 2 to 3 minutes on each side or until browned.

PLACE chicken in 13×9-inch baking dish coated with nonstick cooking spray. Sprinkle Parmesan cheese over chicken. Pour marinara sauce over chicken and top with mozzarella cheese. Bake, covered, 45 minutes or until chicken is no longer pink in center.

Makes 6 servings

Herb Roasted Chicken

Juice from ½ lemon
2 cloves garlic, minced
3 tablespoons chopped mixed fresh
  herbs* or 3 teaspoons mixed dried
  herbs, divided
1 GALIL® Whole Chicken
  (about 3¾ pounds)
4 teaspoons olive oil, divided
½ teaspoon salt
½ teaspoon freshly ground black pepper,
  divided
2 pounds small new potatoes (halved if
  medium, quartered if large)
2 cups chicken broth

*Use any combination of basil, marjoram, oregano, parsley,
rosemary, sage, tarragon and thyme.

Preheat oven to 400°F. Place lemon juice, garlic and ⅓
of the herbs in chicken cavity. Rub surface of chicken
with 1 teaspoon oil. Sprinkle salt, ¼ teaspoon pepper
and ⅓ of the herbs over chicken. Tie chicken legs
together with kitchen string.

Place potatoes, remaining 3 teaspoons oil, ⅓ of the
herbs and ¼ teaspoon pepper in large bowl; toss well.
Place chicken, breast side down, on rack in large
roasting pan. Arrange potatoes around chicken; place
in oven. *Reduce temperature to 350°F.* Bake,
uncovered, 1 hour. Baste chicken with pan juices and
rotate potatoes after 30 minutes of baking.

Turn chicken, breast side up, and baste with pan juices. Rotate potatoes. Bake 30 minutes or until internal temperature of chicken reaches 180°F on meat thermometer inserted in thickest part of thigh. Transfer chicken to cutting board; tent with foil. Let stand 5 to 10 minutes.

Transfer potatoes to serving dish; keep warm. Skim fat from pan juices; discard fat. Transfer pan juices to medium saucepan; stir in chicken broth. Cook, scraping bottom of pan, over medium heat until sauce thickens slightly. Pour sauce into small serving bowl. Serve with chicken and potatoes.

Makes 6 servings

Mexican Style Chicken

1   **package (6 ounces) STOVE TOP®**
    Stuffing Mix for Chicken
4   **boneless skinless chicken breast halves**
    (about 1¼ pounds)
1   **cup salsa**
1   **cup (4 ounces) KRAFT® Natural**
    Shredded Cheddar Cheese

1. STIR stuffing crumbs, seasoning packet, 1½ cups *hot* water and ¼ cup margarine, cut-up, just until moistened.

2. SPOON stuffing in 12×8-inch baking dish. Top with chicken. Pour salsa over chicken; sprinkle with cheese.

3. BAKE at 375°F for 40 minutes or until chicken is cooked through.   *Makes 4 servings*

Chicken Cacciatore

1 broiler-fryer chicken (3 to 3½ pounds),
    cut into 8 pieces
1 tablespoon olive oil
4 ounces fresh mushrooms, finely
    chopped
1 medium onion, chopped
1 clove garlic, minced
½ cup dry white wine
1½ tablespoons white wine vinegar
½ cup chicken broth
1 teaspoon dried basil leaves, crushed
½ teaspoon dried marjoram leaves,
    crushed
½ teaspoon salt
⅛ teaspoon pepper
1 can (14½ ounces) whole peeled
    tomatoes, undrained
8 Italian- or Greek-style black olives
1 tablespoon chopped fresh parsley
    Hot cooked pasta

1. Rinse chicken; drain and pat dry with paper towels.
Heat oil in large skillet over medium heat. Add as many
chicken pieces in single layer without crowding to hot
oil. Cook 8 minutes per side or until chicken is brown;
remove chicken with slotted spatula to Dutch oven.
Repeat with remaining chicken pieces.

2. Add mushrooms and onion to drippings remaining in skillet. Cook and stir over medium heat 5 minutes or until onion is soft. Add garlic; cook and stir 30 seconds. Add wine and vinegar; cook over medium-high heat 5 minutes or until liquid is almost evaporated. Stir in broth, basil, marjoram, salt and pepper. Remove from heat.

3. Press tomatoes and juice through sieve into onion mixture; discard seeds. Bring to a boil over medium-high heat; boil, uncovered, 2 minutes.

4. Pour tomato-onion mixture over chicken. Bring to a boil; reduce heat to low. Cover and simmer 25 minutes or until chicken is tender and juices run clear when pierced with fork. Remove chicken with slotted spatula to heated serving dish; keep warm.

5. Bring tomato-onion sauce to a boil over medium-high heat; boil, uncovered, 5 minutes. Cut olives in half; remove and discard pits.

6. Add olives and parsley to sauce; cook 1 minute more. Pour sauce over chicken and pasta.

Makes 4 to 6 servings

Coq au Vin

2 slices bacon, cut into ½-inch pieces
1 chicken (3½ pounds), cut up
1 medium onion, coarsely chopped
1 cup mushrooms cut into halves
1 red bell pepper, coarsely chopped
¾ cup red wine or dry white wine
1 cup chicken broth, divided
2 cloves garlic, minced
1 teaspoon dried thyme leaves
¼ teaspoon black pepper
¼ cup all-purpose flour
   Hot cooked noodles or rice

COOK bacon in large skillet or Dutch oven over medium heat until crisp. Remove with slotted spoon; set aside. Add chicken pieces to skillet; cook 10 minutes or until golden brown, turning occasionally to brown evenly.

ADD onion, mushrooms, bell pepper, wine, ¾ cup chicken broth, garlic, thyme and black pepper; bring to a boil. Reduce heat to low. Cover and simmer 25 minutes.

COMBINE remaining ¼ cup broth and flour; stir until smooth. Stir into chicken mixture. Simmer uncovered 5 minutes or until thickened. Season to taste with salt and black pepper. Top with reserved bacon. Serve with noodles.   *Makes 4 servings*

Chicken Paprika

----

3 tablespoons all-purpose flour
1 tablespoon paprika
¼ teaspoon salt
⅛ teaspoon black pepper
4 chicken breasts, skinned
    (about 1½ pounds)
1 teaspoon olive oil
1 medium onion, chopped
1 cup chicken broth
¼ cup sour cream
    Hot cooked spaetzle or noodles

COMBINE flour, paprika, salt and pepper on sheet of waxed paper. Coat chicken breasts with flour mixture. Reserve remaining flour mixture.

HEAT oil in large skillet over medium heat until hot. Add chicken; cook about 10 minutes or until browned. Remove chicken from skillet.

ADD onion to same skillet; cook 2 minutes. Stir in remaining flour mixture. Gradually stir in chicken broth; cook and stir until mixture comes to a boil. Return chicken to skillet. Reduce heat to low. Cover and simmer 25 minutes or until chicken is no longer pink in center and juices run clear.

REMOVE chicken to platter. Spoon off fat from gravy in skillet. Add sour cream to skillet; stir to combine. Serve chicken with gravy and spaetzle.

Makes 4 servings

Classic Chicken Marsala

2 tablespoons unsalted butter
1 tablespoon vegetable oil
4 boneless skinless chicken breast halves
     (about 1¼ pounds total)
4 slices mozzarella cheese (1 ounce each)
12 capers, drained
4 flat anchovy fillets, drained
1 tablespoon chopped fresh parsley
1 clove garlic, minced
3 tablespoons marsala
⅔ cup heavy or whipping cream
  Dash salt
  Dash pepper
  Hot cooked pasta (optional)

1. Heat butter and oil in large skillet over medium-high heat until melted and bubbly. Add chicken; reduce heat to medium. Cook, uncovered, 5 to 6 minutes per side until chicken is tender and golden brown. Remove chicken with slotted spatula to work surface. Top each chicken piece with 1 cheese slice, 3 capers and 1 anchovy fillet.

2. Return chicken to skillet. Sprinkle with parsley. Cover and cook over low heat 3 minutes or until cheese is semi-melted and juices from chicken run clear. Remove chicken with slotted spatula to heated serving dish; keep warm.

3. Add garlic to drippings in skillet; cook and stir over medium heat 30 seconds. Stir in marsala; cook and stir 45 seconds, scraping up any brown bits in skillet.

4. Stir in cream. Cook and stir 3 minutes or until sauce thickens slightly. Stir in salt and pepper. Spoon sauce over chicken. Serve with pasta. *Makes 4 servings*

Peanut Chicken

4   half boneless chicken breasts, skinned
2   tablespoons vegetable oil
1   can (14½ ounces) DEL MONTE®
    FreshCut™ Diced Tomatoes with
    Garlic & Onion
2   cloves garlic, minced, *or* ¼ teaspoon
    garlic powder
¼   teaspoon ground ginger *or* 1 teaspoon
    grated ginger root
⅛   to ¼ teaspoon crushed red pepper flakes
3   tablespoons chunky peanut butter

1. Cook chicken in hot oil in large skillet over medium-high heat about 4 minutes on each side or until chicken is no longer pink in center. Remove chicken from skillet.

2. Add tomatoes, garlic, ginger and red pepper flakes to skillet; cook 2 minutes. Stir in peanut butter.

3. Return chicken to skillet; heat through. Sprinkle with chopped cilantro and peanuts and garnish, if desired. *Makes 4 servings*

Chicken Fricassee

3   pounds chicken pieces (breasts, legs, thighs)

Flour

Nonstick cooking spray

3   cups defatted low-sodium chicken broth

1   bay leaf

1   pound whole baby carrots

¾   cup onion wedges (about 1 medium)

1   tablespoon margarine

3   tablespoons flour

¾   cup skim milk

1   tablespoon lemon juice

3   tablespoons minced fresh dill *or*
    2 teaspoons dried dill weed

1   teaspoon sugar

½   teaspoon salt

6   cups hot cooked noodles

1. Coat chicken pieces very lightly with flour. Spray large nonstick skillet with cooking spray; heat over medium heat until hot. Cook chicken 10 to 15 minutes or until browned on all sides. Drain fat from skillet.

2. Add chicken broth and bay leaf to skillet; heat to a boil. Reduce heat to low and simmer, covered, about 1 hour or until chicken is no longer pink in center and juices run clear, adding carrots and onion during last 20 minutes of cooking.

3. Transfer chicken and vegetables with slotted spoon to platter; keep warm. Heat broth to a boil; boil until broth is reduced to 1 cup. Discard bay leaf.

4. Melt margarine in small saucepan over low heat; stir in 3 tablespoons flour. Cook and stir 1 to 2 minutes. Stir in broth, milk and lemon juice; heat to a boil. Boil until thickened, stirring constantly. Stir in dill, sugar and salt. Arrange chicken over noodles on serving plates; top with sauce.   *Makes 6 servings*

Szechuan Chicken Tenders

        2 **tablespoons soy sauce**
        1 **tablespoon chili sauce**
        1 **tablespoon dry sherry**
        2 **cloves garlic, minced**
        ¼ **teaspoon red pepper flakes**
        16 **chicken tenders (about 1 pound)**
        1 **tablespoon peanut oil**
           Hot cooked rice

COMBINE soy sauce, chili sauce, sherry, garlic and red pepper in shallow dish. Add chicken; coat well.

HEAT oil in large nonstick skillet over medium heat until hot. Add chicken; cook 6 minutes, turning once, until chicken is browned and no longer pink in center.

SERVE chicken with rice.   *Makes 4 servings*

Almond Butter Chicken

2 **boneless skinless chicken breasts,
  halved (about 1¼ pounds)**
2 **tablespoons all-purpose flour**
½ **teaspoon salt**
½ **teaspoon pepper**
1 **egg, beaten**
1 **package (2¼ ounces) sliced almonds**
¼ **cup butter**
  Orange Sauce (recipe follows)

Place each chicken breast half between 2 pieces of
plastic wrap. Pound to ¼-inch thickness. Coat chicken
with flour. Sprinkle with salt and pepper. Dip one side
of each chicken breast into egg; press with almonds.
Melt butter in large skillet over medium-high heat.
Cook chicken, almond side down, 3 to 5 minutes or
until almonds are toasted; turn chicken over. Reduce
heat to medium-low; cook 10 to 12 minutes or until
chicken is tender and juices run clear. Serve, almond
side up, with Orange Sauce. Garnish as desired.

Makes 4 servings

Orange Sauce

1 **tablespoon brown sugar**
2 **teaspoons cornstarch**
  Juice of 1 orange (about ½ cup)
2 **tablespoons butter**
1 **teaspoon grated orange peel**

Combine brown sugar and cornstarch in saucepan. Add juice, butter and orange peel. Cook over medium heat, stirring constantly, until thickened.   *Makes ⅔ cup*

Favorite recipe from **Wisconsin Milk Marketing Board**

Chicken Piccata

1 **package GALIL® Chicken Breast Cutlets
(1½ to 1¾ pounds)**
¼ **cup all-purpose flour**
½ **cup parve bread crumbs**
½ **teaspoon dried basil leaves**
¼ **teaspoon salt**
¼ **teaspoon freshly ground black pepper**
1 **egg, beaten**
3 **tablespoons olive oil**
¼ **cup kosher dry white wine**
2 **tablespoons fresh lemon juice**

Cut chicken breasts into halves. Place chicken breast halves between 2 pieces of plastic wrap; pound to ½-inch thickness. Place flour on small plate. Combine bread crumbs, basil, salt and pepper on another small plate. Roll each breast half in flour, then in egg. Coat with bread crumb mixture.

Heat oil in medium nonstick skillet over medium-high heat. Add chicken; cook 4 minutes. Turn; reduce heat to medium. Cook 4 to 5 minutes or until chicken is no longer pink in center. Transfer chicken to serving platter; keep warm. Add wine and lemon juice to skillet; cook and stir over high heat 2 minutes. Spoon sauce over chicken. *Makes 4 servings*

Chicken Italiano

¼ cup all-purpose flour
1½ to 2 pounds (6 to 8) boneless, skinless
    chicken breast halves
3 tablespoons olive or vegetable oil,
    divided
2 cups (2 small) sliced onions
1¾ cups (14½-ounce can) chicken broth
1½ cups (3 medium) peeled sliced carrots
⅔ cup (6-ounce can) CONTADINA® Dalla
    Casa Buitoni Italian Paste with
    Roasted Garlic
1 teaspoon salt
1 teaspoon Italian herb seasoning
⅛ teaspoon crushed red pepper (optional)
1½ cups (2 medium) sliced zucchini

PLACE flour in pie plate; roll chicken in flour to coat.
Heat *2 tablespoons* oil in large skillet over medium-
high heat. Add chicken; cook for 3 to 4 minutes on
each side or until golden brown. Remove chicken.

HEAT *remaining* oil in skillet. Add onions; cook for 3
to 4 minutes or until tender. Stir in broth, carrots,
tomato paste, salt, Italian herb seasoning and crushed
red pepper. Return chicken to skillet; spoon sauce over
chicken. Bring to a boil. Reduce heat to low; cook,
covered, for 25 to 30 minutes or until chicken is no
longer pink in center. Add zucchini; cook for 5
minutes.

SERVE over pasta, if desired.

Makes 6 to 8 servings

Easy Chicken Ragoût

- 2 tablespoons all-purpose flour
- ½ teaspoon poultry seasoning
- ¼ teaspoon salt
- ¼ teaspoon black pepper
- 4 boneless skinless chicken thighs (about 1½ pounds)
- 1 tablespoon olive oil
- 1 can (15 ounces) whole tomatoes, undrained
- 1 can (14½ ounces) chicken broth
- 2 cups quartered mushrooms
- 1 cup baby carrots
- 1 large onion, diced
- ½ to ¾ teaspoon dried thyme leaves
- 1 bay leaf
- 2 cups cooked long-grain and wild rice

COMBINE flour, poultry seasoning, salt and pepper on sheet of waxed paper. Coat chicken with flour mixture.

HEAT oil in large saucepan over medium heat. Add chicken; cook 10 minutes or until evenly browned. Remove chicken; drain fat.

RETURN chicken to saucepan. Add tomatoes with juice, broth, mushrooms, carrots, onion, thyme and bay leaf. Bring to a boil, stirring to break up tomatoes. Reduce heat to low. Cover and simmer 30 minutes or until vegetables are tender and chicken is no longer pink in center, stirring occasionally. Discard bay leaf. Serve over hot rice. *Makes 4 servings*

Creole Chicken

1 tablespoon plus 1½ teaspoons vegetable oil
2½ to 3 pounds chicken pieces (Best of Fryer)
1 tablespoon butter or margarine
1 medium onion, thinly sliced
2 teaspoons LAWRY'S® Garlic Powder with Parsley
1½ teaspoons LAWRY'S® Seasoned Salt
1 teaspoon LAWRY'S® Seasoned Pepper
1 can (8 ounces) tomato sauce
½ cup red wine
3 medium tomatoes, chopped
2 medium-sized red and/or green bell peppers, sliced into strips
3 cups hot cooked white rice
Fresh cilantro leaves (garnish)

In large skillet, heat oil. Add chicken; cook until browned on all sides. Remove chicken from skillet; set aside. In same skillet, heat butter. Add onion; sauté until tender. Add Garlic Powder with Parsley, Seasoned Salt and Seasoned Pepper. Return chicken to skillet. Add all remaining ingredients except rice and cilantro. Reduce heat to low; cover. Simmer 30 to 40 minutes or until chicken is no longer pink in center. Serve over rice. *Makes 4 to 6 servings*

Chicken Marengo

2 tablespoons olive or vegetable oil

2½ to 3 pounds chicken parts or 1½ pounds (about 6) boneless chicken breast halves, skin removed

1 cup (3 ounces) sliced fresh mushrooms

½ cup chopped onion

½ cup chopped green bell pepper

1 clove garlic, finely chopped

1¾ cups (14.5-ounce can) CONTADINA® Dalla Casa Buitoni Recipe Ready Diced Tomatoes, undrained

⅔ cup (6-ounce can) CONTADINA® Dalla Casa Buitoni Italian Paste with Tomato Pesto

½ cup dry red wine

½ cup chicken broth

½ teaspoon salt

⅛ teaspoon ground black pepper

HEAT oil in large skillet over medium-high heat. Add chicken; cook for 3 to 4 minutes on each side or until browned. Remove chicken, leaving drippings in skillet. Add mushrooms, onion, bell pepper and garlic to skillet; cook for 5 minutes. Add tomatoes and juice, tomato paste, wine, broth, salt and pepper. Return chicken to skillet; bring to a boil. Reduce heat to low; cook, covered, for 30 to 40 minutes or until chicken is no longer pink in center.

SERVE over hot cooked pasta or rice.

Makes 6 servings

Greek Chicken

1 package (about 1¼ pounds) PERDUE®
   FIT 'N EASY® Fresh Skinless and
   Boneless OVEN STUFFER® Roaster
   Thighs
1½ teaspoons dried oregano leaves
   Salt and ground pepper to taste
1 tablespoon olive oil
2 cups fresh or frozen green beans
1 cup canned artichoke hearts packed in
   water, drained
1 cup frozen pearl onions, thawed
1 large garlic clove, minced
1½ teaspoons grated fresh lemon peel
1 cup reduced-sodium chicken broth
½ cup white wine
2 cups hot, cooked orzo or other small
   pasta

Remove excess fat from thighs. Flatten thighs slightly
and sprinkle with seasonings. In large nonstick skillet
over medium-high heat, heat oil. Add thighs and cook
8 to 10 minutes until browned on both sides, turning
once. Stir in remaining ingredients; reduce heat to
medium-low. Cover and simmer 10 to 15 minutes until
chicken is cooked through and vegetables are tender-
crisp. Serve over orzo.   *Makes 5 servings*

Roasted Chicken with Maple Glaze

1 (3-pound) broiler-fryer chicken
1 small orange, cut into wedges
1 small onion, cut into wedges
¾ cup apple cider
¼ cup maple syrup
¾ teaspoon cornstarch
¼ teaspoon pumpkin pie spice

PREHEAT oven to 325°F. Remove giblets and neck from chicken; reserve for another use. Rinse chicken under cold water and pat dry with paper towels.

PLACE orange and onion wedges in cavity of chicken. Tie legs together with wet cotton string and place breast-side up on rack in shallow roasting pan coated with nonstick cooking spray. Insert meat thermometer into meaty part of thigh not touching bone.

COMBINE apple cider, maple syrup, cornstarch and pumpkin pie spice in small saucepan; bring to a boil over medium heat, stirring constantly. Cook 1 minute; brush apple cider mixture over chicken.

BAKE chicken 1½ to 2 hours or until meat thermometer registers 180°F, basting frequently with remaining apple cider mixture.

REMOVE string from chicken legs; discard. Remove orange and onion wedges from chicken cavity; discard. Transfer chicken to serving platter. Let stand 10 minutes before carving.   *Makes 12 servings*

Chicken Florentine with Lemon Mustard Sauce

- 2 whole boneless skinless chicken breasts, halved (1 pound)
- ¼ cup EGG BEATERS® Healthy Real Egg Product
- ½ cup plain dry bread crumbs
- 1 teaspoon dried basil leaves
- 1 teaspoon garlic powder
- 2 tablespoons margarine, divided
- ⅓ cup water
- 2 tablespoons GREY POUPON® Dijon Mustard
- 2 tablespoons lemon juice
- 1 tablespoon sugar
- 1 (10-ounce) package frozen chopped spinach, cooked, well drained and kept warm

Pound chicken breasts to ¼-inch thickness. Pour Egg Beaters® into shallow bowl. Combine bread crumbs, basil and garlic. Dip chicken breasts into Egg Beaters, then coat with bread crumb mixture. In large nonstick skillet, over medium-high heat, melt 1 tablespoon margarine. Add chicken; cook for 5 to 7 minutes on each side or until browned and no longer pink in center. Remove chicken from skillet; keep warm. In same skillet, melt remaining margarine; stir in water, mustard, lemon juice and sugar. Simmer 1 minute or until thickened. To serve, arrange chicken on serving platter. Top with spinach; drizzle with lemon-mustard sauce.   *Makes 4 servings*

Braised Chicken Thighs with Fruited Rice and Lentils

- 1 tablespoon olive oil
- 6 skinless chicken thighs
- 3½ cups canned chicken broth
- ¾ cup uncooked basmati rice
- 1 medium onion, chopped
- 2 tablespoons balsamic vinegar
- 2 teaspoons sugar
- 1 teaspoon ground cinnamon
- 1 teaspoon ground cumin
- ¼ teaspoon black pepper
- 1 cup uncooked red lentils
- ⅔ cup quartered dried apricots
- ½ cup raisins
- ¼ cup chopped fresh cilantro or parsley

1. Heat oil in heavy, large saucepan over medium-high heat. Add chicken; cook 10 minutes or until browned and no longer pink in center, turning once. Remove chicken with tongs to clean serving plate; set aside.

2. Add broth, rice, onion, vinegar, sugar, cinnamon, cumin and pepper to saucepan; bring to a boil over high heat. Reduce heat to low; simmer, covered, 15 minutes. Stir in lentils, apricots and raisins.

3. Arrange chicken on top of rice mixture in saucepan. Cover; simmer 40 to 45 minutes until liquid is absorbed and rice and lentils are tender. Transfer chicken to serving plates. Stir cilantro into rice mixture. Spoon rice mixture around chicken.

Makes 6 servings

Sautéed Chicken Breasts in Cream Sauce

2 tablespoons margarine

2 whole chicken breasts, split, skinned, boned and cut into strips

½ medium onion, chopped

1½ cups thinly sliced mushrooms

1 cup thinly sliced celery

½ teaspoon pepper

½ teaspoon dried basil leaves, crushed

¼ teaspoon dried chervil leaves, crushed

⅛ teaspoon dried thyme leaves, crushed

⅓ to ¾ cup dry white wine or sherry, divided

1 package (8 ounces) cream cheese, cubed

¼ cup milk

2½ cups (8 ounces) corkscrew pasta, cooked and drained

1. Melt margarine in large skillet over medium heat until foamy. Add chicken strips, onion, mushrooms, celery, pepper, basil, chervil and thyme. Cook 5 minutes or until chicken is tender, stirring occasionally. Add 2 tablespoons wine; reduce heat and simmer 5 minutes.

2. Combine cream cheese and milk in small saucepan; stir over low heat until smooth. Blend in enough remaining wine to make sauce of pouring consistency. Place hot pasta on serving platter. Top with chicken-vegetable mixture and cream sauce.

Makes 4 to 6 servings

Chicken Royale

6 boneless skinless chicken breast halves
6 ounces cream cheese, softened
¼ cup dried chives
6 slices bacon
1 cup sliced mushrooms
½ cup dry white wine
1 can (10¾ ounces) reduced-calorie
  condensed cream of mushroom soup
1 package (6 ounces) rice pilaf

PREHEAT oven to 350°F. Place chicken breasts
between two layers of plastic wrap. Pound chicken
breasts to ¼-inch thickness with meat mallet or
rolling pin.

COMBINE cream cheese and chives in small bowl.
Shape cheese mixture into 6 logs. Place 1 log in center
of each chicken breast; roll up jelly-roll style, tucking
in sides. Secure with wooden toothpick. Place seam
side down in 13×9-inch baking dish coated with
nonstick cooking spray. Bake 45 minutes or until
chicken is no longer pink in center.

Meanwhile, **HEAT** medium skillet over medium heat
until hot; add bacon. Cook 5 to 10 minutes or until
crisp. Transfer bacon to paper towel to drain. Crumble
bacon. Drain all but 1 tablespoon bacon drippings from
skillet. Add mushrooms; cook and stir 2 to 3 minutes
or until mushrooms are tender. Remove mushrooms
from skillet.

ADD wine to skillet. Cook about 10 minutes or until reduced to about ¼ cup. Add soup, reserved bacon and mushrooms; cook and stir 2 to 3 minutes. Reduce heat to low, cover and keep warm.

PREPARE rice pilaf according to package directions. Spoon rice onto serving plate. Remove toothpicks from chicken rolls; discard. Place chicken rolls on top of rice. Spoon mushroom sauce over top.

Makes 6 servings

All-American Fried Chicken

½ cup all-purpose flour
1 to 2 teaspoons LAWRY'S® Seasoned
    Salt
1 to 2 teaspoons LAWRY'S® Seasoned
    Pepper
2½ to 3 pounds chicken pieces
    Vegetable oil, for frying

In paper or plastic bag, combine flour, Seasoned Salt and Seasoned Pepper. Wash chicken; pat dry and place in flour mixture to coat. Coat only a few pieces at a time.

In large skillet, pour oil to coat pan. When hot, brown chicken, a few pieces at a time, and remove as browned. Repeat as needed. When all chicken is browned, drain fat and return chicken to skillet. Reduce heat; cover and simmer about 25 minutes or until chicken is tender. Uncover during last 10 minutes to crisp skin.

Makes 4 servings

Chicken with Cucumbers and Dill

2 whole chicken breasts, split, skinned
  and boned
1 teaspoon salt, divided
¾ teaspoon pepper, divided
4 tablespoons butter, divided
2 cucumbers, peeled
½ teaspoon dried dill weed, crushed
¼ cup lemon juice

1. Sprinkle chicken breasts with ½ teaspoon salt and
½ teaspoon pepper.

2. Melt 2 tablespoons butter in large skillet over
medium heat until foamy. Add chicken to skillet in
single layer. Cook 10 minutes or until chicken is no
longer pink in center, turning once.

3. Remove chicken to paper-towel-lined baking sheets,
using tongs or slotted spoon; keep warm in preheated
200°F oven. Drain drippings from skillet; reserve.

4. Cut cucumbers lengthwise in half; remove and
discard seeds. Cut cucumbers into ¼-inch slices.

5. Add remaining 2 tablespoons butter to large skillet;
heat until melted. Add cucumbers; stir to coat.
Sprinkle remaining ½ teaspoon salt and ¼ teaspoon
pepper over cucumbers; cook 2 minutes. Stir in dill.
Push cucumbers to side of skillet.

6. Return chicken and drippings to skillet. Cook
2 minutes or until chicken is heated through. Place
chicken on serving platter; arrange cucumbers around
chicken.

7. Cook drippings in skillet over medium heat until light brown. Pour lemon juice and drippings over chicken. *Makes 4 servings*

Roasted Rosemary Chicken Legs

- ¼ **cup finely chopped onion**
- 2 **tablespoons margarine or butter, melted**
- 1 **tablespoon chopped fresh rosemary** *or*
  1 teaspoon dried rosemary leaves
- 2 **cloves garlic, minced**
- ½ **teaspoon salt**
- ¼ **teaspoon black pepper**
- 4 **chicken legs (about 1½ pounds)**
- ¼ **cup white wine or chicken broth**

PREHEAT oven to 375°F.

COMBINE onion, margarine, rosemary, garlic, salt and pepper in small bowl; set aside. Run finger under skin of chicken to loosen. Rub onion mixture under and over skin. Place chicken skin-side up in small shallow roasting pan. Pour wine over chicken.

ROAST chicken 50 to 60 minutes or until chicken is browned, no longer pink in center and juices run clear, basting often with pan juices. *Makes 4 servings*

Apricot Chicken Oriental

2 tablespoons butter or margarine
2 whole chicken breasts, split, skinned and boned
12 dried apricots, chopped
1 jar (10 ounces) apricot preserves
1 cup water
½ cup soy sauce
1 can (8 ounces) sliced water chestnuts, drained and liquid reserved
1 teaspoon ground ginger
1 teaspoon garlic powder
Apricot Rice (recipe follows)
1 red or green bell pepper, cut into strips
3 ribs celery, diagonally sliced
2 cups sliced mushrooms
1 bunch green onions, sliced
1 package (6 ounces) frozen pea pods

1. Melt butter in large skillet over medium heat until foamy. Add chicken to skillet in single layer; cook 10 minutes or until chicken is browned, turning once.

2. Stir in apricots, preserves, water, soy sauce, liquid from water chestnuts, ginger and garlic powder. Simmer 25 minutes or until chicken is tender.

3. Meanwhile, prepare Apricot Rice.

4. Add water chestnuts, bell pepper, celery, mushrooms, green onions and pea pods to skillet with chicken; cook and stir 5 minutes or until vegetables are heated through.

5. Place equal amounts of rice on each serving plate. Arrange chicken and vegetables over rice.

Makes 4 servings

Apricot Rice

2½ **cups water**
¼ **cup finely chopped dried apricots**
¼ **teaspoon salt**
1 **cup long-grain rice**

1. Combine water, apricots and salt in medium saucepan. Bring to a boil; stir in rice.

2. Cover; reduce heat and simmer 20 minutes. Remove from heat; let stand 5 minutes.   *Makes 3 cups rice*

Chicken in Lemon Sauce

¼ **cup butter or margarine**
4 **whole chicken breasts, split, skinned and boned**
½ **teaspoon grated lemon peel**
2 **tablespoons fresh lemon juice**
2 **tablespoons dry white wine**
¼ **teaspoon salt**
⅛ **teaspoon white pepper**
1 **cup heavy cream**
⅓ **cup grated Parmesan cheese**
1 **cup sliced mushrooms**

1. Melt butter in large skillet over medium heat until foamy. Add chicken to skillet in single layer. Cook 10 minutes or until chicken is brown and no longer pink in center, turning once.

2. Remove chicken to broilerproof baking dish; set aside.

3. Drain drippings from skillet.

4. Add lemon peel, lemon juice and wine to skillet; cook and stir over medium heat 1 minute. Stir in salt and white pepper.

5. Gradually pour cream into skillet, stirring constantly. Simmer over medium-low heat until hot; *do not boil*. Pour cream sauce over chicken; sprinkle with cheese and mushrooms.

6. Broil chicken about 6 inches from heat source until lightly browned. Arrange chicken breasts and sauce on serving platter. *Makes 8 servings*

Roast Chicken Spanish Style

1 (4½- to 5-pound) whole roasting
   chicken
   Salt and freshly ground black pepper
1 clove garlic, cut in half
1 tablespoon FILIPPO BERIO® Olive Oil
½ teaspoon dried oregano leaves
1 medium onion, sliced
4 plum tomatoes, diced
2 medium green bell peppers, seeded and
   cut into chunks
1 (10-ounce) package whole mushrooms,
   cleaned and trimmed

Preheat oven to 450°F. Remove and discard giblets and
neck from chicken. Rinse chicken under cold water;
drain well and pat dry with paper towels. Sprinkle
inside and outside of chicken with salt and black
pepper. Rub outside of chicken with garlic. In small
bowl, combine olive oil and oregano; brush over
outside of chicken. Place chicken, breast side up, in
shallow roasting pan. Roast 30 minutes or until skin is
browned. *Reduce oven temperature to 375°F.* Add
onion and tomatoes. Cover pan with foil; bake an
additional 1 hour to 1 hour and 15 minutes or until
legs move freely and juices run clear, adding bell
peppers and mushrooms about 20 minutes before
chicken is done. Let stand 10 minutes before carving.
Makes 6 servings

Tex-Mex Chicken Fajitas

6 boneless, skinless chicken breast halves
    (about 1½ pounds), cut into strips
½ cup LAWRY'S® Mesquite Marinade with
    Lime Juice*
3 tablespoons plus 1½ teaspoons
    vegetable oil, divided
1 small onion, sliced and separated into
    rings
1 medium-sized green bell pepper, cut
    into strips
¾ teaspoon LAWRY'S® Garlic Powder with
    Parsley
½ teaspoon hot pepper sauce
1 medium tomato, cut into wedges
2 tablespoons chopped fresh cilantro
    Flour tortillas, warmed
1 medium lime, cut into wedges

*1 package (1.27 ounces) Lawry's Spices & Seasonings for Fajitas,
¼ cup lime juice and ¼ cup vegetable oil can be substituted.

Pierce chicken several times with fork; place in large
resealable plastic bag or bowl. Pour Mesquite Marinade
with Lime Juice over chicken; seal bag or cover bowl.
Refrigerate at least 30 minutes. Heat 1 tablespoon plus
1½ teaspoons oil in large skillet. Add onion, bell pepper,
Garlic Powder with Parsley and hot pepper sauce; sauté
5 to 7 minutes or until onion is crisp-tender. Remove
vegetable mixture from skillet; set aside.

Heat remaining 2 tablespoons oil in same skillet. Add chicken; sauté 8 to 10 minutes or until chicken is no longer pink in center, stirring frequently. Return vegetable mixture to skillet with tomato and cilantro; heat through. *Makes 4 to 6 servings*

Presentation: Serve with flour tortillas and lime wedges. Top with dairy sour cream, guacamole, salsa and pitted ripe olives as desired.

Classic Fried Chicken

   ¾ **cup all-purpose flour**
   1 **teaspoon salt**
   ¼ **teaspoon pepper**
   1 **frying chicken (2½ to 3 pounds), cut up,**
      or chicken pieces
   ½ **cup CRISCO® all-vegetable shortening**
      or ½ CRISCO® Stick

1. Combine flour, salt and pepper in paper or plastic bag. **Add** a few pieces of chicken at a time. **Shake** to coat.

2. Heat shortening to 365°F in electric skillet or on medium-high heat in large heavy skillet. **Fry** chicken 30 to 40 minutes without lowering heat. **Turn** once for even browning. **Drain** on paper towels.

Makes 4 servings

Southwest Chicken Sandwiches

4 **boneless, skinless chicken breast halves**
(¾ to 1 pound)
¾ **cup LAWRY'S® Mesquite Marinade with**
Lime Juice
½ **teaspoon LAWRY'S® Garlic Powder with**
Parsley
½ **cup chunky-style salsa**
¼ **cup mayonnaise**
4 **sandwich rolls, split**
Lettuce leaves
1 **tomato, thinly sliced**
1 **avocado, peeled, pitted and thinly sliced**

Pierce chicken several times with fork. Place in large
resealable plastic bag or shallow dish. In small bowl,
combine Mesquite Marinade with Lime Juice and
Garlic Powder with Parsley. Add to chicken; seal bag or
cover dish. Refrigerate at least 30 minutes. Remove
chicken from marinade; discard marinade. Broil or
grill chicken breasts, 5 inches from heat source, 7 to
10 minutes on each side or until chicken is no longer
pink in center. In small bowl, combine salsa and
mayonnaise; spread onto cut sides of rolls. Top bottom
half of each roll with lettuce, chicken, tomato and
avocado; cover with top half of roll.

Makes 4 servings

Note: For extra flavor, brush chicken with additional
Mesquite Marinade with Lime Juice while cooking.

Grilled Chicken Breast and Peperonata Sandwiches

1 tablespoon olive oil or vegetable oil
1 medium red bell pepper, sliced into
   strips
1 medium green bell pepper, sliced into
   strips
¾ cup onion slices (about 1 medium)
2 cloves garlic, minced
¼ teaspoon salt
¼ teaspoon black pepper
4 boneless skinless chicken breast halves
   (about 1 pound)
4 small French rolls, split and toasted

1. Heat oil in large nonstick skillet over medium heat until hot. Add bell peppers, onion and garlic; cook and stir 5 minutes. Reduce heat to low; cook and stir about 20 minutes or until vegetables are very soft. Stir in salt and black pepper.

2. Grill chicken, on covered grill over medium-hot coals, 10 minutes on each side or until chicken is no longer pink in center. Or, broil chicken, 6 inches from heat source, 7 to 8 minutes on each side or until chicken is no longer pink in center.

3. Place chicken in rolls. Divide pepper mixture evenly; spoon over chicken.   *Makes 4 servings*

Bistro Turkey Sandwiches

¼ cup reduced-calorie mayonnaise
2 tablespoons finely chopped fresh basil
2 tablespoons chopped drained sun-dried
     tomatoes in oil
2 tablespoons finely chopped pitted
     calamata olives
⅛ teaspoon crushed red pepper
1 loaf focaccia bread, quartered and split
     or 8 slices sourdough bread
1 jar (7 ounces) roasted red bell peppers,
     rinsed, drained
4 romaine or red leaf lettuce leaves
2 packages (4 ounces each) HEBREW
     NATIONAL® Sliced Oven Roasted or
     Smoked Turkey Breast

Combine mayonnaise, basil, sun-dried tomatoes, olives
and crushed red pepper in small bowl; mix well. Spread
evenly over cut sides of bread. Remove excess liquid
from roasted red bell peppers with paper towels. Layer
roasted peppers, lettuce and turkey breast between
bread slices.   *Makes 4 servings*

Spicy Sesame Turkey Sandwich

½ cup mayonnaise
1½ teaspoons LAWRY'S® Pinch of Herbs, divided
1½ teaspoons LAWRY'S® Lemon Pepper, divided
1 teaspoon sesame oil
1 teaspoon fresh lemon juice
4 or 5 turkey cutlets (about 1¼ pounds)
½ cup all-purpose flour
2 tablespoons toasted sesame seeds
¼ to ½ teaspoon cayenne pepper
¼ cup milk
¼ cup vegetable oil
6 whole wheat buns, toasted
1 tomato, cut into 6 slices
6 sprigs watercress

In small bowl, combine mayonnaise, ½ teaspoon Pinch of Herbs, ½ teaspoon Lemon Pepper, sesame oil and lemon juice; cover. Refrigerate until ready to serve. Cut turkey into 6 equal pieces. In large resealable plastic bag, combine flour, sesame seeds, cayenne pepper, remaining Pinch of Herbs and remaining Lemon Pepper. Dip each cutlet into milk. Add turkey, a few pieces at a time, to bag; seal. Shake until well coated. In large, heavy skillet, heat oil over medium heat. Add turkey; cook 5 to 8 minutes or until no longer pink in center, turning over after 3 minutes. Spread buns with mayonnaise mixture. Top bottom halves of buns with turkey; cover with tomato, watercress and tops of rolls.

Makes 6 servings

Roast Turkey and Gravy

1 **PERDUE® Fresh Young Turkey
(12 to 16 pounds)**
2 **tablespoons butter or margarine,
melted
Poultry seasoning to taste
Salt and ground pepper to taste**
1 **onion, peeled (optional)
Fresh fruit and herbs (optional)**
4 **tablespoons all-purpose flour**
1 **can (about 14 ounces) chicken broth**
2 **tablespoons sherry or port wine
(optional)**

Preheat oven to 325°F. Remove neck and giblets from
inside turkey; discard fat from cavities. Rinse turkey
inside and out under cold running water; pat dry.
Brush turkey with butter and season, inside and out,
with poultry seasoning, salt and pepper. Place onion in
large body cavity; fold back wing tips. Check that legs
are secure in plastic holder and BIRD-WATCHER®
Thermometer is flush against breast. Place turkey,
breast side up, in roasting pan.

Roast turkey, uncovered, 3 to 4 hours or until
thermometer pops up and juices run clear when thigh
is pierced, basting occasionally. Remove and discard
thermometer and plastic leg holder. Remove turkey to
serving platter and allow to stand in warm place 15 to
20 minutes before carving. Garnish with fresh fruit and
herbs.

To prepare gravy, pour pan juices into heatproof bowl.
With spoon, skim off 4 tablespoons clear yellow
drippings from top of juices and return to roasting pan.
If using a disposable pan, transfer to saucepan. Skim
off and discard remaining yellow drippings and reserve
degreased pan juices.

Stir flour into drippings in pan and place over medium
heat. Cook 3 to 4 minutes until mixture is deep golden
brown, stirring constantly. Add reserved pan juices,
chicken broth and sherry. Cook 3 to 4 minutes until
gravy is smooth and thickened, stirring constantly.
Season with salt and pepper.

Makes 8 to 12 servings

Turkey Scaloppine

1 **pound turkey cutlets or 4 boneless, skinless chicken breast halves (¾ to 1 pound)**
2 **tablespoons all-purpose flour**
1½ **teaspoons LAWRY'S® Seasoned Salt, divided**
1 **teaspoon LAWRY'S® Lemon Pepper**
3 **tablespoons olive oil, divided**
1 **medium green bell pepper, cut into strips**
1 **cup sliced butternut squash or zucchini**
½ **cup sliced fresh mushrooms**
1 **teaspoon cornstarch**
½ **teaspoon LAWRY'S® Garlic Powder with Parsley**
¼ **cup dry white wine**
⅓ **cup chicken broth**
1 **tablespoon plus 1½ teaspoons lemon juice**

Place turkey between two sheets of waxed paper; pound to ⅛-inch thickness. In large resealable plastic bag, combine flour, ¾ teaspoon Seasoned Salt and Lemon Pepper. Add turkey, a few pieces at a time, to plastic bag; seal bag. Shake until well coated. In large skillet, heat 2 tablespoons oil. Add turkey; cook about 5 minutes on each side or until no longer pink in center. Remove from skillet; keep warm. In same skillet, heat remaining 1 tablespoon oil. Add bell pepper, squash and mushrooms; sauté until bell peppers are crisp-tender. Reduce heat to low. In small bowl, combine cornstarch, Garlic Powder with Parsley and remaining ¾ teaspoon Seasoned Salt; blend well. Stir in combined wine, broth and lemon juice. Add to skillet. Bring just to a boil, stirring constantly. Simmer 1 minute. Garnish, if desired.   *Makes 4 servings*

Presentation: On platter, layer vegetables, turkey or chicken and top with sauce.

Turkey Piccata

⅓ cup all-purpose flour
½ teaspoon salt
½ teaspoon black pepper
1 boneless turkey breast (1 pound), cut into 4 slices
3 tablespoons olive oil, divided
1½ cups sliced fresh mushrooms
2 cloves garlic, crushed
½ cup chicken broth
2 tablespoons lemon juice
½ teaspoon dried oregano leaves
3 tablespoons pine nuts
2 tablespoons chopped fresh parsley

1. Combine flour, salt and pepper in resealable plastic food storage bag. Add turkey; shake to evenly coat with flour mixture. Set aside.

2. Heat 2 tablespoons oil in large skillet over medium-high heat until hot. Add turkey; cook 3 minutes on each side or until lightly browned and no longer pink in center. Remove from skillet to serving plate. Cover with aluminum foil and keep warm.

3. Add remaining 1 tablespoon oil to skillet. Heat over medium-high heat until hot. Add mushrooms and garlic. Cook and stir 2 minutes. Add broth, lemon juice and oregano. Bring to a boil. Reduce heat to medium; simmer, uncovered, 3 minutes.

4. Spoon sauce mixture over turkey. Sprinkle with pine nuts and parsley. Serve immediately.

Makes 4 servings

Honey Dijon Cornish Hens

2 **whole Cornish hens, split
    (about 2½ pounds total) or
    1 (2½-pound) chicken, cut up**
⅔ **cup GREY POUPON® Dijon Mustard**
⅓ **cup honey**
¼ **cup lemon juice**
2 **tablespoons minced onion**
¾ **teaspoon minced fresh rosemary leaves**
½ **cup COLLEGE INN® Chicken Broth or
    Lower Sodium Chicken Broth**
1 **teaspoon cornstarch**
6 **lemon slices, cut into halves
    Hot cooked long grain and wild rice**

Place cornish hens or chicken pieces on rack in roasting pan. Bake at 350°F for 30 minutes.

Meanwhile, in small bowl, blend mustard, honey, lemon juice, onion and rosemary. Use ⅓ cup mustard mixture to brush over hens or chicken. Bake for 30 to 40 minutes more or until done.

In small saucepan, blend remaining mustard mixture, chicken broth and cornstarch. Cook over medium heat until mixture thickens and begins to boil. Add lemon slices; cook for 1 minute. Keep warm.

Serve hens or chicken with rice and heated mustard sauce. Garnish as desired.   *Makes 4 servings*

Bounty of

BEEF & VEAL

Peppered Beef Tenderloin Roast

1 (3- to 4-pound) beef tenderloin,
    fat trimmed
5 cloves garlic, finely chopped
2 tablespoons finely chopped fresh
    rosemary
1 tablespoon green peppercorns in brine,
    drained and finely chopped
1 teaspoon freshly ground black pepper
1 teaspoon salt
2 tablespoons olive oil or vegetable oil
1¼ cups beef stock

Place beef on sheet of plastic wrap. Combine remaining
ingredients except oil and beef stock; rub over roast.
Wrap tightly and refrigerate at least 4 hours, no longer
than 48 hours. Return to room temperature before
cooking. Preheat oven to 425°F. In large ovenproof
skillet or roasting pan, heat oil over medium-high
heat. Place roast in skillet; brown on all sides (about 4
minutes per side). Carefully lift roast with large carving
fork and place roasting rack in skillet; place roast on
rack. Do not cover. Insert meat thermometer in
thickest part of roast. Roast until meat thermometer
registers 155°F. (Roasts will usually increase about 5°F
after removal from oven.) Remove to cutting board and
let rest in warm place 15 minutes before carving. Place
skillet with pan drippings over high heat until hot. Stir
in beef stock. Cook, stirring occasionally, until reduced
to about ¾ cup. Strain and serve in sauce pitcher.

Makes 10 to 12 servings

Favorite recipe from **California Beef Council**

Mustard Crusted Rib Roast

- 1 (3-rib) standing beef rib roast, trimmed* (6 to 7 pounds)
- 3 tablespoons Dijon-style mustard
- 1½ tablespoons chopped fresh tarragon *or* 1½ teaspoons dried tarragon leaves
- 3 cloves garlic, minced
- ¼ cup dry red wine
- 2 shallots, finely chopped, *or* ⅓ cup finely chopped onion
- 1 tablespoon all-purpose flour
- 1 cup canned single-strength beef broth

*Ask meat retailer to remove chine bone for easier carving. Trim fat to ¼-inch thickness.

1. Preheat oven to 450°F. Place roast, bone side down (the bones take the place of a meat rack), in shallow roasting pan. Combine mustard, chopped tarragon and garlic in small bowl; spread over all surfaces of roast, but not on bottom. Insert meat thermometer into thickest part of roast, not touching bone or fat. Roast in oven 10 minutes.

2. *Reduce oven temperature to 325°F.* Roast about 20 minutes per pound or until thermometer registers 120° to 130°F for rare or 135° to 145°F for medium.

3. Transfer roast to cutting board; tent with foil. Let stand in warm place 15 minutes for easier carving. (Temperature of roast will rise about 10° during stand time.)

4. To make gravy, pour fat from roasting pan, reserving 1 tablespoon in medium saucepan. Add wine to roasting pan; place over 2 burners. Cook over medium heat 2 minutes or until slightly thickened, stirring to scrape up browned bits.

5. Add shallots to drippings in saucepan; cook and stir over medium heat 4 minutes or until softened. Add flour; cook and stir 1 minute. Add broth and reserved wine mixture; cook 5 minutes or until sauce thickens, stirring occasionally. Pour through strainer into gravy boat, pressing with back of spoon on shallots; discard.

6. Carve roast into ½-inch-thick slices. Serve with gravy.   *Makes 6 to 8 servings*

Roasted Herb & Garlic Tenderloin

- 1 **well-trimmed beef tenderloin roast (3 to 4 pounds)**
- 1 **tablespoon black peppercorns**
- 2 **tablespoons chopped fresh basil** *or* **2 teaspoons dried basil leaves, crushed**
- 1½ **tablespoons chopped fresh thyme** *or* **1½ teaspoons dried thyme leaves, crushed**
- 1 **tablespoon chopped fresh rosemary** *or* **1 teaspoon dried rosemary, crushed**
- 1 **tablespoon minced garlic Salt and black pepper (optional)**

1. Preheat oven to 425°F.

2. To hold shape of roast, tie roast with cotton string at 1½-inch intervals.

3. Place peppercorns in small heavy resealable plastic food storage bag. Squeeze out excess air; seal bag tightly. Pound peppercorns with flat side of meat mallet or rolling pin until cracked.

4. Place roast on meat rack in shallow roasting pan. Combine cracked peppercorns, basil, thyme, rosemary and garlic in small bowl; rub over top surface of roast.

5. Insert meat thermometer into thickest part of roast.

6. Roast in oven 40 to 50 minutes until thermometer registers 125° to 130°F for rare or 135° to 145°F for medium-rare, depending on thickness of roast.

7. Transfer roast to carving board; tent with foil. Let stand 10 minutes before carving. Remove string; discard.

8. To serve, carve crosswise into ½-inch-thick slices with large carving knife. Season with salt and pepper.

Makes 10 to 12 servings

Marinated Beef Tenderloin

¾ cup dry vermouth
¼ cup olive oil
¼ cup chopped shallots
1 teaspoon LAWRY'S® Garlic Powder with
    Parsley
1 teaspoon dried rosemary
1 teaspoon LAWRY'S® Seasoned Salt
1 teaspoon LAWRY'S® Seasoned Pepper
¾ teaspoon dried thyme, crushed
1½ pounds beef tenderloin

In small bowl, combine all ingredients except meat. Pierce meat several times with fork. In large resealable plastic bag or glass baking dish, place meat and marinade. Seal bag or cover dish. Marinate in refrigerator at least 1 hour or overnight, turning occasionally. Bake at 400°F, uncovered, 50 minutes to 1 hour or until internal meat temperature reaches 180°F. Let stand 5 minutes before slicing.

Makes 4 to 6 servings

Pot Roast Carbonnade

------

  6 **thick slices applewood or other smoked
       bacon (about 6 ounces)**
  2 **tablespoons all-purpose flour**
  ¾ **teaspoon salt**
  ½ **teaspoon freshly ground black pepper**
  1 **well-trimmed round bone* beef chuck
       pot roast (about 3½ pounds)**
  3 **large Spanish onions (about 2 pounds),
       thinly sliced**
  2 **tablespoons light brown sugar**
  1 **can (about 14 ounces) single-strength
       beef broth**
  1 **bottle or can (12 ounces) beer
       (not dark)**
  2 **teaspoons dried thyme leaves, crushed**
  2 **bay leaves**
      **Additional freshly ground black pepper
       (optional)**

*A well-trimmed, 3-pound *boneless* beef chuck pot roast may be
substituted; however, the bone in the pot roast will give the sauce
more flavor.

1. Preheat oven to 350°F.

2. Cook bacon in Dutch oven over medium heat until
crisp. Transfer bacon to paper towel with tongs,
reserving drippings in Dutch oven. Crumble bacon; set
aside.

3. Combine flour, salt and ½ teaspoon pepper in small bowl; spread on sheet of waxed paper. Place pot roast on flour mixture; roll to coat well.

4. Place pot roast in drippings in Dutch oven. Brown over medium-low heat about 4 to 5 minutes per side, holding roast with tongs to brown all edges; remove to platter. Set aside.

5. Pour off all but 2 tablespoons drippings. Add onions to drippings in Dutch oven; cover and cook 10 minutes over medium heat, stirring once. Uncover; sprinkle with sugar. Cook onions, uncovered, over medium-high heat 10 minutes more or until golden brown and tender, stirring frequently.

6. Add broth, beer, dried thyme and bay leaves to Dutch oven; bring to a boil. Return pot roast with any accumulated juices to Dutch oven. Remove from heat; spoon sauce over top. Cover and bake 2 to 2¼ hours until meat is fork-tender. Transfer meat to carving board; tent with foil.

7. Remove bay leaves; discard. Skim fat from juices with large spoon; discard. Place ½ of juice mixture in food processor; process until smooth. Repeat with remaining juice mixture; return pureed mixture to Dutch oven. Stir reserved bacon into sauce; cook over medium heat until heated through.

8. Discard bone from roast; carve roast into ¼-inch-thick slices with large carving knife. Spoon sauce over roast. Sprinkle with additional pepper, if desired.

Makes 8 servings

Savory Pot Roast

⅔ cup A.1. ORIGINAL® or A.1. BOLD®
   Steak Sauce
1 (0.9-ounce) envelope dry onion-
   mushroom soup mix
1 cup water, divided
1 (2½-pound) boneless beef chuck roast
6 medium potatoes, quartered
6 medium carrots, peeled, cut into 1-inch
   pieces
2 tablespoons all-purpose flour

In small bowl, blend steak sauce, soup mix and ¾ cup water; set aside.

Line shallow baking pan or dish with heavy-duty foil, overlapping edges. Place roast in center of foil; place potatoes and carrots around roast. Pour steak sauce mixture evenly over beef and vegetables. Seal foil loosely over top of beef; secure side edges tightly. Bake at 350°F 2 hours or until beef is tender. Remove beef to heated serving platter. Using slotted spoon, remove vegetables to same platter; keep warm. Remove and discard foil.

For gravy, dissolve flour in remaining ¼ cup water. Stir into pan liquid; cook until thickened, stirring occasionally. Slice beef; serve with vegetables and gravy. *Makes 8 servings*

Salisbury Steaks with Mushroom-Wine Sauce

1 **pound lean ground sirloin**
¾ **teaspoon garlic salt or seasoned salt**
¼ **teaspoon pepper**
2 **tablespoons butter or margarine**
1 **package (8 ounces) sliced button mushrooms *or* 2 packages (4 ounces each) sliced exotic mushrooms**
2 **tablespoons sweet vermouth or ruby port wine**
1 **jar (12 ounces) *or* 1 can (10½ ounces) beef gravy**

1. Heat large heavy nonstick skillet over medium-high heat 3 minutes or until hot.* Meanwhile, combine ground beef, garlic salt and pepper; mix well. Shape mixture into four ¼-inch-thick oval patties.

2. Place patties in skillet as they are formed; cook 3 minutes per side or until browned. Transfer to plate; keep warm. Pour off any drippings.

3. Melt butter in skillet; add mushrooms and cook 2 minutes, stirring occasionally. Add vermouth; cook 1 minute. Add gravy; mix well.

4. Return meat to skillet; simmer uncovered over medium heat 3 minutes for medium or until desired doneness, turning meat and stirring sauce once.

Makes 4 servings

*If pan is not heavy, use medium heat.

Beef Wellington

6   center cut beef tenderloin steaks, cut
      1 inch thick (about 2½ pounds)
¾   teaspoon salt, divided
½   teaspoon freshly ground black pepper,
      divided
2   tablespoons butter or margarine
8   ounces fresh crimini or button
      mushrooms, finely chopped
¼   cup chopped shallots or onion
2   tablespoons ruby port or sweet
      Madeira wine
1   package (17¼ ounces) frozen puff
      pastry, thawed
1   egg, separated
½   cup (4 ounces) purchased liver paté,
      liver paté with cognac or chicken liver
      mousse*
2   teaspoons water

*You can find paté in the gourmet or deli section of most
supermarkets or in specialty food stores.

1. Sprinkle steaks with ½ teaspoon salt and ¼ teaspoon
pepper.

2. Heat large nonstick skillet over medium-high heat
until hot; add ½ of steaks. Cook about 3 minutes per
side or until well browned and instant-read
thermometer inserted into steaks registers 110°F (very
rare). Transfer to clean plate; set aside. (Steaks are
seared to hold in their juices while baking.) Repeat
with remaining steaks. (If meat is tied, remove string;
discard.)

3. Melt butter in same skillet over medium heat; add mushrooms and shallots. Cook and stir 5 minutes. Add port, remaining ¼ teaspoon salt and ¼ teaspoon pepper. Bring to a boil. Reduce heat to medium-low; simmer 10 minutes or until liquid evaporates, stirring often. Remove from heat; cool completely.

4. Roll out each pastry sheet to 18×10-inch rectangle on lightly floured surface with lightly floured rolling pin. Cut each sheet into 3 (10×6-inch) rectangles. Cut small amount of pastry from corners to use as decorations, if desired.

5. Beat egg white in small bowl with whisk until foamy; brush over each pastry rectangle with pastry brush. Place 1 cooled steak on each pastry rectangle. Spread paté over steaks, dividing evenly; top with mushroom mixture, pressing lightly so mushrooms adhere to paté. Carefully turn each steak over, placing mushroom side down. Fold pastry over steak. Fold edge of bottom dough over top; press edges to seal. Place on ungreased baking sheet.

6. Beat egg yolk and water in small bowl; brush evenly over pastry covering steaks with pastry brush. Cut pastry scraps into decorative shapes and decorate pastry, if desired. Brush decorations with egg yolk mixture. Cover loosely with plastic wrap; refrigerate 1 to 4 hours until cold.

7. Preheat oven to 400°F. Remove plastic wrap. Bake 20 to 25 minutes until pastry is puffed and golden brown and instant-read thermometer inserted into centers of steaks registers 140°F for medium-rare. Let stand 10 minutes before serving.   *Makes 6 servings*

Steak Diane

2 large well-trimmed boneless beef top
loin steaks, 1 inch thick, cut in half
crosswise (about 1¼ pounds total), or
1 boneless beef top sirloin steak, cut
into 4 serving pieces

½ teaspoon freshly ground black pepper,
divided

3 tablespoons butter, divided

2 tablespoons Dijon-style mustard

2 tablespoons Worcestershire sauce

8 ounces fresh oyster or crimini
mushrooms, wiped clean

½ cup chopped shallots or sweet onion

2 tablespoons brandy or cognac

⅔ cup heavy cream

1½ teaspoons chopped fresh thyme *or*
½ teaspoon dried thyme leaves, crushed

1. Sprinkle steaks with ¼ teaspoon pepper. Melt 1
tablespoon butter in large skillet over medium-high
heat. Add steaks. Cook 2 minutes per side or until
browned. Reduce heat to medium; cook 3 to 4 minutes
more per side for medium-rare or to desired doneness.

2. Transfer steaks to large shallow dish; spread mustard
over both sides of steaks. Spoon Worcestershire sauce
over steaks.

3. Slice oyster mushrooms in half; slice crimini mushrooms.

4. Melt remaining 2 tablespoons butter in same skillet over medium heat. Add shallots; cook and stir 4 minutes. Add mushrooms; cook 5 minutes or until mushrooms are softened. Add brandy to skillet; carefully ignite brandy with lighted long match or barbecue starter flame. Let flames burn off alcohol 30 seconds or until flames subside.

5. Stir in cream, thyme and remaining ¼ teaspoon pepper. Cook about 3 minutes or until sauce thickens. Return steaks and Worcestershire mixture to skillet. Cook 3 minutes or until heated through, turning once. Spoon sauce over steaks.   *Makes 4 servings*

Mushroom and Onion Smothered Swiss Steak

4 (4- to 6-ounce) beef cubed steaks
2 tablespoons margarine
4 cups sliced fresh mushrooms (about 12 ounces)
1 large onion, cut into wedges
2 tablespoons all-purpose flour
1½ cups milk
½ cup A.1. ORIGINAL® or A.1. BOLD® Steak Sauce
   Hot cooked rice, optional

In large skillet, over high heat, cook steaks in margarine 5 minutes on each side or to desired doneness. Remove from skillet; keep warm.

In same skillet, sauté mushrooms and onion until tender. Stir in flour until well blended. Add milk; cook until mixture thickens and begins to boil, stirring constantly. Stir in steak sauce. Serve sauce over steaks and rice if desired.   *Makes 4 servings*

Steak au Pôivre

- **1** tablespoon LAWRY'S® Seasoned Pepper
- **2** teaspoons LAWRY'S® Seasoned Salt
- **1** (2½-pound) beef sirloin roast or steak, 2 inches thick
- **2** tablespoons butter
- **2** tablespoons olive oil
- **¼** cup dry white wine
- **2** tablespoons beef consommé or bouillon
- **¼** cup cognac or brandy

Press Seasoned Pepper and Seasoned Salt into both sides of steak with back of spoon. In large skillet, heat butter and oil. Add steak; cook 8 to 10 minutes on each side or to desired doneness, adding more oil, if necessary. Remove steak from skillet to serving plate; set aside. Reduce heat to low. Add wine and consommé to skillet; heat until warmed. Turn off heat. Remove skillet from heat. Add cognac or brandy; carefully ignite. Pour flaming sauce over steak. Serve immediately. *Makes 4 to 6 servings*

Korean-Style Beef

½ cup dry white wine or water
½ cup soy sauce
¼ cup honey
2 green onions, chopped
1 to 2 tablespoons sesame oil
1 tablespoon grated fresh gingerroot
1 clove garlic, minced
1 flank steak (about 1½ pounds)
  Chives for garnish (optional)

Combine wine, soy sauce, honey, green onions, sesame oil, gingerroot and garlic in large baking dish. Add flank steak. Marinate, covered, in refrigerator about 1 hour, turning at least once. Remove beef from marinade; discard marinade.

On top rack of preheated oven broiler or low rack of charcoal grill over hot coals, cook to desired degree of doneness. Slice diagonally to serve. Serve with vegetables, if desired. Garnish with chives.

Makes 6 to 8 servings

Favorite recipe from **National Honey Board**

German Beef Roulade

1½ pounds flank steak
4 teaspoons GREY POUPON® Dijon Mustard
6 slices bacon, diced
¾ cup chopped onion
⅓ cup chopped dill pickle
¼ cup all-purpose flour
1 (13¾-fluid ounce) can COLLEGE INN® Beef Broth

With meat mallet or rolling pin, flatten meat to approximately a 10×8-inch rectangle. Spread mustard over meat.

In large skillet, over medium-high heat, cook bacon and onion until bacon is crisp; pour off fat, reserving ¼ cup. Spread bacon mixture over meat; sprinkle with pickle. Roll up meat from short end; secure with string.

In large skillet, over medium-high heat, brown beef roll in reserved fat; place in 13×9×2-inch baking dish. Stir flour into fat in skillet until smooth; gradually stir in beef broth. Cook and stir over medium heat until thickened. Pour sauce over beef roll. Cover; bake at 325°F for 1½ hours or until done. Let stand 10 minutes before slicing. Skim fat from sauce; strain and serve sauce with meat.   *Makes 6 servings*

Carne Asada

1½ to 1¾ pounds flank or boneless sirloin
    tip steak
½ cup lime juice
6 cloves garlic, chopped
1 teaspoon ground black pepper
  Salt
1 large green bell pepper, cut lengthwise
    into 1-inch strips
8 corn tortillas, warmed
  Salsa

1. Combine steak, lime juice, garlic and ground pepper in large heavy-duty resealable freezer bag; seal. Refrigerate overnight, turning at least once.

2. To complete recipe, preheat broiler. Remove steak from bag and place on broiler pan. Sprinkle with salt to taste. Add bell pepper to same bag; seal. Turn to coat with marinade; set aside. Broil steak 5 to 7 minutes per side or until well-browned, turning once. Add pepper strips to broiler pan; broil until softened.

3. Transfer steak to cutting board; slice across the grain into thin strips. Place steak on warm tortillas. Top with pepper strips and salsa. Serve immediately.

Makes 4 servings

Beef Sirloin in Rich Italian Sauce

1 pound top sirloin, cut into thin strips
2 tablespoons all-purpose flour
2 tablespoons olive oil
2 cloves garlic, finely chopped
1¾ cups (14-ounce can) CONTADINA®
   Dalla Casa Buitoni Pasta Ready
   Chunky Tomatoes with Mushrooms,
   undrained
2 tablespoons chopped fresh parsley
2 tablespoons dry red wine (optional)
   Hot cooked pasta or rice (optional)

PLACE meat and flour in plastic bag or small bowl; toss to coat lightly.

HEAT oil in large skillet over medium-high heat. Add garlic; cook for 1 minute. Add meat; cook for 3 to 4 minutes or until no longer pink.

STIR in tomatoes and juice, parsley and wine; bring to a boil. Reduce heat to low; cook, covered, for 5 to 6 minutes. Serve over pasta or rice.

Makes 4 servings

Beef Fajitas

½ cup A.1. ORIGINAL or A.1. BOLD
   Steak Sauce
¼ cup REGINA® Red Wine Vinegar
¼ cup vegetable oil, divided
2 teaspoons WRIGHT'S® Concentrated
   Natural Hickory Seasoning
1 clove garlic, minced
½ teaspoon liquid hot pepper seasoning
1 (1-pound) boneless beef sirloin steak,
   thinly sliced
1 large green bell pepper, cut into strips
1 large onion, cut into wedges
8 flour tortillas, heated
   Sour cream and shredded Cheddar
   cheese

In nonmetal large bowl, combine steak sauce, vinegar,
2 tablespoons oil, hickory seasoning, garlic and hot
pepper seasoning; add steak, stirring to coat. Cover;
refrigerate 1 to 2 hours, stirring occasionally.

Remove steak from marinade; reserve marinade. In
large skillet, over medium-high heat, sauté steak in
remaining 2 tablespoons oil 5 to 6 minutes or until no
longer pink. Using slotted spoon, remove steak to clean
large bowl; keep warm.

In same skillet, sauté pepper and onion 5 to 6 minutes
or until tender-crisp. Add reserved marinade; heat to a
boil. Reduce heat; simmer 5 minutes. Stir in steak;
heat through. Serve in warm tortillas topped with sour
cream and cheese. *Makes 4 servings*

Steak Fajitas Suprema

2 tablespoons vegetable oil, divided
1 medium-sized red bell pepper, thinly
    sliced
1 medium onion, very thinly sliced
1 pound beef sirloin steak, thinly sliced
1 package (1.27 ounces) LAWRY'S®
    Spices & Seasonings for Fajitas
¼ cup water
1 can (15 ounces) pinto beans, drained
6 medium flour or corn tortillas
1 cup (4 ounces) shredded Cheddar
    cheese (optional)
    Salsa (optional)
    Dairy sour cream (optional)
    Sliced peeled avocado (optional)

In large skillet, heat 1 tablespoon oil. Add bell pepper
and onion; sauté until crisp-tender. Remove vegetables
from skillet; set aside. In same skillet, heat remaining 1
tablespoon oil. Add meat. Cook 5 to 7 minutes or to
desired doneness; drain fat. Add Spices & Seasonings
for Fajitas, water and pinto beans; blend well. Bring to
a boil. Reduce heat to low; simmer, uncovered, 3 to 5
minutes or until thoroughly heated, stirring
occasionally. Return vegetables to skillet; heat 1
minute.   *Makes 4 to 6 servings*

Presentation: Serve in warm tortillas. If desired, add
shredded Cheddar cheese, salsa, sour cream and
avocado to the inside for extra flavor.

Hint: Partially frozen meat is easier to slice thinly.

Classic Brisket Tzimmes

2 first cut (about 2½ pounds each) *or*
    1 whole HEBREW NATIONAL®
    Fresh Brisket (about 5 to 6 pounds),
    well trimmed
1 teaspoon salt
½ teaspoon freshly ground black pepper
2 tablespoons vegetable oil
1 large onion, chopped
3 cloves garlic, minced
2 cups beef or chicken broth
½ cup orange juice
2 tablespoons light brown sugar
2 tablespoons fresh lemon juice
1 tablespoon tomato paste
1 teaspoon dried thyme leaves
1 teaspoon ground cinnamon
¼ teaspoon ground cloves
6 to 8 medium carrots, peeled, sliced
3 medium sweet potatoes, peeled, cut into
    ½-inch-thick slices
8 ounces dried pitted prunes

Preheat oven to 325°F. Place brisket in large roasting pan; sprinkle with salt and pepper. Heat oil in medium saucepan over medium-high heat. Add onion and garlic; cook and stir 8 minutes. Stir in broth, orange juice, brown sugar, lemon juice, tomato paste, thyme, cinnamon and cloves. Bring to a boil, stirring occasionally. Pour evenly over brisket. Cover; bake 1½ hours.

Add carrots, sweet potatoes and prunes to pan. Cover; bake 1 to 1½ hours or until brisket and vegetables are fork-tender. Transfer brisket to cutting board; tent with foil. Spoon pan juices over fruit and vegetables; transfer to serving platter. Skim fat from pan juices; discard fat.

Slice brisket across the grain into ¼-inch-thick slices; transfer to serving platter. Spoon sauce over brisket and vegetables.   *Makes 10 to 12 servings*

Note: Recipe may be prepared up to 1 day in advance. Reheat sliced brisket and sauce in large skillet over medium heat. Microwave vegetables in large microwave-safe bowl on HIGH 3 to 5 minutes or until heated through.

Texas-Style Barbecued Brisket

1   beef brisket (3 to 4 pounds)
3   tablespoons Worcestershire sauce
1   teaspoon liquid smoke
1   tablespoon ground mild red chili or
      chili powder
1   teaspoon celery salt
1   teaspoon coarsely ground black pepper
2   cloves garlic, minced
2   bay leaves
    Barbecue Sauce (recipe follows)

Trim and discard excess fat from meat; place in heavy self-sealing plastic bag. Combine Worcestershire sauce, liquid smoke, ground chili, celery salt, pepper, garlic and bay leaves in small bowl. Spread half of the mixture onto each side of meat with large spoon; seal bag. Refrigerate 24 hours. Preheat oven to 300°F. Remove meat from bag and place on large piece of heavy-duty foil. Pour marinade over meat; seal foil. Place in large roasting pan. Bake 4 hours. Prepare Barbecue Sauce during last ½ hour of baking.

Remove meat from oven. Open foil; carefully pour juices into 2-cup measure. Discard bay leaves; skim fat from juices. Stir 1 cup of juices into Barbecue Sauce. Save remaining juices for other use or discard. Pour barbecue sauce mixture over meat. Reseal foil; continue baking 1 hour. Remove meat from foil; cut across the grain into ¼-inch slices. Serve 2 to 3 tablespoons barbecue sauce mixture over each serving.
                              Makes 10 to 12 servings

Barbecue Sauce

3 tablespoons vegetable oil
1 medium onion, chopped
2 cloves garlic, minced
1 cup ketchup
½ cup molasses
¼ cup cider vinegar
2 teaspoons ground mild red chili or chili
     powder
½ teaspoon dry mustard

Heat oil in 3-quart pan over medium heat. Add onion
and garlic; cook until onion is tender. Add remaining
ingredients. Simmer 5 minutes, then remove from
heat until needed.

Oven-Barbecued Beef Brisket

1 (3- to 4-pound) beef brisket
1 (15-ounce) can tomato sauce
⅓ cup A.1. THICK & HEARTY® Steak
   Sauce
2 tablespoons firmly packed light brown
   sugar
1 tablespoon lemon juice
1 teaspoon WRIGHT'S® Concentrated
   Natural Hickory Seasoning
1 teaspoon garlic powder
¼ teaspoon liquid hot pepper seasoning
1 tablespoon all-purpose flour
2 tablespoons water

Place brisket, fat side up, in large roasting pan; set aside.

Blend tomato sauce, steak sauce, sugar, juice, hickory seasoning, garlic powder and hot pepper seasoning; pour over brisket. Cover with lid or foil. Bake at 350°F 3 hours or until tender, basting occasionally. Place pan liquid in large saucepan. Dissolve flour in water; add to pan liquid. Cook until thickened, stirring occasionally. Slice beef; serve with thickened sauce.

Makes 4 to 6 servings

Corned Beef with Horseradish Sauce

1 **HEBREW NATIONAL®** Pickled Corned
    Beef (about 7 pounds)
1 **pound fresh baby carrots**
5 **to 6 new potatoes**
1 **pound fresh green beans, trimmed**
⅔ **cup mayonnaise**
1 **tablespoon fresh lemon juice**
3 **tablespoons grated fresh or prepared**
    horseradish

Preheat oven to 350°F. Place corned beef in large
roasting pan; add water to cover. Cover; bake 2 hours.

Add carrots and potatoes to pan. Cover; bake 30
minutes. Add green beans to pan. Cover; bake 15 to 20
minutes or until corned beef and vegetables are fork-
tender.

Combine mayonnaise, lemon juice and horseradish in
small bowl. Cover; refrigerate until ready to serve.

Place corned beef on cutting board. Cut fat from
corned beef; discard fat. Slice corned beef across the
grain into ¼-inch-thick slices. Serve with vegetables
and horseradish sauce for dipping.

Makes 8 servings

Wonderful Meat Loaf

 4 tablespoons unsalted butter
 ¾ cup finely chopped onion
 ½ cup finely chopped celery
 ½ cup finely chopped green bell pepper
 ¼ cup finely chopped green onions
 2 tablespoons plus ½ teaspoon CHEF
      PAUL PRUDHOMME'S® Meat Magic®
 1 tablespoon Worcestershire sauce
 2 teaspoons minced garlic
 2 bay leaves
 ½ cup evaporated milk
 ½ cup ketchup
 1½ pounds ground beef
 ½ pound ground pork
 2 large eggs, lightly beaten
 1 cup very fine dry bread crumbs

Preheat oven to 350°F. Melt butter in 1-quart saucepan over medium heat. Add onion, celery, bell pepper, green onions, Meat Magic®, Worcestershire sauce, garlic and bay leaves. Cook and stir until mixture starts sticking excessively, about 6 minutes, stirring occasionally and scraping pan bottom well. Stir in milk and ketchup. Cook about 2 minutes, stirring occasionally. Cool to room temperature. Discard bay leaves.

Place ground beef and pork in ungreased 13×9-inch baking pan. Add eggs, cooked vegetable mixture and bread crumbs. Mix by hand until thoroughly combined. In center of pan, shape mixture into 12×6×1½-inch loaf. Bake, uncovered, 25 minutes. Increase heat to 400°F; bake until no longer pink in center, about 35 minutes longer. Serve immediately.

Makes 6 servings

Easy Meat Loaf

2 pounds lean ground beef or turkey
1 package (6¼ ounces) STOVE TOP® Stuffing Mix for Beef
1 cup water
½ cup catsup, divided
2 eggs, beaten

1. MIX all ingredients except ¼ cup of the catsup.

2. SHAPE meat mixture into oval loaf in 12×8-inch baking dish; top with remaining ¼ cup catsup.

3. BAKE at 375°F for 1 hour or until center is no longer pink.

Makes 6 to 8 servings

Potato Topped Meat Loaf

------

1 jar (12 ounces) HEINZ® HomeStyle
   Mushroom or Brown Gravy
1½ pounds lean ground beef
1 cup soft bread crumbs
¼ cup finely chopped onion
1 egg, slightly beaten
½ teaspoon salt
   Dash pepper
2½ cups hot mashed potatoes
1 tablespoon melted butter or margarine
   Paprika

Measure ¼ cup gravy from jar; combine with beef,
bread crumbs, onion, egg, salt and pepper. Shape into
8×4×1½-inch loaf in shallow baking pan. Bake in
350°F oven 1 hour. Remove from oven and carefully
drain fat. Spread potatoes over top and sides of meat
loaf. Drizzle melted butter over potatoes; garnish with
paprika. Return meat loaf to oven; bake additional 20
minutes. Let stand 5 minutes. Heat remaining gravy
and serve with meat loaf slices.   *Makes 6 servings*

Spinach Meatloaf Dijon

1½ pounds lean ground beef
¾ cup plain dry bread crumbs
½ cup GREY POUPON® Dijon Mustard,
      divided
2 eggs
1 (10-ounce) package frozen chopped
      spinach, thawed and well drained
1 cup shredded Swiss cheese (4 ounces)
½ cup minced onion
2 teaspoons chopped fresh dill weed
1 teaspoon coarsely ground black pepper
1 clove garlic, minced
2 tablespoons honey

In large bowl, combine ground beef, bread crumbs, 5 tablespoons mustard, eggs, spinach, cheese, onion, dill, pepper and garlic. Shape mixture into 9×5-inch loaf; place in greased 13×9×2-inch baking pan. Bake at 350°F for 60 to 70 minutes or until done. Blend remaining mustard and honey; brush on meatloaf during last 10 minutes of baking time. Remove from oven and let stand 10 minutes. Slice and serve.

Makes 6 to 8 servings

Italian-Style Meat Loaf

1½ pounds lean ground beef or turkey
 8 ounces hot or mild Italian sausage
 1 cup CONTADINA® Dalla Casa Buitoni
    Seasoned Bread Crumbs
 1 cup (8-ounce can) CONTADINA® Dalla
    Casa Buitoni Tomato Sauce, divided
 1 cup (1 small) chopped onion
 ½ cup chopped green bell pepper
 1 egg

COMBINE meat, sausage, bread crumbs, ¾ *cup* tomato sauce, onion, bell pepper and egg in large bowl; mix well. Press into ungreased 9×5-inch loaf pan.

BAKE in preheated 350°F oven for 60 minutes; drain. Spoon *remaining* tomato sauce over meat loaf. Bake for additional 15 minutes or until no longer pink in center. Cool in pan on wire rack for 10 minutes before serving. *Makes 8 servings*

Paprika Meatballs

1 **pound lean ground beef**
1 **cup soft bread crumbs**
1 **egg**
1 **small onion, chopped**
1 **package (1 ounce) HIDDEN VALLEY**
   RANCH® Milk Recipe Original
   Ranch® salad dressing mix
   Vegetable oil
1 **cup (½ pint) sour cream**
1 **small tomato, chopped**
½ **teaspoon paprika**

In large bowl, combine beef, bread crumbs, egg, onion and 1 tablespoon of the salad dressing mix until blended. Shape into 24 (1½-inch) meatballs. Heat oil in medium skillet and lightly brown meatballs on all sides. Reduce heat, cover and cook until done, about 5 minutes; drain. In small bowl, whisk together sour cream, tomato, paprika and remaining salad dressing mix. Pour into skillet and heat through.

Makes 4 servings

Italian Meatballs

1½ pounds meat loaf mix* or lean ground
    beef
⅓ cup dry bread crumbs
⅓ cup milk
⅓ cup grated onion
¼ cup (1 ounce) freshly grated Parmesan
    cheese
1 egg
2 cloves garlic, minced
1½ teaspoons dried basil leaves
1 teaspoon salt
1 teaspoon dried oregano leaves
½ teaspoon rubbed sage
¼ teaspoon crushed red pepper flakes
   Marinara Sauce (recipe follows)
   Additional grated Parmesan cheese
      (optional)

*Meat loaf mix is a combination of ground beef, pork and veal; see
your meat retailer or make your own with 1 pound lean ground beef,
¼ pound pork and ¼ pound veal.

1. Preheat oven to 400°F. Spray broiler pan with
nonstick cooking spray.

2. Combine all ingredients except Marinara Sauce
and additional cheese in large bowl. Mix lightly but
thoroughly. Shape to form meatballs using ⅓ cup
meat mixture for each meatball; place meatballs on
prepared pan.

3. Bake 25 to 30 minutes until instant-read
thermometer inserted into meatballs registers 145°F.

4. Meanwhile, prepare Marinara Sauce. Add cooked meatballs to Marinara Sauce; simmer, uncovered, about 10 minutes or until meatballs are cooked through and no longer pink in centers, turning meatballs in sauce once. (Internal temperature should register 160° to 165°F.)

5. Serve meatballs in shallow bowls; top with sauce. Serve with additional cheese.

Makes 5 to 6 servings

Marinara Sauce

1½ tablespoons olive oil
3 cloves garlic, minced
1 can (28 ounces) Italian plum tomatoes, undrained
¼ cup tomato paste
2 teaspoons dried basil leaves
½ teaspoon sugar
¼ teaspoon salt
¼ teaspoon crushed red pepper flakes

Heat oil in large skillet over medium heat. Add garlic; cook and stir 3 minutes. Stir in remaining ingredients. Bring to a boil. Reduce heat to low; simmer, uncovered, 10 minutes. *Makes about 3½ cups*

Tip: If serving with pasta, double sauce recipe.

Mesquite-Filled Burgers

1 **pound ground beef**
½ **cup LAWRY'S® Mesquite Marinade with**
     Lime Juice
½ **cup chopped green bell pepper**
½ **cup finely chopped onion**
¼ **cup unseasoned bread crumbs**
½ **teaspoon LAWRY'S® Seasoned Pepper**
½ **cup (2 ounces) shredded cheddar**
     cheese
4 **hamburger buns, toasted**
     Lettuce leaves
     Tomato slices

In large bowl, combine ground beef, Mesquite
Marinade with Lime Juice, bell pepper, onion, bread
crumbs and Seasoned Pepper. Let stand 20 minutes.
Shape meat into eight thin patties. In center of each of
four patties, place a layer of cheese; top with remaining
patties. Press edges tightly together to seal. Broil, 4
inches from heat source, 5 to 8 minutes on each side
or to desired doneness.   *Makes 4 servings*

Presentation: Serve burgers on toasted buns with
lettuce and tomato.

Hint: Ground turkey is an excellent substitute for the
ground beef.

Philadelphia Cheese Steak Sandwiches

- 2 cups sliced red or green bell peppers (about 2 medium)
- 1 small onion, thinly sliced
- 1 tablespoon vegetable oil
- ½ cup A.1. ORIGINAL® or A.1. BOLD® Steak Sauce
- 1 teaspoon prepared horseradish
- 8 ounces thinly sliced beef sandwich steaks
- 4 long sandwich rolls, split horizontally
- 4 ounces thinly sliced part-skim mozzarella cheese

In medium saucepan, over medium heat, sauté peppers and onion in oil until tender. Stir in steak sauce and horseradish; keep warm.

In lightly greased medium skillet, over medium-high heat, cook sandwich steaks to desired doneness. Divide steaks among roll bottoms; top evenly with warm pepper mixture and cheese. Broil sandwich bottoms 4 inches from heat source 3 to 5 minutes or until cheese melts; place roll tops over cheese. Serve immediately.

Makes 4 servings

Southwestern Sloppy Joes

- 1 **pound lean ground round**
- 1 **cup chopped onion**
- ¼ **cup chopped celery**
- ¼ **cup water**
- 1 **can (10 ounces) diced tomatoes and green chilies**
- 1 **can (8 ounces) no-salt-added tomato sauce**
- 4 **teaspoons brown sugar**
- ½ **teaspoon ground cumin**
- ¼ **teaspoon salt**
- 9 **whole wheat hamburger buns**

1. Heat large nonstick skillet over high heat. Add beef, onion, celery and water. Reduce heat to medium. Cook and stir 5 minutes or until meat is no longer pink. Drain fat.

2. Stir in tomatoes and green chilies, tomato sauce, brown sugar, cumin and salt; bring to a boil over high heat. Reduce heat; simmer 20 minutes or until mixture thickens. Serve on whole wheat buns.

Makes 9 (⅓-cup) servings

Note: Green chilies add some heat to these Sloppy Joes, but if you prefer them plain, just add an equal amount of tomatoes without chilies.

Short Ribs Contadina®

2   tablespoons olive or vegetable oil
4   pounds beef short ribs
1   cup (1 small) coarsely chopped onion
2⅔ cups water
1⅓ cups (two 6-ounce cans) CONTADINA®
    Dalla Casa Buitoni Italian Paste with
    Tomato Pesto
½   teaspoon salt
¼   teaspoon ground black pepper
2   cups (2 large) carrots, cut into 2-inch
    pieces

HEAT oil in large pot over medium-high heat. Add ribs; cook for 2 to 3 minutes on each side or until browned. Add onion; cook for 1 minute.

COMBINE water, tomato paste, salt and pepper in medium bowl; pour over ribs. Bring to a boil. Reduce heat to low; cook, covered, for 1½ hours. Add carrots; cook for 30 minutes or until ribs are tender.

Makes 6 servings

Smoky Barbecued Beef Sandwiches

2 large onions, sliced
1 well-trimmed first cut whole beef
  brisket (about 3 pounds)
½ teaspoon salt
¾ cup beer (not dark)
½ cup firmly packed light brown sugar
½ cup ketchup
1 tablespoon plus 1½ teaspoons
  Worcestershire sauce
1 tablespoon plus 1½ teaspoons soy sauce
2 cloves garlic, minced
2 whole canned chipotle peppers in adobo
  sauce, finely chopped*
1 teaspoon adobo sauce from can**
6 hoagie or kaiser rolls, split and toasted

*Canned chipotle peppers can be found in the Mexican section of
most supermarkets or gourmet food stores.

**For spicier flavor, add 1 to 2 teaspoons additional sauce.

1. Preheat oven to 325°F. Separate onion slices into
rings; place in bottom of large roasting pan.

2. Place brisket, fat side up, over onions; sprinkle with
salt. Combine remaining ingredients except rolls in
2- or 4-cup glass measuring cup; pour over brisket.

3. Cover with heavy-duty foil or roasting pan lid. Roast
in oven 3 to 3½ hours until brisket is fork-tender.

4. Transfer brisket to cutting board, leaving sauce in pan; tent brisket with foil. Let stand 10 minutes. (Brisket and sauce may be prepared to this point; cool and cover separately. Refrigerate up to 1 day before serving.)

5. Skim fat from pan juices with large spoon; discard. Transfer juices to large saucepan. Cook over medium heat until thickened, stirring frequently.

6. Trim fat from brisket; carve across grain into thin slices with carving knife. Return slices to sauce; cook until heated through, coating slices with sauce. Serve slices and sauce in rolls.   *Makes 6 servings*

Beef Kabobs with Zucchini and Cherry Tomatoes

MARINADE
- ¼ cup FILIPPO BERIO® Olive Oil
- 2 tablespoons chopped fresh parsley
- 2 tablespoons red wine vinegar
- 1 clove garlic, minced
- ½ teaspoon salt
- ⅛ teaspoon freshly ground black pepper

KABOBS
- 1 pound lean beef top sirloin or top round steak, well trimmed and cut into 1-inch cubes
- 1 small zucchini, cut into ½-inch-thick slices
- 12 cherry tomatoes
- 6 metal skewers

In medium glass bowl or dish, whisk together olive oil, parsley, vinegar, garlic, salt and pepper. Add steak, zucchini and tomatoes; toss until lightly coated. Cover; marinate in refrigerator 2 hours or overnight. Drain meat and vegetables, reserving marinade. Alternately thread beef and vegetables onto skewers, ending with cubes of beef.

Brush barbecue grid with olive oil. Grill kabobs, on covered grill, over hot coals 6 to 8 minutes for medium-rare or until desired doneness is reached, turning and brushing with reserved marinade halfway through grilling time. Or, broil kabobs, 4 to 5 inches from heat, 6 to 8 minutes for medium-rare or until desired doneness is reached, turning and brushing with reserved marinade halfway through broiling time.

Makes 6 servings

Chicken Kabobs with Pineapple, Corn and Red Peppers: For marinade, substitute 2 tablespoons pineapple juice for red wine vinegar. For kabobs, use 1 pound boneless skinless chicken breasts, cut into 1½-inch cubes, 2 cobs fresh or frozen corn, cut into 12 pieces, 12 cubes fresh or canned pineapple and 1 large red bell pepper, seeded and cut into 12 chunks. Alternately thread chicken, vegetables and pineapple onto skewers, ending with cube of chicken. Marinate kabobs as directed. Grill or broil kabobs as directed, 6 to 8 minutes or until chicken is no longer pink in center and juices run clear.

Shrimp Kabobs with Green Onions and Sweet Potatoes: For marinade, substitute 2 tablespoons lime juice for red wine vinegar. For kabobs, use 1 pound raw large shrimp, shelled and deveined, 12 green onions with tops, trimmed and cut into 2-inch pieces and 3 small sweet potatoes, peeled and cut into twelve 1-inch chunks, cooked in boiling water 15 minutes and drained. Alternately thread shrimp and vegetables onto skewers, ending with shrimp. Marinate kabobs as directed. Grill or broil kabobs as directed, 5 to 7 minutes or until shrimp are opaque.

Veal Parmesan

3 tablespoons olive or vegetable oil, divided
¼ cup finely chopped onion
1 clove garlic, finely chopped
1 cup (8-ounce can) CONTADINA® Dalla Casa Buitoni Tomato Sauce
1 tablespoon chopped fresh oregano *or* 1 teaspoon dried oregano, crushed
1 egg
½ cup CONTADINA® Dalla Casa Buitoni Seasoned Bread Crumbs
¼ cup (1 ounce) grated Parmesan cheese
1 pound thin veal cutlets
4 ounces thinly sliced mozzarella cheese

HEAT *1 tablespoon* oil in medium saucepan over medium-high heat. Add onion and garlic; cook for 2 to 3 minutes or until tender. Stir in tomato sauce and oregano. Bring to a boil; reduce heat to low. Cook for 5 to 10 minutes or until heated through. Keep warm.

PLACE egg in shallow dish; beat lightly. Combine bread crumbs and Parmesan cheese in separate shallow dish. Dip veal in egg; coat with crumb mixture.

HEAT *remaining* oil in large skillet over medium heat. Add veal; cook for 1 to 2 minutes on each side or until golden brown. Drain on paper towels. Place veal in 13×9-inch baking dish; sprinkle with mozzarella cheese.

BAKE in preheated 350°F. oven for 5 to 6 minutes or until cheese is melted. Serve sauce over veal.

Makes 4 servings

Veal with Mushrooms

¼ cup all-purpose flour
    Salt and freshly ground black pepper
6 veal cutlets, ½ inch thick
    (about 2 pounds)
¼ cup FILIPPO BERIO® Olive Oil
½ cup beef broth
8 ounces fresh mushrooms, cleaned and
    quartered or 1 (4-ounce) can whole
    mushrooms, drained and quartered
5 tablespoons dry white wine

In small shallow bowl, combine flour with salt and pepper to taste. Lightly coat cutlets in flour mixture. In large skillet, heat olive oil over medium-high heat until hot. Add cutlets; cook 5 minutes or until brown, turning occasionally. Add beef broth. Cover; reduce heat to low and cook 10 minutes. Add mushrooms and wine. Cover; cook an additional 10 minutes or until veal is cooked through and tender. Uncover; simmer 5 minutes. *Makes 6 servings*

Veal Scaloppine

4 **veal cutlets, cut ⅜ inch thick**
   (about 4 ounces each)
¼ **cup butter or margarine**
½ **pound fresh mushrooms, thinly sliced**
2 **tablespoons olive oil**
1 **small onion, finely chopped**
¼ **cup dry sherry**
2 **teaspoons all-purpose flour**
½ **cup beef broth**
¼ **teaspoon salt**
⅛ **teaspoon pepper**
2 **tablespoons heavy or whipping cream**

1. Place each veal cutlet between sheets of waxed paper
on cutting board. Pound veal with meat mallet to
¼-inch thickness. Pat dry with paper towels; set aside.

2. Heat butter in large skillet over medium heat until
melted and bubbly. Cook and stir mushrooms in hot
butter 3 to 4 minutes until light brown. Remove
mushrooms with slotted spoon to small bowl; set aside.

3. Add oil to butter remaining in skillet; heat over
medium heat. Add veal; cook 2 to 3 minutes per side
until light brown. Remove veal with slotted spatula to
plate; set aside.

4. Add onion to same skillet; cook and stir 2 to 3 minutes until soft. Stir sherry into onion mixture. Bring to a boil over medium-high heat; boil 15 seconds. Stir in flour; cook and stir 30 seconds. Remove from heat; stir in broth. Bring to a boil over medium heat, stirring constantly. Stir in reserved mushrooms, salt and pepper. Add reserved veal to sauce mixture; reduce heat to low. Cover and simmer 8 minutes or until veal is tender. Remove from heat.

5. Push veal to one side of skillet. Stir cream into sauce mixture; mix well. Cook over low heat until heated through. Serve immediately.   *Makes 4 servings*

Classic Veal Florentine

6 ounces fresh spinach
6 tablespoons butter or margarine,
    divided
2 cloves garlic, minced
1 can (14½ ounces) whole peeled
    tomatoes, undrained
¼ cup dry white wine
¼ cup water
1 tablespoon tomato paste
½ teaspoon sugar
¾ teaspoon salt, divided
¼ teaspoon pepper, divided
¼ cup all-purpose flour
4 veal cutlets, cut ⅜ inch thick
    (about 4 ounces each)
1 tablespoon olive oil
4 ounces mozzarella cheese, shredded

1. To steam spinach, rinse spinach thoroughly in large bowl of water; drain but do not squeeze dry. Trim and discard stems. Stack leaves; cut crosswise into coarse shreds. Place spinach in large saucepan over medium heat. Cover and steam 4 minutes or until tender, stirring occasionally. Add 2 tablespoons butter; cook and stir until butter is absorbed. Remove from pan; set aside.

2. To make tomato sauce, heat 2 tablespoons butter in medium saucepan over medium heat until melted and bubbly. Add garlic; cook and stir 30 seconds. Press tomatoes and juice through sieve into garlic mixture; discard seeds. Add wine, water, tomato paste, sugar, ½ teaspoon salt and ⅛ teaspoon pepper to tomato mixture. Bring to a boil; reduce heat to low. Simmer, uncovered, 10 minutes, stirring occasionally. Remove from heat; set aside.

3. Mix flour, remaining ¼ teaspoon salt and ⅛ teaspoon pepper in small plastic bag. Pound veal with meat mallet to ¼-inch thickness. Pat dry with paper towels. Shake veal, 1 cutlet at a time, in seasoned flour to coat evenly.

4. Heat oil and remaining 2 tablespoons butter in large skillet over medium heat until bubbly. Add veal to skillet; cook 2 to 3 minutes per side until light brown. Remove from heat. Spoon off excess fat. Top veal with reserved spinach, then cheese.

5. Pour reserved tomato mixture into skillet, lifting edges of veal to let sauce flow under. Cook over low heat until bubbly. Cover and simmer 8 minutes or until heated through.   *Makes 4 servings*

Osso Buco

3 pounds veal shanks (about 4 shanks)
¾ teaspoon salt, divided
½ teaspoon freshly ground black pepper
½ cup all-purpose flour
2 tablespoons olive oil
1 cup finely chopped carrot
1 cup chopped onion
1 cup finely chopped celery
2 cloves garlic, minced
½ cup dry white wine
1 can (14½ ounces) peeled, diced
      tomatoes, undrained
1 cup single-strength beef broth
1 tablespoon chopped fresh basil or
      rosemary
1 bay leaf
   Parmesan Gremolata (recipe follows)

1. Season veal shanks with ½ teaspoon salt and pepper. Place flour in shallow bowl; dredge veal shanks, 1 at a time, in flour, shaking off excess.

2. Heat oil in large Dutch oven over medium-high heat until hot. Brown veal shanks 20 minutes, turning ¼ turn every 5 minutes and holding with tongs to brown all edges. Remove to plate.

3. Preheat oven to 350°F. Add carrot, onion, celery and garlic to Dutch oven; cook 5 minutes or until vegetables are soft.

4. To deglaze Dutch oven, pour wine over carrot mixture. Cook over medium-high heat 2 to 3 minutes, stirring to scrape up any browned bits. Add tomatoes with liquid, broth, basil, bay leaf and remaining ¼ teaspoon salt to Dutch oven; bring to a boil. Return veal shanks to Dutch oven; cover and bake 2 hours.

5. Meanwhile, prepare Parmesan Gremolata.

6. Remove bay leaf; discard. Remove veal shanks to individual serving bowls; spoon vegetable mixture over each serving. Sprinkle with Parmesan Gremolata.

Makes 4 to 6 servings

Parmesan Gremolata

1 **lemon**
⅓ **cup freshly grated Parmesan cheese**
¼ **cup chopped fresh parsley**
1 **clove garlic, minced**

Grate lemon peel with finest side of box-shaped grater, being careful to remove only yellow portion and not any of the bitter, white pith. Grate entire lemon peel over small bowl. Add cheese, parsley and garlic; mix well. Cover; refrigerate. *Makes about ⅓ cup*

Veal Cordon Bleu

4 thin veal cutlets or veal scaloppine
(4 ounces each)
Salt and black pepper
1 egg, beaten
1 tablespoon milk
4 slices prosciutto or cooked ham
(½ ounce each)
2 slices Swiss or Gruyère cheese
(1 ounce each), cut in half
1 cup seasoned fine dry bread crumbs
½ cup all-purpose flour
2 tablespoons olive oil

1. Place each veal cutlet between sheets of waxed paper on cutting board. Pound each cutlet with meat mallet to ⅛- to ¼-inch thickness. (Omit step if using scaloppine.)

2. Lightly sprinkle 1 side of each cutlet with salt and pepper. Whisk together egg and milk in small bowl.

3. Place 1 prosciutto slice and 1 cheese slice half in center of each veal piece. Brush tops of cheese and edges of veal with milk mixture. Fold long edges of veal over prosciutto and cheese, pressing gently to adhere. Beginning at short ends, roll veal jelly-roll fashion. Secure with wooden picks.

4. Place bread crumbs and flour on separate plates. Roll veal in flour, then dip in milk mixture. Roll veal in bread crumbs, pressing to coat well. Place on ungreased baking sheet; cover and refrigerate 1 hour.

5. Heat oil in large skillet over medium-high heat until hot. Add veal; cook 20 minutes, turning veal ¼ turn every 5 minutes, or until veal is tender. Remove toothpicks; discard.   *Makes 4 servings*

Grilled Salami Sandwich

½ cup drained HEBREW NATIONAL®
    Sauerkraut
½ teaspoon caraway seeds
4 slices rye bread
2 tablespoons prepared oil and vinegar
    based coleslaw dressing, divided
4 ounces HEBREW NATIONAL® Beef
    Salami or Lean Beef Salami Chub,
    thinly sliced
1 tablespoon parve margarine, divided

Combine sauerkraut and caraway seeds in small bowl. Heat medium nonstick skillet over medium heat. For each sandwich, spread 1 bread slice with 1 tablespoon coleslaw dressing. Cover with salami, sauerkraut mixture and second bread slice. Spread outside of sandwich with margarine. Cook in skillet 6 minutes or until lightly browned on each side. Repeat with remaining ingredients.   *Makes 2 servings*

Pork & Lamb

O'PLENTY

Savory Pork Roast

2 tablespoons lemon juice
1 tablespoon olive oil
2 teaspoons LAWRY'S® Seasoned Salt
1 teaspoon LAWRY'S® Garlic Salt
1 teaspoon dried thyme, crushed
1 (5-pound) boneless pork roast
1 to 2 tablespoons all-purpose flour
½ cup water

In small bowl, combine lemon juice, oil, Seasoned Salt,
Garlic Salt and thyme. In shallow roasting pan, place
meat; brush with seasoning mixture. Bake, uncovered,
in 350°F oven 2 hours or until internal meat
temperature reaches 160°F. Remove meat to serving
platter, reserving drippings in pan; keep meat warm.
Combine flour and water; add to drippings in pan.
Cook over medium heat until thickened, stirring
constantly.   *Makes 6 to 8 servings*

Presentation: Serve gravy over slices of roast—great
with mashed potatoes.

Honey Pepper Pork Roast

1 boneless pork loin roast (about
    2½ pounds)
¼ cup honey
2 tablespoons Dijon-style mustard
2 tablespoons crushed mixed peppercorns
½ teaspoon dried thyme, crushed, *or*
    1½ teaspoons minced fresh thyme
½ teaspoon salt
    Honey Cranberry Relish (recipe
    follows)

Carefully score roast ½ inch deep completely around roast, taking care not to cut string holding roast together. Combine honey, mustard, peppercorns, thyme and salt in small bowl; mix well. Place roast on rack in roasting pan. Spoon or brush ⅔ of honey mixture over pork to coat.

Roast at 325°F 30 minutes; brush with remaining honey mixture. Roast 20 to 30 minutes longer or until meat thermometer registers 155° to 160°F. Let stand, tented with foil, 10 minutes before slicing. Serve with Honey Cranberry Relish.   *Makes 8 servings*

Honey Cranberry Relish

1 medium orange
1 package (12 ounces) fresh or frozen
    whole cranberries
¾ cup honey

Quarter and slice unpeeled orange, removing seeds.
Coarsely chop orange and cranberries. Place in
medium saucepan and stir in honey. Bring to a boil
over medium-high heat and cook 3 to 4 minutes. Cool.

Makes 2¼ cups

Favorite recipe from **National Honey Board**

Regal Crown Roast of Pork

 1 **(16 rib) pork crown roast**
    Salt and pepper
 ⅔ **cup sliced leek**
 ½ **cup sliced celery**
 4 **tablespoons butter or margarine**
 1 **large apple, cored and diced**
12 **Thick-style KAVLI® crispbreads**
 1 **cup finely diced JARLSBERG® cheese**
 ½ **cup dried cherries or dried cranberries**
 ¼ **cup chopped parsley**
 2 **teaspoons salt**
 ½ **teaspoon ground pepper**
 ½ **cup white wine or unsweetened apple**
    juice
    Pan Sauce (recipe follows)
    Steamed baby carrots and leek bundles
    (optional)

Preheat oven to 325°F. Rub roast with salt and pepper.
Place in shallow roasting pan; insert meat
thermometer in thickest part of roast not touching
bone. Roast 1 hour and 45 minutes or until
thermometer registers 150°F.

While roast cooks, prepare stuffing. Cook leek and
celery in butter 5 minutes; stir in apple and cook
3 minutes longer. Remove from heat. Crush or cut
crispbreads into ½-inch pieces (about 2 cups). Place in
large bowl; add cheese, cherries, parsley, salt, pepper
and apple mixture; mix well. Sprinkle with wine; toss
until evenly moistened.

Remove roast from oven. Spoon stuffing into center, mounding it. (Spoon any extra stuffing into small buttered casserole to bake along with roast.) Return roast to oven and roast about 1 hour or until thermometer registers 160°F or slightly under. (Meat will continue to cook as it stands.) Remove roast to serving platter and keep warm. Let rest at least 10 minutes. Prepare Pan Sauce. To serve, carve between ribs. Decorate platter with steamed baby carrots and bundles of small leeks. Serve with Pan Sauce.

Makes 8 servings

Pan Sauce: Deglaze roasting pan with 1 cup water and ½ cup white wine; strain into small saucepan. Skim off fat. Bring to a boil. Blend 2 tablespoons flour with 3 to 4 tablespoons cold water to make a smooth paste. Add to boiling liquid, stirring constantly, until thickened. Lower heat and simmer on low 5 minutes. Add salt and pepper to taste.

Makes about 1½ cups

Fruited Boneless Pork Loin

- 1 **cup pitted prunes**
- 1 **cup dried apricots**
- 1 **(3-pound) boneless pork loin roast**
- 1 **clove garlic, cut into thin strips**
- 3 **tablespoons FILIPPO BERIO® Olive Oil, divided**
   Salt and freshly ground black pepper
- 2 **onions, each cut into 6 wedges**
- 2 **tart apples (such as Granny Smith), peeled, cored and each cut into 8 wedges**
- 8 **fresh sage leaves, chopped***
- 1 **tablespoon lime or lemon juice**
- 1 **cup plus 2 tablespoons chicken broth, divided**
- 3 **tablespoons all-purpose flour**
- ½ **cup reserved prune/apricot liquid**
- ¼ **cup Madeira wine**

*Omit sage if fresh is unavailable. Do not substitute dried sage leaves.

Cover prunes and apricots with cold water; soak at least 2 hours or overnight. Drain, reserving liquid. Preheat oven to 400°F. With tip of sharp knife, cut slashes at 1-inch intervals in pork. Insert garlic into scored pork flesh. Place pork in large shallow roasting pan; insert meat thermometer into center of thickest part of roast. Drizzle with 2 tablespoons olive oil; season with salt and pepper. Roast 1 hour. Add onions, apples and sage to fruit mixture. Drizzle with lime juice. Spoon around pork in roasting pan; baste pork with juices and remaining 1 tablespoon olive oil. Pour 2 tablespoons broth over pork. Roast 30 to 40 minutes or until meat thermometer registers 160°F, turning and basting fruit mixture frequently with juices. Transfer pork to warm serving platter. Surround with fruit mixture; keep warm. Pour drippings from roasting pan into measuring cup; skim off fat. Return juices to roasting pan. In roasting pan over medium heat, gradually stir flour into juices until smooth. Cook and stir 1 minute. Add remaining 1 cup broth, reserved liquid and Madeira. Bring to a boil, stirring frequently. Reduce heat to low; simmer 5 minutes. Season to taste with additional salt and pepper. Serve hot with pork and fruit mixture. Carve pork into thin slices.

Makes 4 to 6 servings

Pork Loin Roasted in Chili-Spice Sauce

    1   cup chopped onion
    ¼   cup orange juice
    2   cloves garlic
    1   tablespoon cider vinegar
    1½   teaspoons chili powder
    ¼   teaspoon dried thyme leaves
    ¼   teaspoon ground cumin
    ¼   teaspoon ground cinnamon
    ⅛   teaspoon ground allspice
    ⅛   teaspoon ground cloves
    1½   pounds pork loin, fat trimmed
    3   firm large bananas
    2   limes
    1   ripe large papaya, peeled, seeded, cubed
    1   green onion, minced

Preheat oven to 350°F. Combine onion, orange juice
and garlic in food processor; process until finely
chopped. Pour into medium saucepan; stir in vinegar,
chili powder, thyme, cumin, cinnamon, allspice and
cloves. Simmer over medium-high heat about
5 minutes or until thickened. Cut ¼-inch-deep
lengthwise slits down top and bottom of roast at
1½-inch intervals. Spread about 1 tablespoon spice
paste over bottom; place roast in baking pan. Spread
remaining 2 tablespoons spice paste over sides and top,
working mixture into slits. Cover. Bake 45 minutes or
until meat thermometer registers 140°F.

Remove roast from oven; *increase oven temperature to 450°F.* Pour off liquid; discard. Return roast to oven and bake, uncovered, 15 minutes or until spice mixture browns lightly and meat thermometer registers 150°F in center of roast. Remove from oven; tent with foil and let stand 5 minutes before slicing.

Meanwhile, spray 9-inch pie plate or cake pan with nonstick cooking spray. Peel bananas and slice diagonally into ½-inch-thick pieces. Place in pan. Squeeze juice from 1 lime over bananas; toss to coat evenly. Cover; bake in oven while roast stands or until hot. Stir in papaya, juice of remaining lime and green onion. Serve with roast.   *Makes 6 servings*

Roast Pork with Banana Sauce

- 1 pork loin roast (about 3 pounds)
- 1 tablespoon vegetable oil
  LAWRY'S® Seasoned Salt to taste
  LAWRY'S® Seasoned Pepper to taste
- ¼ cup LAWRY'S® Minced Onion with Green Onion Flakes
- ¼ teaspoon LAWRY'S® Garlic Powder with Parsley
- 1 can (4 ounces) diced green chilies
- 2 ripe bananas
- 1½ cups orange juice

Preheat oven to 350°F. In large skillet, brown pork on all sides in hot oil; remove from pan. Season pork with Seasoned Salt, Seasoned Pepper, Minced Onion with Green Onion Flakes and Garlic Powder with Parsley. Place in roasting pan. Purée remaining ingredients in food processor, using steel blade. Pour sauce over roast; cover and bake 1½ to 2 hours, basting frequently. Remove roast to serving platter; keep warm. Skim fat from sauce. Serve sauce in separate bowl.

Makes 6 servings

Fruited Pork Loin

1   **cup dried apricot halves**
½   **cup dry sherry**
1   **(3- to 5-pound) center cut pork rib or**
      loin roast, backbone cracked
1   **cup KARO® Light or Dark Corn Syrup**
1   **tablespoon grated orange peel**
½   **cup orange juice**
¼   **cup soy sauce**

1. In small saucepan, combine apricots and sherry. Cover and cook over medium heat, stirring occasionally, until liquid is absorbed.

2. Trim excess fat from surface of roast. Cut deep slits in meat directly over rib bones; insert 3 or 4 apricots in each slit. Place roast, boneside down, on rack in roasting pan.

3. Roast in 325°F oven 1 to 2 hours* or until meat thermometer registers 160°F.

4. Meanwhile, prepare glaze. In small saucepan, stir corn syrup, orange peel, orange juice and soy sauce. Bring to boil; reduce heat and simmer 5 minutes. Set aside half of glaze to serve with pork loin.

5. Brush pork loin frequently with remaining glaze during last 30 minutes of roasting. Serve with reserved glaze.   *Makes 6 to 10 servings*

*Roast pork loin at 325°F for 20 to 25 minutes per pound.

Spanish Roasted Pork Loin and Eggplant Purée

1 (2½-pound) boneless pork loin roast
2 tablespoons FILIPPO BERIO® Olive Oil
2 cloves garlic, minced
1 tablespoon paprika
1½ teaspoons dried oregano leaves
½ teaspoon salt
¼ teaspoon freshly ground black pepper
Eggplant Purée (recipe follows)

Place pork in large shallow glass dish. In small bowl, combine olive oil, garlic, paprika, oregano, salt and pepper. Spread over all sides of pork. Cover; marinate in refrigerator at least 2 hours or overnight.

Preheat oven to 350°F. Remove pork from refrigerator 1 hour before roasting. Place in large shallow roasting pan; insert meat thermometer into center of thickest part of pork. Roast, uncovered, 1 hour and 15 minutes or until meat thermometer registers 160°F. Transfer pork to carving board; tent with foil. Let stand 5 to 10 minutes before carving. Cut into thin slices. Serve on bed of Eggplant Purée.   *Makes 8 servings*

Eggplant Purée

2 **small eggplants (about 1 pound each)**
11 **tablespoons FILIPPO BERIO® Olive
       Oil, divided**
8 **cloves garlic, unpeeled**
1 **egg yolk**
1 **tablespoon salt**
2 **tablespoons lemon juice**

Preheat oven to 350°F. Cut eggplants in half
lengthwise. Brush cut sides with 2 tablespoons olive
oil. Place, cut side down, on baking sheet. In small
bowl, toss garlic cloves with 1 tablespoon olive oil.
Place garlic cloves on same baking sheet. Bake
30 minutes; remove garlic. Bake eggplant an additional
45 minutes or until tender. Cool slightly.

Scrape flesh from eggplant into blender container or
food processor. Slip off skins from garlic. Add garlic,
egg yolk and salt to blender; process until smooth.
While machine is running, slowly drizzle in remaining
8 tablespoons olive oil. Add lemon juice. Transfer
mixture to medium saucepan. Cook over low heat
10 minutes, stirring often, until hot. *Do not boil.*

Makes about 3 cups

Carne Adovada

8 to 10 dried red New Mexico or
    California chilies
2 cups water
⅓ cup finely chopped onion
1 clove garlic, minced
1 teaspoon dried oregano, crushed
½ teaspoon salt
½ teaspoon ground cumin
1½ pounds lean boneless pork butt *or*
    2 pounds pork chops, cut ½ inch
    thick

Wash chilies; remove stems and seeds. Place in 3-quart pan with water. Cover and simmer 20 minutes or until chilies are very soft. Pour chilies and liquid into blender or food processor container fitted with metal blade; process until puréed. Push purée through wire strainer; discard pulp. Add onion, garlic, oregano, salt and cumin to chili mixture.

If using pork butt, trim excess fat. Cut meat into ½-inch slices, then cut into strips about 1 inch wide and 3 inches long. If using pork chops, trim fat.

Place meat in heavy self-sealing plastic bag. Pour chili mixture over meat; seal bag. Refrigerate 1 to 2 days. Preheat oven to 325°F. Transfer meat and chili mixture to 2½-quart casserole dish; cover. Bake 2 to 2½ hours or until meat is very tender. Skim and discard fat before serving. *Makes 4 to 6 servings*

Pork Tenderloin Diane

1   **pound pork tenderloin, cut into
    8 crosswise pieces**
2   **teaspoons lemon pepper**
2   **tablespoons butter**
2   **tablespoons lemon juice**
1   **tablespoon Worcestershire sauce**
1   **teaspoon Dijon-style mustard**
1   **tablespoon minced parsley or chives**

Pound each tenderloin slice, with meat mallet, to
1-inch thickness; sprinkle with lemon pepper. Heat
butter in heavy skillet; cook tenderloin medallions 3 to
4 minutes on each side or until fork-tender. Remove
medallions to serving platter; keep warm. Add lemon
juice, Worcestershire sauce and mustard to pan juices
in skillet. Cook until heated through. Pour sauce over
medallions and sprinkle with parsley; serve.

Makes 4 servings

Favorite recipe from **National Pork Producers Council**

Pork Tenderloin with Mandarin Salsa

1½ pounds boneless pork loin chops, cut into ¼-inch strips
1 cup orange juice
1 medium green bell pepper, finely chopped
1 can (10½ ounces) mandarin orange segments, drained and chopped
1⅓ cups chopped red onion, divided
½ cup frozen whole kernel corn, thawed
2 tablespoons olive oil, divided
4 teaspoons bottled minced garlic, divided
1½ teaspoons chili powder, divided
1¼ teaspoons salt, divided
1½ teaspoons cumin
¼ teaspoon ground black pepper

1. Combine pork and orange juice in medium bowl. Set aside.

2. Combine bell pepper, mandarin orange segments, ⅓ cup onion, corn, 1 tablespoon oil, 1 teaspoon garlic, ¼ teaspoon chili powder and ¼ teaspoon salt in another medium bowl. Set aside.

3. Heat remaining 1 tablespoon oil in large nonstick skillet over medium-high heat. Add remaining 1 cup onion and 3 teaspoons garlic. Cook and stir 5 minutes or until onion is softened and starting to brown.

4. Meanwhile, drain pork, reserving orange juice marinade. Toss pork, remaining 1¼ teaspoons chili powder, cumin, remaining 1 teaspoon salt and ground pepper in large bowl; add to skillet. Cook and stir

5 minutes or until pork is cooked through and lightly
browned. Add ⅓ cup reserved orange juice marinade to
skillet; bring to a boil. Reduce heat; simmer 1 to
2 minutes or until liquid thickens slightly. Serve
immediately with Mandarin Salsa.

Makes 4 servings

Honey Sesame Tenderloin

1   **pound whole pork tenderloin**
½   **cup soy sauce**
2   **cloves garlic, minced**
1   **tablespoon grated fresh ginger *or***
    1 teaspoon ground ginger
1   **tablespoon sesame oil**
¼   **cup honey**
2   **tablespoons brown sugar**
4   **tablespoons sesame seed**

Combine soy sauce, garlic, ginger and sesame oil. Place
tenderloin in resealable plastic bag; pour soy sauce
mixture over to coat. Marinate 2 hours or overnight in
refrigerator. Preheat oven to 375°F. Remove pork from
marinade; pat dry. Mix together honey and brown
sugar on a plate. Place sesame seed on a separate plate.
Roll pork in honey mixture, coating well; then roll in
sesame seed. Roast in shallow pan 20 to 30 minutes, or
until inserted meat thermometer registers 160°F.
Remove to serving platter; slice thinly to serve.

Makes 4 servings

Favorite recipe from **National Pork Producers Council**

Pork with Sweet Hungarian Paprika

1 teaspoon olive oil, divided
1 onion, sliced
2 cloves garlic, minced
1 tomato, chopped
1 medium red bell pepper, chopped
1 large Anaheim or 1 medium green bell
  pepper, chopped
1 can (10½ ounces) ⅓-less-salt chicken
  broth, divided
2 tablespoons sweet Hungarian paprika
1 pork tenderloin (12 ounces)
3 tablespoons all-purpose flour
⅓ cup sour cream
6 cups cooked enriched egg noodles
  (6 ounces uncooked)

1. Heat ½ teaspoon olive oil in medium saucepan over medium heat until hot. Add onion and garlic. Cook and stir 2 minutes. Add tomato, peppers, ½ cup chicken broth and paprika. Reduce heat to low; cover and simmer 5 minutes.

2. Cut pork crosswise into 8 slices. Pound pork between two pieces of plastic wrap to ¼-inch thickness, using flat side of meat mallet or rolling pin. Heat remaining ½ teaspoon olive oil in nonstick skillet over medium heat until hot. Cook pork 1 minute on each side or until browned. Add onion mixture. Reduce heat to low and simmer 5 minutes. Whisk together remaining chicken broth and flour in small bowl.

3. Remove pork from skillet; keep warm. Stir flour mixture into liquid in skillet. Bring liquid to a boil; remove from heat. Stir in sour cream. Serve sauce over pork and noodles. *Makes 4 servings*

Quick Pork with Orange-Basil Sauce

   1 **pound pork tenderloin, cut into ¼-inch slices**
   1 **teaspoon vegetable oil**
   1 **cup DOLE® Pineapple Orange Juice or Mandarin Tangerine Juice**
   2 **garlic cloves, finely chopped**
   2 **teaspoons cornstarch**
 1½ **teaspoons dried basil leaves**
   1 **teaspoon grated orange peel**
   2 **DOLE® Oranges, sliced**
   1 **DOLE® Green Onion, sliced**

• **Cook** and stir pork over medium-high heat in hot oil in large, nonstick skillet 3 to 5 minutes or until pork is no longer pink. Remove pork; drain.

• **Stir** together juice, garlic, cornstarch, basil and orange peel in skillet until blended. Bring to boil; cook 2 minutes or until sauce thickens slightly. Return pork to skillet; cook 1 minute or until heated through.

• **Place** pork slices and orange slices on 4 dinner plates; sprinkle with green onion. Garnish with fresh basil leaves, if desired. *Makes 4 servings*

Roasted Pork Tenderloin with Fresh Plum Salsa

2 to 3 limes
Fresh Plum Salsa (recipe follows)
1 whole well-trimmed pork tenderloin
(about 1 pound)
⅓ cup soy sauce
1 tablespoon Oriental sesame oil
2 cloves garlic, minced
2 tablespoons firmly packed brown sugar

1. Cut limes crosswise in half; squeeze with citrus reamer to extract juice into measuring cup. Measure 2 tablespoons; set aside. Prepare Fresh Plum Salsa using remaining juice.

2. Place tenderloin in large resealable plastic food storage bag. Combine soy sauce, 2 tablespoons lime juice, oil and garlic in small bowl. Pour over tenderloin. Seal bag tightly, turning to coat. Marinate in refrigerator overnight, turning occasionally.

3. Preheat oven to 375°F. Drain tenderloin, reserving 2 tablespoons marinade. Combine reserved marinade and sugar in small saucepan. Bring to a boil over medium-high heat. Cook 1 minute, stirring once; set aside.

4. To ensure even cooking, tuck narrow end of tenderloin under roast, forming even thickness of meat. Secure with cotton string. Place tenderloin on meat rack in shallow roasting pan. Brush with reserved sugar mixture.

5. Insert meat thermometer into tenderloin. Bake
15 minutes; brush with remaining sugar mixture.
Bake 10 minutes more or until thermometer registers
160°F.

6. Transfer tenderloin to cutting board; tent with foil.
Let stand 10 minutes. Remove string from tenderloin;
discard. Carve tenderloin into thin slices with carving
knife. Serve with Fresh Plum Salsa.

Makes 4 servings

Fresh Plum Salsa

    2 **cups coarsely chopped red plums
       (about 3)**
    2 **tablespoons chopped green onion**
    2 **tablespoons firmly packed brown sugar**
    1 **tablespoon chopped fresh cilantro**
    2 **teaspoons freshly squeezed lime juice
       Dash ground red pepper**

Combine all ingredients in small bowl. Cover;
refrigerate at least 2 hours.   *Makes 1 cup*

Jamaican Pork Skillet

1 tablespoon vegetable oil
4 well-trimmed center cut pork chops,
   cut ½ inch thick
¾ teaspoon blackened or Cajun seasoning
   mix
¼ teaspoon ground allspice
1 cup chunky salsa, divided
1 can (15 ounces) black beans, drained
   and rinsed
1 can (about 8 ounces) whole kernel
   corn, drained, or 1 cup thawed frozen
   whole kernel corn
1 tablespoon fresh lime juice

1. Heat oil in large deep skillet over medium-high heat until hot. Sprinkle both sides of pork chops with blackened seasoning mix and allspice; cook 2 minutes per side or until browned.

2. Pour ½ cup salsa over pork chops; reduce heat to medium. Cover and simmer about 12 minutes or until pork is no longer pink.

3. While pork chops are simmering, combine beans, corn, remaining ½ cup salsa and lime juice in medium bowl; mix well. Serve bean mixture with pork chops.

Makes 4 servings

Pork Chops with Apples and Stuffing

4   pork chops, ½ inch thick
     Salt and pepper
1   tablespoon oil
2   medium apples, cored, cut into
       8 wedges
1   cup apple juice
2   cups STOVE TOP® Cornbread Stuffing
       Mix in the Canister
¼   cup chopped pecans

SPRINKLE chops with salt and pepper. Heat oil in large skillet on medium-high heat. Add chops and apples; cook until chops are browned on both sides.

STIR in apple juice. Bring to boil. Reduce heat to low; cover and simmer 8 minutes or until chops are cooked through. Remove chops from skillet.

STIR stuffing mix and pecans into skillet. Return chops to skillet; cover. Remove from heat. Let stand 5 minutes.   *Makes 4 servings*

Glazed Stuffed Pork Chops

2 medium cooking apples
3 cups prepared cabbage slaw blend
¼ cup raisins
¾ cup apple cider, divided
2 tablespoons maple-flavored pancake
    syrup
4 teaspoons spicy brown mustard, divided
2 lean pork chops (about 6 ounces each),
    1 inch thick
  Nonstick cooking spray
2 teaspoons cornstarch

1. Quarter and core apples. Chop 6 quarters; reserve remaining 2 quarters. Combine chopped apples, slaw blend, raisins, ¼ cup apple cider, syrup and 2 teaspoons mustard in large saucepan. Cover and cook over medium heat 5 minutes or until cabbage is tender.

2. Make a pocket in each pork chop by cutting horizontally through chop almost to bone. Fill each pocket with about ¼ cup cabbage-apple mixture. Keep remaining cabbage-apple mixture warm over low heat.

3. Spray medium nonstick skillet with cooking spray. Heat over medium heat until hot. Brown pork chops about 3 minutes on each side. Add ¼ cup apple cider. Reduce heat to low; cover and simmer 8 minutes or until pork is barely pink in center. Remove pork from skillet; keep warm.

4. Add liquid from remaining cabbage-apple mixture to skillet. Combine remaining ¼ cup apple cider,

2 teaspoons mustard and cornstarch in small bowl
until smooth. Stir into liquid in skillet. Simmer over
medium heat until thickened. Spoon glaze over chops
and cabbage-apple mixture. Slice remaining 2 apple
quarters; divide between servings.

Makes 2 servings

Jerked Pork Chops

- **2 teaspoons onion powder**
- **1 teaspoon sugar**
- **1 teaspoon dried thyme leaves, crushed**
- **½ teaspoon salt**
- **½ teaspoon ground allspice**
- **½ teaspoon ground red pepper**
- **¼ teaspoon ground nutmeg**
- **4 boneless pork loin chops, trimmed of fat**
- **4 cups cooked white rice**
- **2 green onions, finely chopped**

1. Combine onion powder, sugar, thyme, salt, allspice,
ground red pepper and nutmeg in small bowl; mix
well. Rub pork chops on both sides with spice mixture.

2. Spray nonstick skillet with nonstick cooking spray;
heat over medium heat. Cook pork chops about
5 minutes per side or until juicy and barely pink in
center.

3. Serve pork chops over rice; sprinkle with green
onions.

Makes 4 servings

Pork Chops with Apples and Bourbon

4 boneless loin pork chops, cut 1-inch
   thick, fat trimmed
1 clove garlic, halved lengthwise
   Pinch sage
2 tablespoons margarine or butter
¼ teaspoon TABASCO® pepper sauce
1 teaspoon fresh lemon juice
½ cup chopped onion
1 medium apple, preferably Granny
   Smith, peeled, cored and diced
⅓ cup bourbon or apple cider

Pat pork chops dry with paper towel; rub each on both sides with cut sides of garlic. Sprinkle with sage. In large skillet over medium-high heat, combine margarine and TABASCO sauce and heat until mixture sizzles. Add chops; cook 12 to 14 minutes, turning once, or until chops are golden brown on both sides and cooked through. Remove from pan; sprinkle with lemon juice and keep warm.

Add onion to skillet; cook and stir over medium heat 1 minute. Stir in apple; cook 1 minute longer. Add bourbon; cook, stirring, 1 minute. Spoon onion, apple and bourbon sauce over pork chops; serve immediately.

Makes 4 servings

Herbed Tomato Pork Chops and Stuffing

1 tablespoon oil
4 pork chops, ½ inch thick
1 can (8 ounces) stewed tomatoes
1 can (8 ounces) tomato sauce
1 medium green pepper, chopped
½ teaspoon dried oregano leaves
¼ teaspoon ground pepper
2 cups STOVE TOP® Stuffing Mix for Chicken in the Canister
1 cup (4 ounces) shredded mozzarella cheese, divided

HEAT oil in large skillet on medium-high heat. Add chops; brown on both sides.

STIR in tomatoes, tomato sauce, green pepper, oregano and ground pepper. Bring to boil. Reduce heat to low; cover and simmer 15 minutes or until chops are cooked through. Remove chops from skillet.

STIR stuffing mix and ½ cup of the cheese into skillet. Return chops to skillet. Sprinkle with remaining ½ cup cheese; cover. Remove from heat. Let stand 5 minutes.

Makes 4 servings

LAWRY'S® Home-Baked Ribs

 2 tablespoons LAWRY'S® Seasoned Salt
 6 pounds lean baby back ribs
1½ cups lemon juice
 ½ bottle (3.5 ounces) liquid smoke
 1 bottle (16 ounces) barbecue sauce
   Syrup from 1 can (16 ounces) peaches*
   (about ½ cup)

Sprinkle Seasoned Salt onto both sides of ribs. In large resealable bag or shallow glass baking dish, place ribs. Combine lemon juice and liquid smoke; pour over ribs. Seal bag or cover dish. Marinate in refrigerator at least 2 hours or overnight, turning occasionally. Remove ribs from marinade. Place in shallow baking pan. Bake in 350°F oven 1 hour. Reduce oven temperature to 300°F. Combine barbecue sauce and peach syrup; pour over ribs. Bake 30 to 45 minutes longer or until ribs are tender.   *Makes 8 servings*

*Peaches can be refrigerated for later use.

Spareribs with Zesty Honey Sauce

1   **cup chili sauce**
½   **to ¾ cup honey**
¼   **cup minced onion**
2   **tablespoons dry red wine (optional)**
1   **tablespoon Worcestershire sauce**
1   **teaspoon Dijon-style mustard**
3   **pounds pork spareribs**
    Salt and pepper

Combine chili sauce, honey, onion, wine, if desired,
Worcestershire sauce and mustard in small saucepan.
Cook and stir over medium heat until mixture comes
to a boil. Reduce heat to low and simmer, uncovered,
5 minutes.

Sprinkle spareribs with salt and pepper. Place on rack
in roasting pan; cover with foil. Roast at 375°F 35 to
45 minutes. Uncover and brush generously with sauce.
Roast 45 minutes, brushing with sauce every
15 minutes, until spareribs are fully cooked and tender.
Cut spareribs into serving portions and serve with
remaining sauce.   *Makes 4 servings*

Favorite recipe from **National Honey Board**

Honey Glazed Ham

¼ cup honey
3 tablespoons water
1½ teaspoons dry mustard
½ teaspoon ground ginger
¼ teaspoon ground cloves
1 fully cooked ham steak (about 12 to 16 ounces)

Combine honey, water and spices in small bowl. On top rack of preheated oven broiler, broil ham steak on both sides until lightly browned and thoroughly heated. *Or,* pan-fry ham steak on both sides in nonstick skillet over medium-high heat.

Place ham on heated serving dish; set aside. Add honey mixture to pan drippings and bring to a boil. Simmer 1 to 2 minutes, stirring. Brush sauce over ham; serve remaining sauce separately.   *Makes 4 servings*

Favorite recipe from **National Honey Board**

Baked Ham with Sweet and Spicy Glaze

1 (8-pound) bone-in smoked half ham
     Sweet and Spicy Glaze (recipe follows)

Preheat oven to 325°F. Place ham, fat side up, on rack in roasting pan. Insert meat thermometer with bulb in thickest part away from fat or bone. Roast ham in oven about 3 hours.

Prepare Sweet and Spicy Glaze. Remove ham from oven; do not turn oven off. Generously apply glaze over ham; return to oven 30 minutes longer or until meat thermometer registers internal temperature of 160°F. Remove ham from oven and reglaze. Let ham sit about 20 minutes before slicing.

Makes 8 to 10 servings

Sweet and Spicy Glaze

- ¾ **cup packed brown sugar**
- ⅓ **cup cider vinegar**
- ¼ **cup golden raisins**
- 1 **can (8¾ ounces) sliced peaches in heavy syrup, drained, chopped, syrup reserved**
- 1 **tablespoon cornstarch**
- ¼ **cup orange juice**
- 1 **can (8¼ ounces) crushed pineapple in syrup, undrained**
- 1 **tablespoon grated orange peel**
- 1 **garlic clove, crushed**
- ½ **teaspoon crushed red pepper flakes**
- ½ **teaspoon grated fresh ginger**

Combine brown sugar, vinegar, raisins and peach syrup in medium saucepan. Bring to boil over high heat; reduce to low and simmer 8 to 10 minutes. In small bowl, dissolve cornstarch in orange juice; add to brown sugar mixture. Add remaining ingredients; mix well. Cook over medium heat, stirring constantly, until mixture boils and thickens. Remove from heat.

Makes about 2 cups

German-Style Bratwurst & Sauerkraut

    6 slices bacon
    1 small onion, chopped
    1 clove garlic, minced
    1 (32-ounce) jar or can sauerkraut,
         rinsed and well drained
    2 medium potatoes, peeled and sliced
    1½ to 2 cups water
    ½ cup apple juice or dry white wine
    2 tablespoons brown sugar
    1 teaspoon instant chicken bouillon
         granules
    1 teaspoon caraway seeds
    1 dried bay leaf
    1 pound BOB EVANS FARMS® Bratwurst
         (5 links)
    2 medium apples, cored and sliced

Cook bacon in large skillet over medium-high heat
until crisp. Remove bacon; drain and crumble on paper
towel. Set aside. Drain off all but 2 tablespoons
drippings in skillet. Add onion and garlic to drippings;
cook over medium heat until tender, stirring
occasionally. Stir in sauerkraut, potatoes, 1½ cups
water, juice, brown sugar, bouillon, caraway and dried
bay leaf. Add remaining ½ cup water, if necessary, to
cover potatoes. Bring to a boil over high heat.

Meanwhile, make 3 or 4 diagonal ¼-inch-deep cuts into
one side of each bratwurst. Cook bratwurst in large
skillet over medium heat until browned, turning
occasionally. Add bratwurst to sauerkraut mixture.
Reduce heat to low; simmer, covered, 20 to 30 minutes

or until potatoes are just tender, stirring occasionally. Add apples; cook, covered, 5 to 10 minutes or until apples are just tender. Stir in reserved bacon. Remove and discard dried bay leaf. Serve hot. Refrigerate leftovers.   *Makes 5 servings*

Homestyle Meatloaf

½ cup ketchup
2 teaspoons brown sugar
1 teaspoon dry mustard
1 pound BOB EVANS FARMS® Original Recipe Roll Sausage
1 pound lean ground beef
1 cup uncooked quick oats
½ cup chopped onion
1 egg, beaten
1 teaspoon salt
¼ teaspoon black pepper

Preheat oven to 350°F. Combine ketchup, brown sugar and mustard in small bowl; set aside. Combine ⅓ cup ketchup mixture and remaining ingredients in large bowl; mix well. Shape mixture into loaf in large shallow baking dish. Bake 1 hour; remove from oven. Pour remaining ketchup mixture over loaf; bake 10 minutes more. Let stand 5 minutes before slicing. Serve hot. Refrigerate leftovers.

Makes 6 to 8 servings

Ham and Swiss Sandwiches with Citrus Mayonnaise

¼ cup GREY POUPON® Dijon Mustard
¼ cup mayonnaise*
1 tablespoon lime juice
1 tablespoon honey
½ teaspoon grated lime peel
¼ teaspoon ground black pepper
8 (½-inch-thick) slices black bread
1 cup shredded lettuce
8 slices tomato
4 ounces sliced Swiss cheese
12 ounces sliced honey-baked ham

In small bowl, blend mustard, mayonnaise, lime juice, honey, lime peel and pepper. Spread about 1 tablespoon mustard mixture on each bread slice. On each of 4 bread slices, layer ¼ cup lettuce, 2 tomato slices, 1 ounce cheese and 3 ounces ham. Top with remaining bread slices. Serve with remaining mustard mixture.

Makes 4 sandwiches

*Lowfat mayonnaise may be substituted for regular mayonnaise.

Sloppy Joes

1 pound BOB EVANS FARMS® Italian
   Roll Sausage
1 medium onion, chopped
½ green bell pepper, chopped
½ cup ketchup
2 tablespoons Dijon mustard
2 tablespoons cider vinegar
1 tablespoon sugar
1 teaspoon minced garlic
8 sandwich buns, split and toasted

Crumble sausage into medium skillet. Add onion and
pepper. Cook over medium heat until sausage is
browned, stirring occasionally. Drain off any drippings.
Stir in all remaining ingredients except buns. Bring to
a boil. Reduce heat to low; simmer 30 minutes. Serve
hot on buns. Refrigerate leftovers.

Makes 8 servings

Bagel Dogs with Zesty BBQ Sauce

- 1½ cups ketchup
- ⅓ cup finely chopped onion
- ¼ cup packed light brown sugar
- 1 tablespoon cider vinegar
- 1 tablespoon Worcestershire sauce*
- 1 teaspoon hot pepper sauce
  Dash liquid smoke (optional)
- 8 HEBREW NATIONAL® Bagel Dogs

Combine ketchup, onion, sugar, vinegar, Worcestershire, hot sauce and liquid smoke in small saucepan. Bring to a boil over medium-high heat. Reduce heat; simmer 5 minutes, stirring occasionally.

Heat bagel dogs according to package directions. Serve bagel dogs with sauce.   *Makes 8 servings*

*Use a kosher-certified Worcestershire sauce that doesn't contain any fish product.

Reuben Dijon

¼ cup **GREY POUPON® COUNTRY DIJON®** Mustard
¼ cup **mayonnaise***
2 tablespoons **chili sauce**
1 tablespoon **sweet pickle relish**
8 slices **seeded rye bread**
4 ounces **sliced Swiss cheese**
8 ounces **sliced deli corned beef**
½ cup **sauerkraut**
2 tablespoons **margarine or butter, softened**

In small bowl, blend mustard, mayonnaise, chili sauce and pickle relish. Spread mixture on each bread slice. Layer 1 ounce cheese, 2 ounces corned beef and 2 tablespoons sauerkraut on each of 4 bread slices; top with remaining bread slices to form sandwiches. Spread outside of each sandwich with margarine or butter. In large skillet or griddle, over medium heat, brown sandwiches on each side until cheese melts, about 3 to 4 minutes. Cut sandwiches in half and serve immediately.   *Makes 4 sandwiches*

*Lowfat mayonnaise may be substituted for regular mayonnaise.

Barbecued Pork Sandwiches

2 **pork tenderloins (about 1½ pounds total)**
⅓ **cup prepared barbecue sauce**
½ **cup prepared horseradish**
4 **pita bread rounds, cut into halves**
1 **onion, thinly sliced**
4 **romaine lettuce leaves**
1 **red bell pepper, cut lengthwise into ¼-inch-thick slices**
1 **green bell pepper, cut lengthwise into ¼-inch-thick slices**

1. Preheat oven to 400°F. Place pork tenderloins in roasting pan; brush with barbecue sauce.

2. Bake tenderloins 15 minutes; turn and bake 15 minutes or until internal temperature reaches 155°F. Cover with foil; let stand 15 minutes.

3. Slice pork across grain. Spread horseradish on pita bread halves; stuff with pork, onion, lettuce and bell peppers. *Makes 4 servings*

Individual Sausage Melts

1 (10-ounce) package BOB EVANS
   FARMS® Skinless Link Sausage
½ cup sliced fresh mushrooms
⅓ cup chopped green bell pepper
⅓ cup chopped onion
2 cups chopped tomatoes
1 teaspoon dried oregano leaves
¼ teaspoon dried basil leaves
6 English muffins, split and toasted
12 slices part-skim mozzarella cheese

Chop sausage. Heat large nonstick skillet over
medium-high heat until hot. Add sausage, mushrooms,
pepper and onion; cook and stir until vegetables are
tender. Stir in tomatoes, oregano and basil. Reduce
heat to low; simmer 25 minutes or until liquid is
absorbed. Preheat oven to 350°F. Top each muffin half
with ¼ cup filling and 1 slice cheese. Bake just until
cheese melts. Serve hot. Refrigerate leftovers.

Makes 6 servings

Italian Subs

½ cup prepared Italian salad dressing
¼ cup GREY POUPON® Dijon Mustard
1 teaspoon dried oregano leaves
1 (18- to 20-inch) loaf Italian bread, split lengthwise
2 cups shredded lettuce
8 ounces deli sliced ham
4 ounces deli sliced salami
1 (7-ounce) jar roasted red peppers, cut into strips
4 ounces deli sliced Provolone cheese
1 small red onion, thinly sliced

In small bowl, whisk salad dressing, mustard and oregano until blended. Spread dressing mixture over cut sides of bread. Place half the lettuce on bottom half of bread; top with layers of ham, salami, pepper strips, cheese, onion and remaining lettuce. Replace bread top; slice and serve.   *Makes 6 to 8 servings*

Tacos

1   pound **BOB EVANS FARMS®** Original
     Recipe or Zesty Hot Roll Sausage
1   (8-ounce) jar taco sauce
1   package taco shells (10 to 12 count)
2   cups (8 ounces) shredded Cheddar
     cheese
1   large onion, chopped
2   tomatoes, chopped
¼   head iceberg lettuce, shredded

Preheat oven to 350°F. Crumble sausage into medium skillet; cook over medium-high heat until browned, stirring occasionally. Drain off any drippings. Stir in taco sauce. Bring to a boil. Reduce heat to low; simmer 5 minutes. Meanwhile, bake taco shells until warmed and crisp. To assemble tacos, place 2 tablespoons sausage mixture in each taco shell and top evenly with cheese, onion, tomatoes and lettuce. Serve hot. Refrigerate any leftover filling.

Makes 10 to 12 tacos

Sun-Dried Tomato and Pepper Stuffed Leg of Lamb with Garlic Chèvre Sauce

 1 (6- to 7-pound) leg of lamb, boned and
   butterflied
   Salt and black pepper
4½ ounces sun-dried tomatoes in oil,
   drained (about ¾ cup)
 2 red or green bell peppers, roasted,
   peeled and seeded
1½ cups olive oil
 2 tablespoons minced fresh rosemary
 2 tablespoons minced fresh thyme
 3 cloves garlic, minced
 1 teaspoon TABASCO® pepper sauce
   Garlic Chèvre Sauce (recipe follows)

Set lamb, skin side down, on work surface. Pat dry.
Sprinkle with salt and black pepper. Arrange tomatoes
and bell peppers down center of lamb. Roll up lamb;
secure with kitchen string. Set in roasting pan. Whisk
oil, herbs, garlic and TABASCO sauce in small bowl.
Pour over lamb, turning to coat. Cover and refrigerate
24 hours. Preheat oven to 450°F. Place uncovered lamb
in oven and reduce temperature to 325°F. Cook about
2 hours or 20 minutes per pound. Let stand
15 minutes before slicing. Serve with Garlic Chèvre
Sauce. *Makes 8 servings*

Garlic Chèvre Sauce

1 package (4 ounces) goat cheese
½ cup light cream
3 cloves garlic, minced
¼ teaspoon TABASCO® pepper sauce
1 sprig fresh rosemary

Combine goat cheese, cream, garlic and TABASCO sauce in microwavable dish; stir to combine. Microwave, uncovered, at MEDIUM (50% power) 45 seconds. Let stand 5 minutes and refrigerate.

Horseradish-Herb-Crusted Leg of Lamb

1 (6-pound) leg of lamb
2 cups fresh white bread crumbs
⅓ cup chopped parsley
3 garlic cloves, minced
1½ teaspoons dried rosemary leaves
1 teaspoon dried thyme leaves
½ cup BLUE BONNET® Vegetable Oil
Spread, melted
⅓ cup GREY POUPON® Horseradish
Specialty Mustard

Preheat oven to 350°F. Remove fat from lamb with sharp knife. Place on rack in roasting pan. Bake 1 hour. Remove from oven; cool 10 to 15 minutes.

Combine crumbs, parsley, garlic, rosemary and thyme; blend in spread. Spread top and sides of lamb with mustard. Press crumb mixture evenly and firmly into mustard. Lightly cover with foil. Bake 30 minutes. Remove foil; bake 30 to 45 minutes more or until meat thermometer registers internal temperature of 140°F to 160°F, depending on desired doneness. Remove from oven and let stand 10 minutes before slicing.

Makes 10 servings

High-Country Lamb

1 leg of lamb (6 to 7 pounds), boned and
   butterflied
¼ cup olive oil
¼ cup lemon juice
¼ cup dry vermouth
1 teaspoon dried oregano, crushed
1 clove garlic, minced
1 teaspoon salt
½ teaspoon pepper
½ teaspoon ground cumin
⅛ teaspoon hot pepper sauce

Place lamb in heavy self-sealing plastic bag. Combine
remaining ingredients in small bowl. Pour over meat;
seal bag. Refrigerate 4 to 6 hours or overnight, turning
bag occasionally to distribute marinade.

Preheat charcoal grill and grease grill rack. Remove
meat from refrigerator and bring to room temperature.
Remove meat from marinade and drain briefly; reserve
marinade. Place meat on grill 4 to 6 inches above solid
bed of coals (coals should be evenly covered with gray
ashes). Cook, uncovered, 50 minutes or until a meat
thermometer inserted in thickest part registers 140°F
for rare, 160°F for medium or 170°F for well-done,
basting frequently and turning as needed to brown
evenly. To serve, slice meat across grain.

Makes 8 to 10 servings

Herb-Roasted Racks of Lamb

2   whole racks (6 ribs each) lamb loin
      chops (2½ to 3 pounds)
½   cup mango chutney, chopped
2   to 3 cloves garlic, minced
1   cup fresh French or Italian bread
      crumbs
1   tablespoon chopped fresh thyme *or*
      1 teaspoon dried thyme leaves,
      crushed
1   tablespoon chopped fresh rosemary *or*
      1 teaspoon dried rosemary, crushed
1   tablespoon chopped fresh oregano *or*
      1 teaspoon dried oregano

1. Preheat oven to 400°F.

2. Trim fat from racks of lamb. Combine chutney and
garlic in small bowl; spread evenly over meaty side of
lamb. Combine remaining ingredients in separate
small bowl; pat crumb mixture evenly over chutney
mixture.

3. Place lamb racks, crumb sides up, on rack in
shallow roasting pan. Roast in oven about 30 minutes
or until instant-read thermometer inserted into lamb,
but not touching bone, registers 135°F for rare or to
desired doneness.

4. Place lamb on carving board. Slice between ribs into
individual chops with large carving knife. Serve
immediately.   *Makes 4 servings*

Rack of Lamb with Dijon-Mustard Sauce

1   rack of lamb (3 pounds), all visible fat
       removed
1   cup finely chopped fresh parsley
½   cup Dijon-style mustard
½   cup soft whole wheat bread crumbs
1   tablespoon chopped fresh rosemary *or*
       2 teaspoons dried rosemary
1   teaspoon minced garlic

1. Preheat oven to 500°F. Place lamb in large baking pan.

2. Combine parsley, mustard, bread crumbs, rosemary and garlic in small bowl. Spread evenly over top of lamb. Place in center of oven; cook 7 minutes for medium-rare. *Turn off oven but do not open door for at least 30 minutes.* Serve 2 to 3 chops on each plate, depending on size and total number of chops.

Makes 6 servings

Note: If you prefer really rare lamb turn the oven off after just 5 minutes, or if you like your lamb well done leave the oven on for 10 to 12 minutes. You may leave the lamb in the oven for more than 30 minutes; what is crucial is that you turn off the oven at the correct time.

Provençal-Style Lamb Shanks

- 2 tablespoons olive oil
- 4 lamb shanks (about 1 pound each)
- 2 large onions, chopped
- 5 cloves garlic, minced, divided
- 1 can (28 ounces) Italian-style plum tomatoes, undrained and coarsely chopped
- ½ cup dry vermouth
- 1½ teaspoons dried basil leaves, crushed
- 1½ teaspoons dried rosemary, crushed
- 1 teaspoon salt
- ½ teaspoon freshly ground black pepper
- 1 can (19 ounces) cannellini beans, rinsed and drained
- 1½ tablespoons balsamic vinegar (optional)
- 2 tablespoons chopped fresh Italian parsley
- 1 teaspoon grated lemon peel

1. Heat 1 tablespoon oil in Dutch oven over medium heat until hot. Add 2 lamb shanks. Brown on all sides; transfer to large plate. Repeat with remaining 1 tablespoon oil and 2 lamb shanks.

2. Add onions and 4 cloves garlic to drippings in Dutch oven; cook 6 to 8 minutes until onions are tender, stirring occasionally. Add tomatoes with liquid, vermouth, basil, rosemary, salt and pepper; bring to a boil over medium-high heat. Return shanks to Dutch oven. Reduce heat to low; cover and simmer 1½ hours or until shanks are tender.

3. Remove shanks; cool slightly. Skim fat from pan juices with large spoon; discard.

4. Stir beans into pan juices; heat through. Cut lamb from shanks into 1-inch pieces; discard bones and gristle. Return lamb to Dutch oven; heat through. Stir in vinegar.

5. Combine parsley, lemon peel and remaining clove garlic in small bowl. To serve, ladle lamb mixture into 6 individual shallow serving bowls; sprinkle with parsley mixture.

Makes 6 servings (about 10 cups)

Greek Lamb Braised with Vegetables

¼ cup FILIPPO BERIO® Olive Oil
2½ pounds lean boneless lamb, cut into
       1½-inch cubes
1 cup chicken broth
½ cup dry white wine
2 medium carrots, diagonally cut into
       1-inch pieces
2 ribs celery, diagonally cut into 1-inch
       pieces
½ medium bulb fennel, cut into
       ¼-inch-thick slices lengthwise
       through stem
1 (14-ounce) can artichoke hearts,
       drained and cut into quarters
       lengthwise
3 green onions, trimmed and cut into
       1½-inch pieces
   Salt and freshly ground black pepper
8 ounces uncooked orzo pasta
   Chopped fresh parsley

In Dutch oven, heat olive oil over medium-high heat
until hot. Add lamb; cook and stir 5 minutes or until
lightly browned. Add broth and wine; cover. Bring
mixture to a boil. Reduce heat to low, simmer 1½ hours.
Add carrots, celery, fennel, artichokes and green
onions. Simmer 15 to 20 minutes or until lamb and
vegetables are tender.

Season to taste with salt and pepper. Meanwhile, cook orzo according to package directions until al dente (tender but still firm). Drain. Serve lamb mixture over orzo. Top with parsley. *Makes 6 servings*

Broiled Lamb Chops

- 4 **lamb shoulder or blade chops, ¾ inch thick (about 2 pounds)**
- 1 **tablespoon finely minced onion**
- 1 **tablespoon FILIPPO BERIO® Olive Oil**
- 1 **tablespoon dry white wine**
- 1 **clove garlic, minced**
- 1 **teaspoon dried thyme leaves**
- ½ **teaspoon salt**

Place lamb chops in single layer in large shallow glass dish. In small bowl, whisk together onion, olive oil, wine, garlic, thyme and salt. Pour marinade over lamb chops; turn to coat both sides. Cover; marinate in refrigerator 2 hours, turning lamb chops after 1 hour. Remove lamb chops; arrange on broiler pan. Discard marinade. Broil, 4 to 5 inches from heat, 10 to 12 minutes for medium or until desired doneness is reached, turning halfway through broiling time.

Makes 4 servings

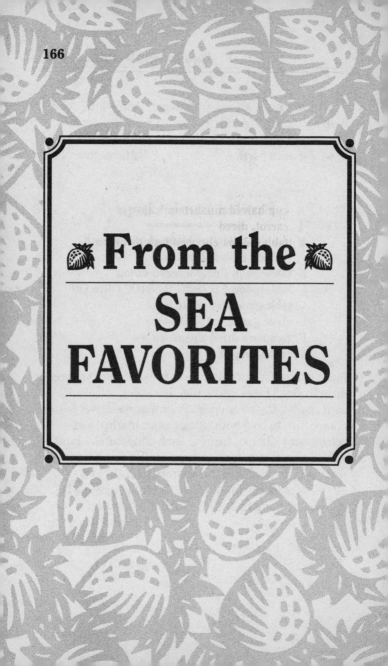

From the
SEA
FAVORITES

Baked Fish with Mushrooms

2 pounds fish fillets (whitefish, haddock
   or perch)
2 tablespoons FILIPPO BERIO®
   Olive Oil
½ cup halved mushroom caps
1 carrot, diced
2 tablespoons chopped leek or onion
1 cup dry white wine
½ cup water or fish stock
¼ teaspoon *each* dried thyme leaves, dried
   marjoram leaves, salt and freshly
   ground black pepper

Preheat oven to 350°F. Grease 13×9-inch baking pan
with olive oil. Add fish. In medium skillet, heat olive oil
over medium heat until hot. Add mushrooms, carrot
and leek; cook and stir 5 minutes or until leek is
softened. Add wine, water, thyme, marjoram, salt and
pepper. Simmer 10 minutes or until vegetables are
tender-crisp. Spoon vegetables over fish, reserving
liquid remaining in skillet. Cover pan with foil.

Bake 15 to 20 minutes or until fish flakes easily when
tested with fork. Meanwhile, transfer reserved liquid
from skillet to small saucepan. Bring to a boil over
high heat. Reduce heat to low; simmer, uncovered, 10
minutes or until liquid is reduced by half. Pour over
fish just before serving. *Makes 6 servings*

Fish Françoise

1   can (14½ ounces) DEL MONTE®
      FreshCut™ Diced Tomatoes with
      Garlic & Onion
1   tablespoon lemon juice
2   cloves garlic, minced
½   teaspoon dried tarragon, crushed
⅛   teaspoon pepper
3   tablespoons whipping cream
      Vegetable oil
1½ pounds firm white fish (such as halibut
      or cod)
      Lemon wedges

1. Preheat broiler; position rack 4 inches from heat.

2. Combine tomatoes, lemon juice, garlic, tarragon and pepper in large saucepan. Cook over medium-high heat about 10 minutes or until liquid has evaporated.

3. Stir in cream. Reduce heat to low. Cook until tomato mixture is very thick; set aside.

4. Brush broiler pan with oil. Arrange fish on pan; season with salt and additional pepper, if desired. Broil 3 to 4 minutes on each side or until fish flakes easily when tested with a fork.

5. Spread tomato mixture over top of fish. Broil 1 minute. Serve with lemon wedges.

Makes 4 servings

Fish with Hidden Valley Ranch® Tartar Sauce

1   cup (½ pint) sour cream
¼   cup chopped sweet pickles
1   package (1 ounce) HIDDEN VALLEY
      RANCH® Milk Recipe Original
      Ranch® salad dressing mix
¾   cup dry bread crumbs
1½ pounds white fish fillets (sole, flounder,
      snapper or turbot)
1   egg, beaten
      Vegetable oil
      French fried shoestring potatoes
      (optional)
      Lemon wedges (optional)

To make sauce, in small bowl, combine sour cream, pickles and 2 tablespoons of the salad dressing mix; cover and refrigerate. On large plate, combine bread crumbs and remaining salad dressing mix. Dip fillets in egg, then coat with bread crumb mixture. Fry fillets in 3 tablespoons oil until golden. (Add more oil to pan if necessary to prevent sticking.) Serve with chilled sauce. Serve with French fries and lemon wedges, if desired.   *Makes 4 servings*

Blackened Fish Fillets

1½ cups (3 sticks) unsalted butter, melted
6 (½- to ¾-inch-thick) redfish or other
  firm-fleshed fish fillets*
  (8 to 10 ounces each), at room
  temperature
3 tablespoons CHEF PAUL
  PRUDHOMME'S® Blackened Redfish
  Magic®

*Redfish and pompano are ideal for this method of cooking. If tilefish is used, you may have to split the fillets in half horizontally to have the proper thickness. If you can't get any of these fish, red snapper, wall-eyed pike or sac-a-lait fillets or salmon or tuna steaks can be substituted. In any case, the fillets or steaks must not be more than ¾-inch thick.

Heat a cast-iron skillet as hot as possible on your kitchen stove, at least 10 minutes. When the coals are glowing, use **very thick pot holders** to carefully transfer the hot skillet to the grill.

Meanwhile, pour 2 tablespoons melted butter in each of 6 small ramekins; set aside and keep warm. Reserve remaining butter. Heat 6 serving plates in 250°F oven.

Dip each fillet in the reserved melted butter so that both sides are well coated; then sprinkle the Blackened Redfish Magic generously and evenly on both sides of the fillets. Place 1 or 2 fillets in the dry, hot skillet and cook uncovered over high heat until the underside becomes deep-brown, almost black (but not burned), about 2 minutes (the time may vary according to the fillet's thickness and the heat of the skillet). Turn the fish over and pour 1 teaspoon butter on top of each.

Cook until fish is done, about 2 minutes more. Repeat with remaining fillets. Serve immediately with a ramekin of butter on each plate.

When cooking more than one batch of fish, the skillet should be thoroughly wiped out in between batches to remove all burned particles and butter—or these will produce a burned taste.   *Makes 6 servings*

Note: If you don't have a commercial hood vent over your stove, this dish will set off every smoke alarm in your neighborhood! It's better to cook it outdoors on a gas grill or a butane burner. Or you can use a charcoal grill, but you'll need to make the coals hotter by giving them extra air. (A normal charcoal fire doesn't get hot enough to blacken the fish properly.)

Bluefish Plaki-Style

2 tablespoons olive oil
1 medium onion, chopped
2 medium carrots, thinly sliced
2 cloves garlic, minced
½ cup dry white wine
1 can (14½ ounces) whole tomatoes,
    drained, juice reserved
2 tablespoons chopped fresh parsley
½ teaspoon salt
⅛ teaspoon black pepper
4 bluefish fillets (about 1½ pounds)

1. Preheat oven to 400°F.

2. Heat oil in medium skillet over medium-high heat. Add onion, carrots and garlic; cook and stir until vegetables are tender. Add wine and scrape any brown bits from bottom of skillet.

3. Add reserved tomato juice to skillet. Coarsely chop tomatoes. Add tomatoes, parsley, salt and pepper. Bring to a simmer. Simmer 15 minutes or until liquid is slightly thickened.

4. Spread one third of vegetable mixture in bottom of shallow 12×8-inch baking dish.

5. Rinse bluefish and pat dry with paper towels. Arrange fish, skin side down, on top of vegetable mixture in dish. Spoon remaining vegetable mixture over fish.

6. Bake 10 to 15 minutes or until fish flakes easily when tested with fork.   *Makes 4 servings*

Rolled Fish with Cream Sauce

1½ pounds white fish fillets (sole, flounder, snapper or turbot)
1 tablespoon lemon juice
¼ teaspoon dill weed
½ cup dry white wine
2 tablespoons sliced green onion
½ cup prepared HIDDEN VALLEY RANCH® Original Ranch® salad dressing
2 teaspoons all-purpose flour
Paprika (optional)

Sprinkle fillets with lemon juice and dill weed. Roll up; secure with wooden picks, if necessary. Place fish rolls in large skillet; add wine and onion. Cover, bring to boil, then simmer until fish is tender and flakes easily when tested with fork, 8 to 10 minutes. Transfer fish rolls to platter and keep warm. Bring drippings to boil; cook until liquid is reduced by half, about 5 minutes. In small bowl, whisk together salad dressing and flour; stir into liquid and heat until thickened and heated through. Pour over fish rolls. Sprinkle with paprika, if desired. *Makes 4 servings*

Fish alla Milanese

⅓ cup plus 2 tablespoons olive oil, divided
2 tablespoons lemon juice
½ teaspoon salt
Dash pepper
1 small onion, finely chopped
1 pound flounder or haddock fillets
(4 to 8 pieces)
2 eggs
1 tablespoon milk
½ cup all-purpose flour
¾ cup fine dry unseasoned bread crumbs
¼ cup plus 2 tablespoons butter or
margarine, divided
1 clove garlic, minced
1 tablespoon chopped fresh parsley
Lemon slices (optional)

1. For marinade, whisk ⅓ cup oil, lemon juice, salt and pepper in small bowl; stir in onion. Pour marinade into 13×9-inch glass baking dish.

2. Rinse fish; pat dry with paper towels. Place fish in baking dish; spoon marinade over fish to coat thoroughly. Marinate, covered, in refrigerator 1 hour, turning fish over occasionally.

3. Combine eggs and milk in shallow bowl; mix well. Spread flour and bread crumbs on separate plates. Remove fish from marinade; pat dry with paper towels. Discard marinade.

4. Dip fish to coat both sides evenly, first in flour, then in egg mixture, then in bread crumbs. Press crumb coating firmly onto fish. Place on waxed paper; refrigerate 15 minutes.

5. Heat remaining 2 tablespoons oil and 2 tablespoons butter in large skillet over medium heat until melted and bubbly; add fish. Cook 2 to 3 minutes per side until fish flakes easily with a fork and topping is light brown. Remove to heated serving plate.

6. Melt remaining ¼ cup butter in medium skillet over medium heat. Add garlic. Cook 1 to 2 minutes until butter turns light brown; stir in parsley. Pour browned butter mixture over fish. Serve immediately with lemon slices, if desired.   *Makes 4 servings*

Flounder Stuffed with Crabmeat Imperial

2 whole baby flounder (about
   1 to 1¼ pounds each)*
1 cup flaked crabmeat
¼ cup mayonnaise
2 tablespoons minced green bell pepper
1 teaspoon Worcestershire sauce
1 teaspoon prepared mustard
1 teaspoon chopped pimiento
   Dash salt and black pepper
2 tablespoons seasoned bread crumbs
1 tablespoon melted butter

*Flat fish are generally sold as fillets. Whole flat fish, such as
flounder, may need to be special ordered from your seafood retailer.
Flounder should be gutted and scaled with head and tail left on.

1. Preheat oven to 375°F.

2. Rinse flounder and pat dry with paper towels. Place
fish on greased baking sheet with head side up. Cut slit
down backbone, which is in the center of the top of the
fish, using sharp utility knife. Repeat with remaining
fish.

3. Starting on 1 side of fish, insert knife horizontally
into slit. Begin cutting, about 1 inch from head,
between flesh and bone, stopping just before tail to
form pocket. Cut another pocket on other side of slit.
Repeat with remaining fish.

4. To make stuffing, combine crabmeat, mayonnaise, bell pepper, Worcestershire, mustard, pimiento, salt and black pepper in small bowl. Spoon mixture evenly into prepared fish pockets.

5. Sprinkle fish with bread crumbs and drizzle with butter.

6. Bake 25 minutes or until fish flakes easily when tested with fork.   *Makes 2 servings*

Dijon-Crusted Fish Fillets

¼ cup GREY POUPON® Dijon Mustard, divided
2 tablespoons margarine or butter, melted
½ cup plain dry bread crumbs
2 tablespoons grated Parmesan cheese
2 tablespoons chopped parsley
4 (4- to 6-ounce) firm fish fillets (salmon, cod or catfish)

In small bowl, blend 2 tablespoons mustard and margarine or butter; stir in bread crumbs, cheese and parsley. Place fish fillets on baking sheet; spread fillets with remaining mustard and top with crumb mixture. Bake at 400°F for 10 to 12 minutes or until fish is golden and flakes easily when tested with fork.

Makes 4 servings

Fish Tajin (Fish Braised in Olive Oil with Vegetables

3 tablespoons FILIPPO BERIO® Olive Oil
4 small potatoes, peeled and cut into ⅛-inch-thick slices
2 large red bell peppers, seeded and cut into strips
3 small tomatoes, peeled and chopped
1 jalapeño pepper, seeded and chopped, or ½ teaspoon chili powder
3 cloves garlic, minced
2 pounds fish steaks, 1 inch thick (cod, haddock, halibut or skate)
1 tablespoon lime or lemon juice
½ cup chopped fresh cilantro

In large skillet or Dutch oven, heat olive oil over medium heat until hot. Carefully layer potatoes in pan; simmer gently 5 minutes. Add bell peppers, tomatoes, jalapeño pepper and garlic; mix well. Add fish, spooning vegetable mixture over fish. Cover; reduce heat to low and cook 10 to 15 minutes or until fish flakes easily when tested with fork. Sprinkle with lime juice. Top with cilantro.   *Makes 8 servings*

Baked Stuffed Snapper

1 **red snapper (1½ pounds)**
2 **cups hot cooked rice**
1 **can (4 ounces) sliced mushrooms,
   drained**
½ **cup diced water chestnuts**
¼ **cup thinly sliced green onions**
¼ **cup diced pimiento**
2 **tablespoons chopped parsley**
1 **tablespoon grated lemon peel**
½ **teaspoon salt**
⅛ **teaspoon ground black pepper
   Vegetable cooking spray**
1 **tablespoon margarine, melted**

Preheat oven to 400°F. Clean and butterfly fish.
Combine rice, mushrooms, water chestnuts, onions,
pimiento, parsley, lemon peel, salt and pepper; toss
lightly. Fill cavity of fish with rice mixture; close with
wooden toothpicks soaked in water. Place fish in 13×9-
inch baking dish coated with cooking spray; brush fish
with margarine. Bake 18 to 20 minutes or until fish
flakes easily with fork. Wrap remaining rice in foil and
bake in oven with fish.   *Makes 4 servings*

Favorite recipe from **USA Rice Council**

Blackened Snapper with Red Onion Salsa

Cajun Seasoning Mix (recipe follows)
Red Onion Salsa (recipe follows)
4 red snapper fillets
 (about 6 ounces each)
2 tablespoons butter

1. Prepare Cajun Seasoning Mix and Red Onion Salsa; set aside.

2. Rinse red snapper and pat dry with paper towels. Sprinkle with Cajun Seasoning Mix.

3. Heat large, heavy skillet over high heat until very hot. Add butter and swirl skillet to coat bottom. When butter no longer bubbles, place fish in pan.

4. Cook fish 6 to 8 minutes or until surface is very brown and fish flakes easily when tested with fork, turning halfway through cooking. Serve with Red Onion Salsa. *Makes 4 servings*

Cajun Seasoning Mix

2 tablespoons salt
1 tablespoon paprika
1½ teaspoons garlic powder
1 teaspoon onion powder
1 teaspoon ground red pepper
½ teaspoon ground white pepper
½ teaspoon black pepper
½ teaspoon dried thyme leaves, crushed
½ teaspoon dried oregano leaves, crushed

Combine all ingredients in small bowl.

Makes about ½ cup

Red Onion Salsa

1 tablespoon vegetable oil
1 large red onion, chopped
1 clove garlic, minced
½ cup chicken broth
¼ cup dry red wine or red wine vinegar
¼ teaspoon dried thyme leaves, crushed
Salt and black pepper to taste

Heat oil in small saucepan over medium-high heat.
Add onion; cover and cook 5 minutes. Add garlic; cook
1 minute. Add remaining ingredients. Cover and cook
about 10 minutes. Uncover and cook until liquid
reduces to ¼ cup. *Makes about ¼ cup*

Grilled Snapper with Pesto

1½ cups packed fresh basil
1½ cups packed fresh cilantro or parsley
¼   cup packed fresh mint
¼   cup olive oil
3   tablespoons lime juice
3   cloves garlic, chopped
1   tablespoon sugar
½   teaspoon salt
4   (6-ounce) snapper or grouper fillets

1. Combine basil, cilantro, mint, oil, lime juice, garlic, sugar and salt in food processor or blender; process until smooth.

2. Spread about ½ teaspoon pesto on each side of fillets. Sprinkle both sides with pepper. Arrange fish in single layer in grill basket coated with nonstick cooking spray. Grill, covered, over medium-hot coals 3 to 4 minutes per side or until fish flakes easily when tested with fork. Serve with remaining pesto.

Makes 4 servings

Note: Snapper is a mild-flavor, low-fat fish. To preserve the moistness in this lean fish, cook only until the thickest part turns opaque and flakes easily when pierced with a fork.

Mediterranean Cod

1   bag (16 ounces) BIRDS EYE® frozen
      Farm Fresh Mixtures Broccoli, Green
      Beans, Pearl Onions and Red Peppers
1   can (14½ ounces) stewed tomatoes
½   teaspoon dried basil
1   pound cod fillets, cut into serving
      pieces
½   cup orange juice
2   tablespoons flour
¼   cup sliced black olives (optional)

• Combine vegetables, tomatoes and basil in large skillet. Bring to boil over medium-high heat.

• Place cod on vegetables. Pour ¼ cup orange juice over fish. Cover and cook 5 to 7 minutes or until fish is tender and flakes with fork.

• Remove cod and keep warm. Blend flour with remaining ¼ cup orange juice; stir into skillet. Cook until liquid is thickened and vegetables are coated.

• Serve fish with vegetables; sprinkle with olives.

Makes about 4 servings

Soleful Roulettes

1 package (6¼ ounces) long-grain and
   wild rice mix
1 package (3 ounces) cream cheese,
   softened
2 tablespoons milk
32 medium fresh spinach leaves
4 sole fillets (about 1 pound)
   Salt and black pepper
¼ cup dry white wine
½ cup water

1. Cook rice mix according to package directions. Place 2 cups cooked rice in large bowl. Cover and refrigerate remaining rice and save for another use. Combine cream cheese and milk in medium bowl. Stir into rice; set aside.

2. Swish spinach leaves in cold water. Repeat several times with fresh cold water to remove sand and grit. Place spinach in heatproof bowl. Pour very hot water (not boiling) over spinach to wilt leaves slightly.

3. Rinse sole and pat dry with paper towels. Place fish on work surface. Sprinkle both sides of each fillet with salt and pepper. Cover each fillet with spinach leaves.

4. Divide rice mixture evenly and spread over top of each spinach-lined fillet. To roll fillets, begin with thin end of fillet, roll up and secure with wooden toothpicks.

5. Combine wine and water in large, heavy saucepan. Stand fillets upright on rolled edges in saucepan; cover. Simmer over low heat. *(Do not boil. This will cause fish to break apart.)* Simmer 10 minutes or until fish flakes easily when tested with fork.

Makes 4 servings

Señor Fish

- ½ **cup all-purpose flour**
- 1 **package (1.0 ounce) LAWRY'S® Taco Spices & Seasonings**
- ¾ **teaspoon LAWRY'S® Garlic Powder with Parsley**
- ½ **teaspoon LAWRY'S® Seasoned Pepper**
- 1 **pound halibut or orange roughy fillets**
- 2 **tablespoons butter or margarine Lemon wedges**

In shallow dish, combine flour, Taco Spices & Seasonings, Garlic Powder with Parsley and Seasoned Pepper. Rinse fish; pat dry with paper towels. Coat both sides of fish with flour mixture. In large nonstick skillet, melt butter. Add fish; cook 5 minutes on each side or until fish flakes easily with fork.

Makes 4 servings

Presentation: Squeeze lemon wedges over fish when serving.

Tuna 'n' Cheese Dogs

2 hot dog buns, toasted if desired
   Butter or margarine (optional)
   Lettuce leaves
1 can (3¼ ounces) STARKIST® Tuna,
   drained and flaked
2 slices (1 ounce each) reduced-calorie
   American cheese, cut into ¼-inch
   squares
2 tablespoons chopped red or green bell
   pepper or celery
1 tablespoon reduced-calorie mayonnaise
   or salad dressing
2 teaspoons orange juice

1. Place each hot dog bun on a plate. Spread with butter if desired. Arrange small lettuce leaves on bottom half of each bun.

2. In a medium bowl stir together tuna, cheese and chopped bell pepper.

3. Stir in mayonnaise and orange juice until well mixed.

4. Spread tuna filling over lettuce on buns.

Makes 2 sandwiches

Tuna with Peppercorns on a Bed of Greens

- **4** **tuna steaks (about 1½ pounds)**
- **Salt**
- **2** **teaspoons coarsely ground black pepper**
- **1** **tablespoon butter**
- **1** **large onion, thinly sliced**
- **¼** **cup dry white wine**
- **1** **tablespoon olive oil**
- **½** **pound fresh kale or spinach, washed, stemmed and cut into 1-inch strips**
- **½** **teaspoon sugar**
- **¼** **teaspoon black pepper**

Preheat oven to 325°F. Rinse tuna and pat dry with paper towels. Lightly sprinkle fish with salt, then press coarsely ground pepper into both sides of steaks. Set aside.

Melt butter in large skillet over medium heat. Add onion; cook and stir 5 minutes or until crisp-tender. Add wine; remove from heat. Spread onion mixture onto bottom of 13×9-inch glass baking dish. Place fish on top of onion mixture.

Bake 15 minutes. Spoon liquid over fish; bake 15 minutes or until fish flakes easily when tested with fork.

Heat oil in medium skillet over medium-high heat. Add kale, sugar and black pepper. Cook and stir 2 to 3 minutes or until tender. Serve fish and onion mixture over kale. *Makes 4 servings*

Tuna Melt

1   can (12 ounces) STARKIST® Solid
     White or Chunk Light Tuna, drained
     and flaked
⅓   cup mayonnaise
1½ tablespoons sweet pickle relish
1½ tablespoons chopped onion
½   tablespoon mustard
3   English muffins, split and toasted
6   tomato slices, halved
6   slices American, Cheddar, Swiss or
     Monterey Jack cheese
    Fresh fruit (optional)

In medium bowl, combine tuna, mayonnaise, pickle
relish, onion and mustard; mix well. Spread about ⅓
cup on each muffin half. Top with tomato slice and
cheese slice. Broil 4 to 5 minutes or until cheese melts.
Serve with fresh fruit, if desired.

Makes 6 servings

Note: For a festive look, cut each slice of cheese into
strips. Arrange in a decorative pattern over sandwiches.

Fresh Tuna with Island Fruit Sauce

4 **tuna or halibut steaks (about 1½ lbs.)**
Vegetable cooking spray
2¼ **cups DOLE® Pine-Orange-Guava Juice**
or Pine-Orange-Banana Juice, divided
1 **teaspoon dried basil leaves, crushed**
1 **can (8 oz.) DOLE® Crushed Pineapple**
2 **teaspoons cornstarch**
1 **teaspoon grated orange peel**

• **Place** fish in large, nonstick skillet sprayed with vegetable cooking spray. Add 1½ cups juice, basil and enough water to cover fish by 1 inch. Cover; bring to simmer over medium heat.

• **Cook** fish in simmering liquid *(do not boil)* 10 to 15 minutes or until fish flakes easily with fork. Meanwhile, combine remaining ¾ cup juice, undrained pineapple, cornstarch and orange peel in small saucepan. Bring to boil, stirring occasionally. Reduce heat to low; cook 2 minutes or until sauce is slightly thickened.

• **Remove** fish carefully with slotted spatula to serving platter. Garnish with orange slices, if desired. Serve with sauce. *Makes: 4 servings*

Southern Fried Catfish with Hush Puppies

Hush Puppy Batter (recipe follows)
4 catfish fillets (about 1½ pounds)
½ cup yellow cornmeal
3 tablespoons all-purpose flour
1½ teaspoons salt
¼ teaspoon ground red pepper
Vegetable oil for frying

1. Prepare Hush Puppy Batter; set aside.

2. Rinse catfish and pat dry with paper towels.

3. Combine cornmeal, flour, salt and red pepper in shallow dish. Dip fish in cornmeal mixture.

4. Heat 1 inch of oil in large, heavy saucepan over medium heat until a fresh bread cube placed in oil browns in 45 seconds (about 365°F). Fry fish, a few pieces at a time, 4 to 5 minutes or until golden brown and fish flakes easily when tested with fork. Adjust heat to maintain temperature. (Allow temperature of oil to return to 365°F between each batch.) Drain fish on paper towels.

5. To make Hush Puppies, place 1 tablespoon of batter into hot oil. Fry a few pieces at a time, 2 minutes or until golden brown. *Makes 4 servings*

Hush Puppy Batter

1½ cups yellow cornmeal
½ cup all-purpose flour
2 teaspoons baking powder
½ teaspoon salt
1 egg
1 cup milk
1 small onion, minced

Combine cornmeal, flour, baking powder and salt in medium bowl. Add egg, milk and onion. Stir until well combined. Allow batter to stand 5 to 10 minutes before frying. *Makes about 24 hush puppies*

Baked Salmon in Foil

2   tablespoons FILIPPO BERIO® Olive
    Oil, divided
1   (10-ounce) package frozen chopped
    spinach, thawed
1   (8-ounce) can stewed tomatoes
1   onion, chopped
1   clove garlic, minced
4   salmon steaks, 1 inch thick
    (about 2 pounds)
4   pieces heavy-duty aluminum foil,
    each 12 inches square
4   thin lemon slices
1   tablespoon chopped fresh parsley
    Salt and freshly ground black pepper

Preheat oven to 375°F. In medium saucepan, heat 1
tablespoon olive oil over medium heat until hot. Add
spinach, tomatoes, onion and garlic. Cook, stirring
occasionally, 5 minutes or until mixture is thick.

In medium skillet, heat remaining 1 tablespoon olive
oil over medium high heat until hot. Add salmon; cook
1 to 2 minutes on each side or until lightly browned.
Remove from heat. Place one fourth of spinach mixture
in center of each piece of foil; top with a salmon steak.
Drizzle liquid from skillet over salmon. Top each with
lemon slice and parsley. Fold edges of each foil square
together. Pinch well to seal, completely enclosing filling.
Place on baking sheet. Bake 15 minutes or until salmon
flakes easily when tested with fork. To serve, cut an "X"
on top of each packet; carefully peel back foil. Season to
taste with salt and pepper.   *Makes 4 servings*

Teriyaki Salmon Steaks

½ cup LAWRY'S® Teriyaki Marinade with
   Pineapple Juice
¼ cup dry sherry
2 tablespoons orange juice
1 tablespoon Dijon-style mustard
4 salmon steaks (about 2 pounds)
1 large tomato, diced
½ cup thinly sliced green onion

In medium bowl, blend together Teriyaki Marinade
with Pineapple Juice, sherry, orange juice and mustard
with wire whisk. In large resealable plastic bag or
shallow glass baking dish, place salmon; cover with
marinade mixture. Seal bag or cover dish. Refrigerate
at least 40 minutes, turning occasionally. In small
bowl, combine tomato and green onion; set aside.
Remove salmon from marinade, reserving marinade.
Broil or grill, 4 inches from heat source, 3 to 5
minutes, brushing once with reserved marinade. Turn
salmon over. Spoon vegetables over salmon; broil or
grill 3 to 5 minutes longer or until thickest part of
salmon flakes easily with fork. Garnish as desired.

Makes 4 servings

Barbecued Glazed Salmon

1 **large onion, thinly sliced**
1 **cup dry white wine or vegetable broth**
1 **cup tomato juice**
½ **cup ketchup**
¼ **cup honey**
1 **tablespoon Worcestershire sauce**
½ **teaspoon finely chopped garlic**
½ **teaspoon chili powder**
   Salt and pepper to taste
4 **salmon steaks (about 6 ounces each)**
   Vegetable oil

Combine onion and wine in medium saucepan; bring to a boil over medium-high heat. Add tomato juice, ketchup, honey, Worcestershire sauce, garlic, chili powder and salt and pepper to taste; stir well. Reduce heat to low and simmer 1 hour. Remove from heat and purée in blender or food processor; set aside.

Place salmon steaks in lightly oiled baking pan and baste with sauce. Bake in preheated 425°F oven about 6 minutes; turn and baste. Bake until fish just flakes when tested with fork. (The salmon steaks should cook about 10 minutes per inch of thickness, measured at the thickest part.)   *Makes 4 servings*

Favorite recipe from **National Honey Board**

Broiled Trout with Piñon Butter

4 whole trout (each about 8 ounces),
   cleaned
¼ cup vegetable oil
¼ cup dry white wine
2 tablespoons minced chives
2 tablespoons chopped parsley
½ teaspoon salt
⅛ teaspoon pepper
¼ cup butter or margarine, softened
¼ cup pine nuts, finely chopped

Place trout in heavy self-sealing plastic bag. Whisk oil, wine, chives, parsley, salt and pepper in small bowl. Pour over fish; seal bag. Marinate 30 minutes or refrigerate up to 2 hours, turning bag occasionally to distribute marinade. Combine butter and pine nuts; stir until well blended. Cover and let stand at room temperature until ready to use.

Preheat broiler and greased broiling pan. Remove fish from marinade and drain briefly; reserve marinade. Place fish on broiling pan. Broil 4 to 6 inches from heat 4 minutes; turn fish over. Brush with marinade; continue broiling 4 to 6 minutes or until fish turns opaque and just begins to flake. Transfer fish to serving platter. Place a dollop of reserved butter mixture on each fish. *Makes 4 servings*

Note: If you prefer to barbecue trout, place fish in a hinged wire broiler and grill, uncovered, 4 to 6 inches above low-glowing coals.

Trout with Apples and Toasted Hazelnuts

⅓ cup whole hazelnuts or walnuts
5 tablespoons butter or margarine,
    divided
1 large Red Delicious apple, cored and cut
    into 16 wedges
2 butterflied rainbow trout fillets
    (about 8 ounces each)
    Salt and black pepper
3 tablespoons all-purpose flour
1 tablespoon lemon juice
1 tablespoon snipped fresh chives

1. Preheat oven to 350°F. To toast hazelnuts, spread in single layer on baking sheet. Bake 8 to 10 minutes or until skins split. Wrap hazelnuts in kitchen towel; set aside 5 minutes to cool slightly. Rub nuts in towel to remove as much of the papery skins as possible. Place hazelnuts in food processor. Process using on/off pulsing action until hazelnuts are coarsely chopped; set aside.

2. Melt 3 tablespoons butter in medium skillet over medium-high heat. Add apple; cook 4 to 5 minutes or until crisp-tender. Remove apple from skillet with slotted spoon; set aside.

3. Rinse trout and pat dry with paper towels. Sprinkle fish with salt and pepper, then coat in flour.

4. Place fish in skillet. Cook 4 minutes or until golden and fish flakes easily when tested with fork, turning halfway through cooking time. Return apple to skillet. Reduce heat to low and keep warm.

5. Melt remaining 2 tablespoons butter in small saucepan over low heat. Stir in lemon juice, chives and hazelnuts. Drizzle fish and apple with hazelnut mixture.   *Makes 2 servings*

Tequila-Lime Prawns

 1 **pound medium shrimp, shelled and deveined**
 3 **tablespoons butter or margarine**
 1 **tablespoon olive oil**
 2 **large garlic cloves, minced**
 2 **tablespoons tequila**
 1 **tablespoon lime juice**
 ¼ **teaspoon salt**
 ¼ **teaspoon crushed red chili pepper**
 3 **tablespoons coarsely chopped cilantro**
    Hot cooked rice (optional)

Pat shrimp dry with paper towels. Heat butter and oil in large skillet over medium heat. When butter is melted, add garlic; cook 30 seconds. Add shrimp; cook 2 minutes, stirring occasionally. Stir in tequila, lime juice, salt and chili pepper. Cook 2 minutes or until most of liquid evaporates and shrimp are pink and glazed. Add cilantro; cook 10 seconds. Serve over hot cooked rice if desired.   *Makes 3 or 4 servings*

Fish & Chips

¾ cup all-purpose flour
½ cup flat beer or lemon-lime carbonated
    beverage
Vegetable oil
4 medium russet potatoes, each cut into
    8 wedges
Salt
1 egg, separated
1 pound cod fillets
Malt vinegar (optional)

1. Combine flour, beer and 2 teaspoons oil in small bowl. Cover; refrigerate 1 to 2 hours.

2. Pour 2 inches of oil into heavy skillet. Heat oil over medium heat until a fresh bread cube placed in oil browns in 45 seconds (about 365°F).

3. Add enough potato wedges as fit without crowding to skillet. Fry potato wedges 2 to 3 minutes. Turn using slotted spoon. Fry 2 to 3 minutes or until outsides are brown. Drain on paper towels; sprinkle lightly with salt. Repeat with remaining potato wedges. (Allow temperature of oil to return to 365°F between frying each batch.) Reserve oil to fry cod.

4. Stir egg yolk into flour mixture.

5. Beat egg white with electric mixer at high speed in narrow bowl until soft peaks form. Fold egg white into flour mixture; set aside.

6. Rinse fish and pat dry with paper towels. Cut fish into 8 pieces. Dip 4 fish pieces into batter and place in reserved oil in hot skillet; fry 2 to 3 minutes. Using slotted spoon; turn. Fry 2 to 3 minutes or until batter is crispy and brown and fish flakes easily when tested with fork. Drain on paper towels. Repeat with remaining fish pieces. (Allow temperature of oil to return to 365°F between frying each batch.)

7. Serve immediately with potato wedges. Sprinkle fish with malt vinegar, if desired.   *Makes 4 servings*

Broiled Shrimp Kabobs

    2   **tablespoons olive oil**
    2   **tablespoons lemon juice**
    ½   **teaspoon bottled minced garlic**
    ½   **teaspoon salt**
    ½   **teaspoon dried oregano leaves**
    ⅛   **teaspoon ground red pepper**
    ½   **pound medium shrimp, peeled**
    1   **red bell pepper, cut into squares**
    1   **medium zucchini, cut into ½-inch slices**

1. Preheat broiler. Whisk together first 6 ingredients in medium bowl. Add shrimp, bell pepper and zucchini; stir until well coated.

2. Alternately thread shrimp, bell pepper and zucchini on skewers. Place on rack of broiler pan. Broil 4 inches from heat 2 minutes per side or until shrimp turn pink and opaque.   *Makes 4 servings*

Crystal Shrimp with Sweet & Sour Sauce

½ cup **KIKKOMAN®** Sweet & Sour Sauce
1 tablespoon water
2 teaspoons cornstarch
½ pound medium-size raw shrimp, peeled and deveined
1 egg white, beaten
2 tablespoons vegetable oil, divided
1 clove garlic, minced
2 carrots, cut diagonally into thin slices
1 medium-size green bell pepper, chunked
1 medium onion, chunked
1 tablespoon sesame seed, toasted

Blend sweet & sour sauce and water; set aside. Measure cornstarch into large plastic food storage bag. Coat shrimp with egg white; drain off excess egg. Add shrimp to cornstarch in bag; shake bag to coat shrimp. Heat 1 tablespoon oil in hot wok or large skillet over medium-high heat. Add garlic; stir-fry 10 seconds, or until fragrant. Add shrimp and stir-fry 2 minutes, or until pink; remove. Heat remaining 1 tablespoon oil in same pan over high heat. Add carrots, green pepper and onion; stir-fry 4 minutes. Add shrimp and sweet & sour sauce mixture. Cook and stir until shrimp and vegetables are coated with sauce. Remove from heat; stir in sesame seed. Serve immediately.

Makes 4 servings

Spicy Broiled Shrimp

¼ cup butter or margarine
2½ teaspoons LAWRY'S® Seasoned Salt
¾ teaspoon LAWRY'S® Garlic Powder with Parsley
2 tablespoons vegetable oil
1 bay leaf, crushed
¾ to 1 teaspoon hot pepper sauce
1 teaspoon dried rosemary, crushed
¼ teaspoon dried basil, crushed
¼ teaspoon dried oregano, crushed
1½ pounds large, fresh shrimp, peeled and deveined

In small saucepan, melt butter over low heat. Add all remaining ingredients except shrimp; cook, uncovered, 5 minutes. Rinse shrimp; pat dry with paper towels. Place on broiler pan. Brush generously with melted butter mixture. Broil, 5 inches from heat source, 5 minutes or until shrimp turn pink, turning and brushing frequently with melted butter mixture. Garnish as desired.   *Makes 4 servings*

Presentation: Spoon any remaining melted butter mixture over cooked shrimp. Serve with lemon wedges and warm bread. This recipe is also great served over hot cooked rice.

Hint: To prepare in skillet, heat butter mixture in skillet as directed above. Add shrimp; sauté 5 to 7 minutes or until shrimp turn pink. Serve as directed.

Shrimp Scampi

- 2 **tablespoons olive oil**
- ½ **cup chopped onion**
- 1 **large clove garlic, finely chopped**
- 1 **cup (1 small) green bell pepper strips**
- 1 **cup (1 small) yellow bell pepper strips**
- 8 **ounces uncooked medium shrimp, peeled, deveined**
- 1¾ **cups (14-ounce can) CONTADINA® Dalla Casa Buitoni Pasta Ready Chunky Tomatoes with Spicy Red Pepper, undrained**
- 2 **tablespoons chopped fresh parsley**
- 1 **tablespoon lime juice**
- ½ **teaspoon salt**
  Hot cooked pasta or rice (optional)

HEAT oil in large skillet over medium-high heat. Add onion and garlic; cook for 1 minute. Add bell peppers; cook for 2 minutes.

STIR in shrimp; cook for 2 minutes or until shrimp turn pink. Add tomatoes and juice, parsley, lime juice and salt; cook for 2 to 3 minutes.

SERVE over pasta. *Makes 4 servings*

Swordfish Messina Style

2 tablespoons olive oil

½ cup chopped fresh parsley *or*
    1 tablespoon dried parsley

2 tablespoons chopped fresh basil *or*
    2 teaspoons dried basil, crushed

2 cloves garlic, finely chopped

1 cup (8-ounce can) CONTADINA® Dalla
    Casa Buitoni Tomato Sauce

¾ cup (about 2 ounces) sliced fresh
    mushrooms

1 tablespoon CROSSE & BLACKWELL®
    Capers

1 tablespoon lemon juice

⅛ teaspoon ground black pepper

3 pounds swordfish or halibut steaks

HEAT oil in small saucepan over medium heat. Add parsley, basil and garlic; cook for 1 to 2 minutes.

STIR in tomato sauce, mushrooms and capers; cook for 5 minutes. Stir in lemon juice and pepper. Place fish in single layer in greased 13×9-inch baking dish; pour sauce over fish.

BAKE, covered, in preheated 400°F oven for 20 minutes or until fish flakes easily when tested with a fork.   *Makes 8 servings*

Boiled Whole Lobster with Burned Butter Sauce

8   tablespoons butter
2   tablespoons chopped fresh parsley
1   tablespoon cider vinegar
1   tablespoon capers
2   live lobsters*

*Purchase live lobsters as close to the time of cooking as possible. Store in refrigerator.

1. Fill 8-quart stockpot with enough water to cover lobsters. Cover stockpot; bring water to a boil over high heat.

2. Meanwhile, to make Burned Butter Sauce, melt butter in medium saucepan over medium heat. Cook and stir butter until it turns dark chocolate brown. Remove from heat. Add parsley, vinegar and capers. Pour into 2 individual ramekins; set aside.

3. Holding lobster by its back, submerge head first in boiling water. Cover and continue to heat. When water returns to a boil, cook lobsters from 10 to 18 minutes, according to size: 1 pound—10 minutes; 1¼ pounds— 12 minutes; 1½ pounds—15 minutes; 2 pounds— 18 minutes. Transfer to 2 large serving platters. Remove bands restraining claws. To remove meat from claws, first break them from the body. Pull off the "thumb" part of the claw. Then, using a metal nutcracker, crack claw gently to avoid damaging the meat. Using seafood fork, gently remove claw meat (it should come out in 1 piece).

4. Crack legs gently with nutcracker. Pick out meat.

5. To remove tail meat, place lobster tail with underside facing up. With kitchen scissors, cut through underside of shell. Pull shell apart and slide your index finger between meat and shell to loosen meat; gently pull out meat from shell.

6. Serve lobster with Burned Butter Sauce.

Makes 2 servings

Jamaican Shrimp & Pineapple Kabobs

½ **cup prepared jerk sauce**
¼ **cup pineapple preserves**
2 **tablespoons minced fresh chives**
1 **pound large shrimp, peeled and**
   deveined
½ **medium pineapple, peeled, cored and**
   cut into 1-inch cubes
2 **large red, green or yellow bell peppers,**
   cut into 1-inch cubes

1. Combine jerk sauce, preserves and chives in small bowl; mix well. Thread shrimp, pineapple and peppers onto 4 metal skewers; brush with jerk sauce mixture.

2. Grill kabobs over medium-hot coals 6 to 10 minutes or until shrimp turn pink and opaque, turning once. Serve with remaining jerk sauce mixture.

Makes 4 servings

Lemon Sesame Scallops

1 tablespoon sesame seeds
1 pound sea scallops
8 ounces whole wheat spaghetti
3 tablespoons sesame oil, divided
¼ cup chicken broth *or* clam juice
½ teaspoon grated lemon peel
3 tablespoons lemon juice
2 tablespoons oyster sauce
1 tablespoon soy sauce
1 tablespoon cornstarch
1 tablespoon vegetable oil
1 yellow bell pepper, cut into strips
2 carrots, peeled and cut into matchstick pieces
4 slices peeled fresh ginger
1 clove garlic, minced
6 ounces fresh snow peas, trimmed, or 1 (6-ounce) package frozen snow peas, thawed
2 green onions, thinly sliced

1. To toast sesame seeds, heat small skillet over medium heat. Add sesame seeds; cook and stir about 5 minutes or until golden. Set aside.

2. Rinse scallops and pat dry with paper towels.

3. Cook spaghetti according to package directions. Drain in colander. Place spaghetti in large bowl; toss with 2 tablespoons sesame oil. Cover to keep warm.

4. Combine broth, lemon peel, lemon juice, oyster sauce, soy sauce and cornstarch in 1-cup glass measure; set aside.

5. Heat remaining 1 tablespoon sesame oil and vegetable oil in large skillet or wok over medium heat. Add bell pepper and carrots; stir-fry 4 to 5 minutes or until crisp-tender. Transfer to large bowl; set aside.

6. Add ginger and garlic to skillet. Stir-fry 1 minute over medium high-heat. Add scallops; stir-fry 1 minute. Add snow peas and onions; stir-fry 2 to 3 minutes or until peas turn bright green and scallops turn opaque. Remove slices of ginger; discard. Transfer scallop mixture to bowl with vegetable mixture, leaving any liquid in skillet.

7. Stir broth mixture; add to liquid in skillet. Cook and stir 5 minutes or until thickened. Return scallop mixture to skillet; cook 1 minute. Serve immediately over warm spaghetti; sprinkle with sesame seeds.

Makes 4 servings

Tarragon Scallops & Zucchini

1¼ pounds sea scallops
6 tablespoons butter or margarine
2 small zucchini, thinly sliced
¼ teaspoon onion powder
2 cups instant white rice
3 large green onions including tops, chopped
3 tablespoons chopped fresh tarragon *or* ¾ teaspoon dried tarragon leaves
¼ teaspoon salt
2 tablespoons lemon juice
2 teaspoons cornstarch

1. Rinse scallops; pat dry with paper towels. Cut large scallops in half.

2. Melt butter in large nonstick skillet over medium heat. Stir in scallops, zucchini and onion powder; cook and stir 2 minutes. Cover; reduce heat. Cook 7 minutes.

3. Meanwhile, prepare rice according to package directions. Combine green onions, tarragon and salt in small bowl. Blend lemon juice and cornstarch in another small bowl, stirring until cornstarch dissolves; set aside.

4. Stir green onion and cornstarch mixtures into skillet. Increase heat to medium; cook and stir 1 minute or until sauce thickens and scallops are opaque. Serve over rice. *Makes 4 servings*

Steamed Maryland Crabs with Corn on the Cob

1 pint water or beer
1 pint cider vinegar or white vinegar
2 dozen live Maryland blue crabs
½ pound seafood seasoning
½ pound salt
4 ears fresh corn, cooked

1. Place water and vinegar in 10-gallon stockpot. Place rack in bottom of pot. Place 1 layer of crabs on rack. Mix seafood seasoning with salt and sprinkle half over crabs. Repeat with remaining crabs, layering with remaining seasoning mixture.

2. Cover pot. Heat on high until liquid begins to steam. Steam about 25 minutes or until crabs turn red and meat is white. Remove crabs to large serving platter using tongs.

3. Cover table with disposable paper cloth. To pick crabs, place crab on its back. With thumb or knife point, pry off "apron" flap (the "pull tab" looking shell in the center) and discard. Lift off top shell and discard. Break off toothed claws and set aside. With knife edge, scrape off 3 areas of lungs and debris over hard semi-transparent membrane covering edible crabmeat.

4. Hold crab at each side; break apart at center. Discard legs. Remove membrane cover with knife, exposing large chunks of meat; remove with fingers or knife. Crack claws with mallet or knife handle to expose meat. Serve with corn on the cob.   *Makes 4 servings*

Devilishly Stuffed Soft-Shell Crab

8   soft-shell crabs, cleaned, fresh or
      frozen
¼   cup *each* chopped onion and celery
2   tablespoons chopped green bell pepper
1   clove garlic, minced
½   cup margarine or butter, melted, divided
1   cup buttery cracker crumbs
2   tablespoons milk
1   egg, beaten
1   tablespoon chopped parsley
½   teaspoon dry mustard
½   teaspoon Worcestershire sauce
¼   teaspoon salt
⅛   teaspoon cayenne pepper

Thaw crabs if frozen. Wash crabs thoroughly; drain well.

Cook onion, celery, green pepper and garlic in ½ of the
margarine until tender.

In medium bowl, combine onion mixture with cracker
crumbs, milk, egg, parsley, mustard, Worcestershire
sauce, salt and cayenne pepper.

Place crabs in shallow, well-greased baking pan.
Remove top shells from crabs and fill each cavity with
1 tablespoon stuffing mixture. Replace top shells.
Brush crabs with remaining melted margarine. Bake in
preheated 400°F oven 15 minutes or until shells turn
red and crabs brown slightly.   *Makes 4 servings*

Favorite recipe from **Florida Department of Agriculture and Consumer
Services, Bureau of Seafood and Aquaculture**

Crab Cakes

1 egg
2 tablespoons mayonnaise
1 teaspoon dry mustard
1 teaspoon LAWRY'S® Seasoned Pepper
½ teaspoon LAWRY'S® Seasoned Salt
¼ teaspoon cayenne pepper
4 cans (4¼ ounces each) crabmeat,
    drained, rinsed and cartilage removed
3 tablespoons finely chopped fresh
    parsley
2 tablespoons soda cracker crumbs
    Vegetable oil for frying (about ½ cup)

In medium, deep bowl, beat egg. Blend in mayonnaise, mustard, Seasoned Pepper, Seasoned Salt and cayenne pepper. Add crabmeat, parsley and cracker crumbs; mix lightly. Divide mixture into eight equal portions; shape each into a ball, about 2 inches in diameter. Flatten each ball slightly; wrap in waxed paper. Refrigerate 30 minutes. In large, deep skillet, heat oil. Carefully add crab cakes, four at a time, to skillet. Fry 8 minutes or until golden brown on all sides, turning frequently. With slotted spoon, remove cakes from oil; drain on paper towels. Serve immediately.   *Makes 8 cakes*

Presentation: Serve with tartar sauce and lemon wedges.

Mussels in Beer Broth over Pasta

2 pounds mussels
  Salt
8 ounces fettucine pasta
2 tablespoons olive oil
12 ounces beer or chicken broth
2 shallots, chopped, or ⅓ cup chopped
    onion
1 clove garlic, minced
¼ teaspoon fennel seeds, crushed
1 bulb fresh fennel, peeled, cubed
1 cup coarsely chopped fresh plum
    tomatoes

1. Discard any mussels that remain open when tapped with fingers.

2. To clean mussels, scrub with stiff brush under cold running water. To debeard, pull threads from shells with fingers. Soak mussels in mixture of ⅓ cup salt to 1 gallon water 20 minutes. Drain water; repeat 2 more times.

3. Cook fettucini according to package directions. Drain in colander. Place fettucine in large bowl; toss with oil. Cover to keep warm.

4. Meanwhile, combine beer, shallots, garlic and fennel seeds in large stockpot. Bring to a boil over high heat. Cover and boil 3 minutes. Add mussels. Cover; reduce heat to medium. Steam 5 to 7 minutes until mussels are opened. Remove from stockpot with slotted spoon; set aside. Discard any unopened mussels.

5. Simmer, uncovered, until liquid is reduced to about 1 cup. Add cubed fennel. Simmer 1 to 2 minutes. Add tomatoes; remove sauce from heat.

6. Place fettucine in 4 pasta bowls. Place mussels over noodles and pour sauce on top. Serve immediately.

Makes 4 servings

Hot Off
THE GRILL

Grilled Pork Tenderloin Medallions

PEPPER & HERB RUB
- 1 tablespoon dried basil leaves
- 1 tablespoon garlic salt
- 1 tablespoon dried thyme leaves
- 1½ teaspoons cracked black pepper
- 1½ teaspoons dried rosemary
- 1 teaspoon paprika

PORK
- 2 tablespoons Pepper & Herb Rub
- 12 pork tenderloin medallions (about 1 pound)

1. For rub, combine basil, salt, thyme, pepper, rosemary and paprika in small jar or resealable plastic food storage bag. Store in cool dry place up to 3 months.

2. To complete recipe, prepare barbecue grill for direct cooking.

3. Sprinkle rub evenly over both sides of pork, pressing lightly. Spray pork with olive-oil-flavored nonstick cooking spray. Place pork on grid over medium-hot coals. Grill, uncovered, 4 to 5 minutes per side or until pork is no longer pink in center.

Makes 4 servings

Barbecued Pork Loin

- 2 teaspoons LAWRY'S® Seasoned Salt
- 1 (3- to 3½-pound) boneless pork loin
- 1 cup orange juice
- ¼ cup soy sauce
- 1 teaspoon LAWRY'S® Garlic Powder with Parsley
- ½ teaspoon LAWRY'S® Seasoned Pepper
  Vegetable oil
  Fresh herb sprigs (garnish)

Sprinkle Seasoned Salt onto all sides of meat. In large resealable plastic bag or shallow glass baking dish, place meat; let stand 10 to 15 minutes. Combine orange juice, soy sauce, Garlic Powder with Parsley and Seasoned Pepper; pour over meat. Seal bag or cover dish. Refrigerate at least 2 hours or overnight, turning occasionally. Heat grill; brush with vegetable oil. Remove meat from marinade, reserving marinade. Add meat to grill; cook 30 minutes or until internal meat temperature reaches 160°F, turning and brushing frequently with reserved marinade. Remove meat from grill; let stand about 10 minutes before thinly slicing. Meanwhile, in small saucepan, bring reserved marinade to a boil; boil 1 minute.

Makes 6 servings

Presentation: Serve sliced meat with extra heated marinade poured over top.

Conventional Directions: Marinate meat as directed. Remove meat from marinade, reserving marinade. Place meat in shallow roasting pan; brush with reserved marinade. Bake, uncovered, in 350°F oven 1 hour or until internal temperature reaches 170°F, brushing frequently with reserved marinade. Discard any remaining marinade.

Grilled Spiced Pork Tenderloin

1 whole pork tenderloin (1¼ pounds)
2 tablespoons lemon juice
1 tablespoon FILIPPO BERIO® Olive Oil
2 cloves garlic, minced
½ teaspoon ground coriander
½ teaspoon ground cumin
½ teaspoon chili powder

Place tenderloin in shallow glass dish. In small bowl, combine lemon juice, olive oil, garlic, coriander, cumin and chili powder. Spread olive oil mixture over all sides of tenderloin. Cover; marinate in refrigerator at least 2 hours or overnight, turning once. Remove tenderloin, reserving marinade.

Brush barbecue grid with olive oil. Grill tenderloin, on covered grill, over hot coals 25 to 30 minutes, turning and brushing with reserved marinade halfway through grilling time, or until tenderloin is juicy and barely pink in center.   *Makes 3 to 4 servings*

Spicy Black Bean Tenderloin

2 **pounds pork tenderloin**
  Black Bean Sauce (recipe follows)
8 **bay leaves**
1 **tablespoon** *each* **black pepper, dried basil leaves, garlic powder, dried thyme leaves and dried oregano leaves**
1 **teaspoon** *each* **ground cloves, dry mustard and salt**
½ **teaspoon ground cumin**
¼ **teaspoon ground cinnamon**
  Hot cooked pasta (optional)

Prepare Black Bean Sauce. Combine all seasonings in blender or food processor; process until bay leaves are fully ground and mixture is smooth.

Prepare grill. Coat tenderloin on all sides with dry rub seasoning. Sear all sides of pork on grill. Place on roasting rack over medium coals. Grill pork about 35 minutes or to an internal temperature of 150°F. Cover and let stand 10 to 15 minutes. To serve, slice tenderloin and fan on serving plates. Drizzle with Black Bean Sauce. Serve with pasta, if desired.

Makes 8 servings

Black Bean Sauce: Heat 2 tablespoons olive oil in large stockpot; add 1 finely chopped yellow onion, 1 finely chopped carrot and 2 crushed garlic cloves. Cook and stir until onion is translucent. Add 2 cups dried black beans and stir well; add 2 quarts chicken stock and 1 pound ham hocks. Bring to a boil over high heat; reduce heat to medium-low and simmer, partially covered, 1½ hours. Remove ham hocks; discard. Process sauce in food processor or blender in batches. Season with salt and pepper to taste. Keep warm until serving.

Favorite recipe from **National Pork Producers Council**

Pork Roast with Honey-Mustard Glaze

Wood chunks or chips for smoking
⅓ cup honey
¼ cup whole-seed or coarse-grind
   prepared mustard
   Grated peel and juice of 1 medium
   orange
1 teaspoon minced fresh ginger *or*
   ¼ teaspoon ground ginger
½ teaspoon salt
⅛ teaspoon ground red pepper
   Apple juice at room temperature
1 boneless pork loin roast
   (3½ to 4 pounds)

Soak about 4 wood chunks or several handfuls of wood chips in water; drain. Mix honey, mustard, grated orange peel and juice, ginger, salt and red pepper in small bowl.

Arrange medium-low KINGSFORD® Briquets on each side of a rectangular metal or foil drip pan. Pour in apple juice to fill pan half full. Add soaked wood (all the chunks; part of the chips) to the fire.

Oil hot grid to help prevent sticking. Place pork on grid directly above drip pan. Grill pork, on covered grill, 20 to 30 minutes per pound until meat thermometer inserted in thickest part registers 155°F. (If your grill has a thermometer, maintain a cooking temperature of about 300°F.) Add a few more briquets to both sides of fire every 45 minutes to 1 hour, or as necessary, to maintain a constant temperature. Add more soaked wood chips every 30 minutes. Brush meat with honey-mustard mixture twice during the last 40 minutes of cooking. Let pork stand 10 minutes before slicing to allow the internal temperature to rise to 160°F. Slice and serve with sauce made from pan drippings (directions follow), if desired.

Makes 6 to 8 servings

To make a sauce from pan drippings: Taste the liquid and drippings left in the drip pan. If the drippings have a mild smoky flavor they will make a nice sauce. (If a strong-flavored wood, such as hickory, or too many wood chips were used, the drippings may be overwhelmingly smoky.) Remove excess fat from drip pan with a bulb baster; discard. Measure liquid and drippings; place in a saucepan. For each cup of liquid, use 1 to 2 tablespoons cider vinegar and 2 teaspoons cornstarch mixed with a little cold water until smooth. Stir vinegar-cornstarch mixture into saucepan. Stirring constantly, bring to a boil over medium heat and boil 1 minute.

Makes 6 to 8 servings

Herbed Citrus Chops

4 pork loin chops
¾ cup orange juice
3 tablespoons LAWRY'S® Chicken Sauté
Country Dijon with Thyme and Dill
2 tablespoons minced onion
1 teaspoon freshly grated orange peel
½ teaspoon dried rosemary, crushed
1 orange, sliced (garnish)
Chopped fresh parsley (garnish)

Pierce pork chops several times with fork; place in
large resealable plastic bag or shallow glass baking
dish. In small bowl, combine orange juice, chicken
sauté, onion, orange peel and rosemary; pour over
chops. Seal bag or cover dish. Refrigerate at least
30 minutes, turning occasionally. Remove chops from
bag, reserving marinade. Grill or broil chops, 4 inches
from heat source, 5 to 7 minutes on each side or until
just slightly pink in center, brushing with reserved
marinade halfway through cooking time.

Makes 4 servings

Succulent BBQ Pork Chops

⅓ cup KIKKOMAN® Teriyaki Baste
 & Glaze
2 tablespoons plum jam
1 teaspoon brown sugar, packed
1 teaspoon grated fresh ginger root
¼ teaspoon grated lemon peel
4 pork loin chops, ¾ inch thick
1½ tablespoons water

Combine teriyaki baste & glaze, plum jam, brown
sugar, ginger and lemon peel; remove and reserve
¼ cup mixture. Place pork chops on grill 4 to 5 inches
from hot coals; brush with remaining baste & glaze
mixture. Cook about 8 minutes or until light pink in
center, turning chops over and brushing occasionally
with baste & glaze mixture. (Or, place chops on rack of
broiler pan; brush with remaining baste & glaze
mixture. Broil 4 to 5 inches from heat 4 minutes on
each side or until light pink in center, brushing
occasionally with baste & glaze mixture.) Meanwhile,
combine reserved ¼ cup baste & glaze mixture with
1½ tablespoons water in small microwave-safe bowl.
Cover. Microwave on Medium-High (70%) 90 seconds,
stirring every 30 seconds; serve with chops.

Makes 4 servings

Peppered Beef Rib Roast

1 tablespoon plus 1½ teaspoons black
    peppercorns
2 cloves garlic, minced
1 boneless beef rib roast (2½ to
    3 pounds), well trimmed
¼ cup Dijon-style mustard
¾ cup sour cream
2 tablespoons prepared horseradish
1 tablespoon balsamic vinegar
½ teaspoon sugar

1. Prepare barbecue grill with rectangular metal or foil
drip pan. Bank briquets on either side of drip pan for
indirect cooking.

2. Meanwhile, to crack peppercorns, place peppercorns
in heavy, small resealable plastic food storage bag.
Squeeze out excess air; seal bag tightly. Pound
peppercorns using flat side of meat mallet or rolling
pin until cracked. Set aside.

3. Pat roast dry with paper towels. Combine garlic and
mustard in small bowl; spread with spatula over top
and sides of roast. Sprinkle pepper over mustard
mixture.

4. Insert meat thermometer into center of thickest
part of roast. Place roast, pepper-side up, on grid
directly over drip pan. Grill roast, on covered grill, over
medium coals 1 hour to 1 hour 10 minutes or until
thermometer registers 150°F for medium-rare or until
desired doneness is reached, adding 4 to 9 briquets to

each side of the fire after 45 minutes to maintain medium coals.

5. Meanwhile, combine sour cream, horseradish, vinegar and sugar in small bowl; mix well. Cover; refrigerate until serving.

6. Transfer roast to carving board; tent with foil. Let stand 5 to 10 minutes before carving. Serve with horseradish sauce.   *Makes 6 to 8 servings*

Cajun-Style Rubbed Steaks

⅓ **cup A.1. ORIGINAL® or A.1. BOLD® Steak Sauce**
¼ **cup margarine, melted**
¾ **teaspoon each garlic powder, onion powder and ground black pepper**
½ **teaspoon ground white pepper**
¼ **teaspoon ground red pepper**
4 **(4- to 6-ounce) beef shell steaks, about ½ inch thick**

In small bowl, blend steak sauce and margarine; set aside.

In another small bowl, combine garlic powder, onion powder and peppers. Brush both sides of steaks with reserved steak sauce mixture, then sprinkle with seasoning mixture. Grill steaks over medium-high heat or broil 4 inches from heat source 5 minutes on each side or to desired doneness. Serve immediately. Garnish as desired.   *Makes 4 servings*

Succulent Grilled Tenderloin

------

2 teaspoons dry mustard
1¼ teaspoons water
¼ cup KIKKOMAN® Soy Sauce
¼ cup dry white wine
2 cloves garlic, pressed
¾ teaspoon ground ginger
1 (3-pound) beef tenderloin roast,
 trimmed

Blend mustard and water in small bowl to make a smooth paste. Cover tightly; let stand 10 minutes. Combine soy sauce, wine, garlic and ginger. Gradually add soy sauce mixture to mustard paste, stirring until blended. Place roast on grill 4 to 5 inches from medium-hot coals; brush with sauce. Cook 30 to 45 minutes, or until meat thermometer inserted into thickest part of roast registers 135°F for rare or 155°F for medium,* turning over and brushing occasionally with sauce. (Or, place roast on rack in shallow pan. Bake at 425°F about 45 minutes, or until meat thermometer inserted into thickest part of roast registers 135°F for rare or 155°F for medium, or to desired doneness, brushing with sauce every 15 minutes.)   *Makes 12 servings*

*Roast will rise 5°F in temperature upon standing.

Tournedos with Mushroom Wine Sauce Dijon

¼ cup chopped shallots
2 tablespoons margarine
1 cup small mushrooms, halved
  (about 4 ounces)
¼ cup GREY POUPON® Dijon Mustard,
  divided
2 tablespoons A.1.® Steak Sauce
2 tablespoons Burgundy wine
1 tablespoon chopped parsley
4 slices bacon
4 (4-ounce) beef tenderloin steaks
  (tournedos), about 1 inch thick
¼ teaspoon coarsely ground black pepper

In small saucepan, over medium heat, sauté shallots in margarine until tender. Add mushrooms; sauté 1 minute. Stir in 2 tablespoons mustard, steak sauce, wine and parsley; heat to a boil. Reduce heat and simmer for 5 minutes; keep warm.

Wrap bacon slice around edge of each steak; secure with toothpicks. Coat steaks with remaining mustard; sprinkle with pepper. Grill steaks over medium heat for 10 to 12 minutes or to desired doneness, turning occasionally. Remove toothpicks; serve steaks topped with warm mushroom sauce.   *Makes 4 servings*

Grilled Peppered London Broil

1¼ cups canned crushed tomatoes
1 medium onion, quartered
1 tablespoon FILIPPO BERIO® Olive Oil
1 tablespoon cider vinegar
1 jalapeño pepper, seeded and chopped, or
    1 tablespoon purchased chopped hot
    pepper
1 clove garlic
½ teaspoon salt
1 teaspoon freshly ground black pepper
1 (2-pound) beef London broil, 2 inches
    thick

Process tomatoes, onion, olive oil, vinegar, jalapeño pepper and garlic in blender container or food processor until smooth. Transfer mixture to small saucepan. Bring to a boil. Reduce heat to low; simmer 2 minutes. Pour marinade into shallow glass dish. Stir in salt and black pepper. Cool slightly. Add London broil to marinade; turn to coat both sides. Cover; marinate in refrigerator at least 4 hours or overnight, turning occasionally. Remove London broil, reserving marinade.

Brush barbecue grid with olive oil. Grill London broil, on covered grill, over hot coals 8 to 10 minutes, brushing frequently with reserved marinade. Turn with tongs. Grill an additional 18 to 20 minutes for medium-rare or until desired doneness is reached.

Makes 6 to 8 servings

Rosemary-Crusted Leg of Lamb

¼ cup Dijon-style mustard
2 large cloves garlic, minced
1 boneless butterflied leg of lamb (sirloin
   half, about 2½ pounds), well trimmed
3 tablespoons chopped fresh rosemary
   leaves *or* 1 tablespoon dried rosemary
   leaves, crushed
   Fresh rosemary sprigs (optional)
   Mint jelly (optional)

1. Prepare barbecue grill for direct cooking.

2. Combine mustard and garlic in small bowl; spread half of mixture with fingers or spatula over one side of lamb. Sprinkle with half of chopped rosemary; pat into mustard mixture. Turn lamb over; repeat with remaining mustard mixture and rosemary.

3. Insert meat thermometer into center of thickest part of lamb.

4. Place lamb on grid. Grill lamb, on covered grill, over medium coals 35 to 40 minutes or until thermometer registers 160°F for medium or until desired doneness is reached, turning every 10 minutes.

5. Meanwhile, soak rosemary sprigs in water. Place rosemary sprigs directly on coals during last 10 minutes of grilling.

6. Transfer lamb to carving board; tent with foil. Let stand 10 minutes before carving into thin slices. Serve with mint jelly. *Makes 8 servings*

Swordfish with Honey-Lime Glaze

- ½ cup lime juice
- 3½ tablespoons honey
- 2 cloves garlic, minced
- ½ to 1 serrano or jalapeño chili pepper, fresh or canned, seeded and minced
- 1½ teaspoons cornstarch
  Salt
- 2 tablespoons finely chopped fresh cilantro (optional)
- 6 swordfish steaks (at least ¾ inch thick)
  Black pepper
- 2 cups diced seeded tomatoes (about 1½ pounds)

To make Honey-Lime Glaze, combine lime juice, honey, garlic, chili pepper, cornstarch and ½ teaspoon salt in a small saucepan. Boil about 1 minute until slightly thickened, stirring constantly. Stir in cilantro, if desired. Reserve half of Honey-Lime Glaze in a small bowl; cool. Rinse steaks; pat dry with paper towels. Season fish with salt and pepper. Brush fish with some of the remaining glaze.

Oil hot grid to help prevent sticking. Grill fish, on covered grill, over medium KINGSFORD® Briquets, 6 to 10 minutes. Halfway through cooking time, brush top with glaze, then turn and continue grilling until fish turns from transparent to opaque throughout. (Grilling time depends on the thickness of fish; allow 3 to 5 minutes for each ½ inch of thickness.) Stir tomatoes into reserved, cooled glaze and serve as a topping for fish. *Makes 6 servings*

Teriyaki Fish Grill

- ½ cup KIKKOMAN® Teriyaki Marinade & Sauce
- ½ cup vegetable oil
- ½ cup dry white wine
- ¼ cup water
- 2 tablespoons lemon juice
- ½ teaspoon dried dill weed, crumbled
- 6 fish steaks (sole, halibut, sea bass, rock fish or flounder), 1 inch thick
- 2 tablespoons dried parsley flakes

Combine teriyaki sauce, oil, wine, water, lemon juice and dill weed; pour over fish in shallow pan. Turn fish over to coat both sides well. Marinate 30 minutes, turning fish over occasionally. Reserving marinade, remove fish; sprinkle both sides of fish with parsley. Place on grill 5 inches from hot coals. Cook 10 to 15 minutes, or until fish flakes easily with fork, turning over and brushing occasionally with reserved marinade. (Or, place fish on rack of broiler pan; brush with reserved marinade. Broil 4 to 5 inches from heat 5 minutes; turn over. Brush with reserved marinade. Broil 5 minutes longer, or until fish flakes easily with fork.) Pour remaining marinade into small saucepan. Bring to boil; serve with fish.   *Makes 6 servings*

Lemony Lobster Supreme

- **4** frozen lobster tails (about 8 ounces each), thawed
- **½** cup butter or margarine, melted
- **½** teaspoon grated lemon peel
- **2** tablespoons lemon juice
- **2** tablespoons dry sherry
- **1** tablespoon KIKKOMAN® Soy Sauce
- **½** teaspoon parsley flakes
- **¼** teaspoon ground ginger
- **⅛** teaspoon paprika

Cut along underside of tails with scissors. Peel back soft undershell; discard. Bend tails to crack shell or insert long skewers lengthwise between shell and meat to prevent curling. Combine butter, lemon peel, lemon juice, sherry, soy sauce, parsley, ginger and paprika; brush lobster meat with sauce. Place tails, meat side up, on grill 4 to 5 inches from hot coals. Cook 5 to 8 minutes; turn tails over. Brush shells with sauce. Cook 5 to 10 minutes longer, or until meat becomes opaque. (Or, place tails, meat side up, on rack of broiler pan. Broil 4 to 5 inches from heat 5 to 8 minutes. Turn tails over; brush shells with sauce. Broil 5 to 10 minutes longer, or until meat becomes opaque.) Serve immediately with remaining sauce.

Makes 4 servings

Hot, Spicy, Tangy, Sticky Chicken

1 chicken (3½ to 4 pounds), cut up
1 cup cider vinegar
1 tablespoon Worcestershire sauce
1 tablespoon chili powder
1 teaspoon salt
1 teaspoon black pepper
1 teaspoon hot pepper sauce
¾ cup K.C. MASTERPIECE® Barbecue
    Sauce (about)

Place chicken in shallow glass dish or large heavy plastic bag. Combine vinegar, Worcestershire sauce, chili powder, salt, pepper and hot pepper sauce in small bowl; pour over chicken pieces. Cover dish or close bag. Marinate in refrigerator at least 4 hours, turning several times.

Oil hot grid to help prevent sticking. Place dark meat pieces on grill 10 minutes before white meat pieces (dark meat takes longer to cook). Grill chicken, on covered grill, over medium KINGSFORD® Briquets, 30 to 45 minutes, turning once or twice. Turn and baste with K.C. MASTERPIECE® Barbecue Sauce last 10 minutes of cooking. Remove chicken from grill; baste with sauce. Chicken is done when meat is no longer pink by bone.   *Makes 4 servings*

Castillian Grilled Chicken

3 tablespoons KIKKOMAN® Lite Soy
  Sauce
2 tablespoons water
1 tablespoon olive oil
1 clove garlic, pressed
½ teaspoon dried oregano leaves,
  crumbled
¼ teaspoon ground cumin
¼ to ½ teaspoon ground red pepper
  (cayenne)
6 boneless, skinless chicken breast halves

Blend lite soy sauce, water, oil, garlic, oregano, cumin
and pepper; pour over chicken in large plastic food
storage bag. Press air out of bag; close top securely.
Refrigerate 1 hour, turning bag over occasionally.
Remove chicken from marinade; place on grill 4 to
5 inches from hot coals. Cook chicken 5 minutes on
each side, or until no longer pink in center. (Or, place
chicken on rack of broiler pan. Broil 4 to 5 inches from
heat 5 to 6 minutes on each side, or until no longer
pink in center.)   *Makes 6 servings*

Grilled Marinated Chicken

8 chicken legs (thighs and drumsticks
   attached)
6 ounces frozen lemonade concentrate,
   thawed
2 tablespoons white wine vinegar
1 tablespoon grated lemon peel
2 cloves garlic, minced

1. Remove skin and all visible fat from chicken. Place chicken in 13×9-inch glass baking dish. Combine all remaining ingredients in small bowl, blending well. Pour over chicken. Cover and refrigerate 3 hours or overnight, turning chicken occasionally.

2. Spray cold grid with nonstick cooking spray. Heat grill until coals are glowing. Place chicken on grill; cook 10 to 15 minutes per side or until juices run clear when pierced with fork and chicken is no longer pink near bone. (Do not overcook or chicken will be dry.)

Makes 8 servings

Lemon-Garlic Roasted Chicken

> 1   **chicken (3½ to 4 pounds)**
>   **Salt and black pepper**
> 2   **tablespoons butter or margarine,**
>   **softened**
> 2   **lemons, cut into halves**
> 4   **to 6 cloves garlic, peeled, left whole**
> 5   **to 6 sprigs fresh rosemary**
>   **Garlic Sauce (recipe follows)**
>   **Additional rosemary sprigs and lemon**
>   **wedges for garnish**

Rinse chicken; pat dry with paper towels. Season with salt and pepper, then rub the skin with butter. Place lemons, garlic and rosemary in cavity of chicken. Tuck wings under back and tie legs together with cotton string.

Arrange medium-low KINGSFORD® Briquets on each side of a rectangular metal or foil drip pan. Pour in hot tap water to fill pan half full. Place chicken, breast side up, on grid, directly above the drip pan. Grill chicken, on covered grill, about 1 hour until a meat thermometer inserted in the thigh registers 175° to 180°F or until the joints move easily and juices run clear when chicken is pierced. Add a few briquets to both sides of the fire, if necessary, to maintain a constant temperature.

While the chicken is cooking, prepare Garlic Sauce. When chicken is done, carefully lift it from the grill to a wide shallow bowl so that all the juices from the cavity run into the bowl. Transfer juices to a small bowl or gravy boat. Carve chicken; serve with Garlic Sauce and cooking juices. Garnish with additional rosemary sprigs and lemon wedges.   *Makes 4 servings*

Garlic Sauce

- 2 tablespoons olive oil
- 1 large head of garlic, cloves separated and peeled
- 2 (1-inch-wide) strips lemon peel
- 1 can (14½ ounces) low-salt chicken broth
- ½ cup water
- 1 sprig each sage and oregano or 2 to 3 sprigs parsley
- ¼ cup butter, softened

Heat oil in a saucepan; add garlic cloves and lemon peel; sauté over medium-low heat, stirring frequently, until garlic just starts to brown in a few spots. Add broth, water and herbs; simmer to reduce mixture by about half. Discard herb sprigs and lemon peel. Transfer broth mixture to blender or food processor; process until smooth. Return garlic purée to the saucepan and whisk in butter over very low heat until smooth. Sauce can be rewarmed before serving.

Makes about 1 cup

Grilled Turkey Cutlets with Fresh Salsa

4 or 5 turkey cutlets (about 1¼ pounds)
1 bottle (12 ounces) LAWRY'S® Herb &
  Garlic Marinade with Lemon Juice,
  divided
1 large tomato, chopped
¼ cup chopped mild green chile peppers
  or 1 can (2.25 ounces) diced green
  chiles, drained (optional)
¼ cup sliced green onion
1 tablespoon red wine vinegar
1 tablespoon chopped fresh cilantro
½ teaspoon LAWRY'S® Garlic Salt
  Flour tortillas, warmed

Preheat grill. Pierce turkey several times with fork;
place in large resealable plastic bag or shallow glass
dish. Add 1 cup Herb & Garlic Marinade with Lemon
Juice; seal bag or cover dish. Refrigerate at least
30 minutes, turning occasionally. Meanwhile, prepare
salsa by combining tomato, chile peppers, green onion,
vinegar, cilantro, Garlic Salt and ¼ cup Herb & Garlic
Marinade with Lemon Juice; cover. Refrigerate until
ready to serve. Remove turkey from marinade. Grill,
5 inches from heat source, 7 to 10 minutes or until
turkey is no longer pink in center, turning over at least
once. Remove from grill; top with salsa. Serve with
tortillas.   *Makes 4 servings*

Barbecued Turkey Breast

1 **bone-in turkey breast (about 5 pounds)**
¼ **cup firmly packed dark brown sugar**
2 **tablespoons paprika**
1 **tablespoon minced garlic**
1 **teaspoon salt**
1 **teaspoon black pepper**
½ **teaspoon ground red pepper**
1½ **cups K.C. MASTERPIECE® Barbecue Sauce (about)**

Rinse turkey; pat dry with paper towels. Combine brown sugar, paprika, garlic, salt and peppers in small bowl; rub sugar mixture on inside and outside of turkey breast.

Arrange medium KINGSFORD® Briquets on each side of a rectangular metal or foil drip pan. Pour in hot tap water to fill pan half full. Oil hot grid to help prevent sticking. Place turkey breast on grid directly above drip pan. Grill turkey, on a covered grill, 20 to 24 minutes per pound until a meat thermometer inserted in the thickest part registers 170°F. If your grill has a thermometer, maintain a cooking temperature of about 300°F. Add a few more briquets to both sides of the fire after 45 minutes to 1 hour, or as necessary, to maintain a constant temperature. Warm about 1 cup barbecue sauce in a small saucepan to serve with turkey. Brush remaining ½ cup sauce on turkey during the last 20 to 30 minutes of cooking. Let turkey stand 10 minutes before slicing.   *Makes 6 to 8 servings*

Smoked Turkey

Wood chunks or chips for smoking
1 turkey (8 to 14 pounds), thawed if
   frozen, neck and giblets removed
1 lemon
½ cup butter or margarine, melted
⅓ cup finely chopped mixed fresh herbs*
2 cloves garlic, minced
1 teaspoon Dijon mustard
½ teaspoon salt
½ teaspoon black pepper

*Substitute ½ teaspoon *each* dried thyme, oregano, rosemary, basil
and rubbed sage *plus* 2 tablespoons finely chopped fresh parsley for
the mixed fresh herbs.

Soak 4 to 6 wood chunks or several handfuls of wood
chips in water; drain. Rinse turkey; pat dry with paper
towels. Tuck wing tips under back and tie legs together.
Squeeze 1½ tablespoons juice from lemon; mix with
butter, chopped herbs, garlic, mustard, salt and pepper
in a small bowl. Place remaining lemon in cavity of
turkey.

Arrange medium-low KINGSFORD® Briquets on each
side of a rectangular metal or foil drip pan. Pour in hot
tap water to fill pan half full. Add soaked wood (all the
chunks; part of the chips) to the fire.

Oil hot grid to help prevent sticking. Place turkey,
breast side up, on grid, directly over drip pan. Smoke-
cook turkey, on a covered grill, 11 to 14 minutes per
pound until a meat thermometer inserted in the thigh
registers 180°F or until joints move easily and juices

run clear when turkey is pierced. Baste turkey three or four times with butter mixture during grilling. If your grill has a thermometer, maintain a cooking temperature of about 300°F. Add a few more briquets to both sides of the fire every 45 minutes to 1 hour, or as necessary, to maintain a constant temperature. Add more soaked wood chips every 30 to 45 minutes. Let turkey stand 10 to 20 minutes before slicing.

Makes 8 to 14 servings

Many Peppered Fillets

 1   **package (about ¾ pound) PERDUE®
      FIT 'N EASY® Fresh Skinless and
      Boneless Turkey Breast Fillets**
 1   **tablespoon olive oil
      Salt and ground black pepper to taste**
 2   **cups sliced bell peppers**
 1   **cup sliced onion**
 2   **cups hot, cooked couscous or brown
      rice**
 1   **tablespoon minced fresh parsley
      (optional)**

Prepare outdoor grill for cooking or preheat broiler. Rub fillets with oil and lightly season with salt and pepper. Grill fillets 5 to 6 inches from heat source 3 minutes. Turn fillets over and cover with peppers and onions. Grill 5 to 6 minutes longer until turkey is cooked through. Serve with couscous tossed with parsley, if desired. *Makes 4 servings*

Brats 'n' Beer

1 can or bottle (12 ounces) beer
   (not dark) or nonalcoholic beer
4 fresh bratwurst (about 1 pound)
1 large sweet or Spanish onion
   (about ½ pound), thinly sliced and
   separated into rings
1 tablespoon olive or vegetable oil
¼ teaspoon salt
¼ teaspoon pepper
4 hot dog rolls, preferably bakery-style or
   onion, split
   Coarse-grain or sweet-hot mustard
   (optional)
   Drained sauerkraut (optional)

1. Prepare barbecue grill for direct cooking.

2. Pour beer into heavy medium saucepan with
ovenproof handle. (If not ovenproof, wrap heavy-duty
foil around handle.) Set saucepan on one side of grid.

3. Pierce each bratwurst in several places with tip of
sharp knife. Carefully add bratwurst to beer; simmer,
on uncovered grill, over medium coals 15 minutes,
turning once.*

4. Meanwhile, place onion rings on 18×14-inch sheet
of heavy-duty foil. Drizzle with oil; sprinkle with salt
and pepper. Close foil securely. Place on grid next to
saucepan. Grill onions, on uncovered grill, 10 to
15 minutes or until onions are tender.

5. Transfer bratwurst with tongs to grid; remove saucepan using heavy-duty mitt. Discard beer. Grill bratwurst, on covered grill, 9 to 10 minutes or until browned and cooked through, turning halfway through grilling time.

6. If desired, place rolls, cut-side down, on grid to toast lightly during last 1 to 2 minutes of grilling. Place bratwurst in rolls. Open foil packet carefully. Top each bratwurst with onions. Serve with mustard and sauerkraut.   *Makes 4 servings*

*If desired, bratwurst may be simmered on rangetop. Pour beer into medium saucepan. Bring to a boil over medium-high heat. Carefully add bratwurst to beer. Reduce heat to low and simmer, uncovered, 15 minutes, turning once.

Beef Kabobs with Apricot Glaze

1 can (15¼ ounce) DEL MONTE® Apricot
   Halves, undrained
1 tablespoon cornstarch
1 teaspoon Dijon mustard
½ teaspoon dried basil, crushed
1 pound sirloin steak, cut into 1½-inch
   cubes
1 small green bell pepper, cut into ¾-inch
   pieces
4 medium mushrooms, cut in half
4 to 8 skewers

1. Drain apricot syrup into small saucepan. Blend in
cornstarch until dissolved. Cook over medium heat,
stirring constantly, until thickened. Stir in mustard
and basil. Set aside.

2. Thread meat, apricots, green pepper and
mushrooms alternately onto skewers; brush with
apricot syrup mixture. Grill kabobs over hot coals (or
broil) about 5 minutes on each side or to desired
doneness, brushing occasionally with additional syrup
mixture.   *Makes 4 servings*

Tip: To prevent burning of wooden skewers, soak
skewers in water for 10 minutes before assembling
kabobs.

Scallop Kabobs

1   pound Florida Calico Scallops, fresh or
    frozen
2   cups cherry tomatoes
2   cups fresh small mushrooms
1   can (13½ ounces) pineapple chunks,
    drained
1   green pepper, cut into 1-inch squares
¼   cup vegetable oil
¼   cup lemon juice
¼   cup chopped parsley
¼   cup soy sauce
½   teaspoon salt
⅛   teaspoon pepper

Thaw scallops, if frozen. Rinse with cold running water
to remove any remaining shell particles.

Place tomatoes, mushrooms, pineapple, green pepper
and scallops in a medium bowl. Combine oil, lemon
juice, parsley, soy sauce, salt and pepper; pour over
scallop mixture. Let stand 30 minutes, stirring
occasionally.

Using long skewers, alternate scallops, tomatoes,
mushrooms, pineapple and green pepper until skewers
are filled. Cook about 4 inches from moderately hot
coals for 6 minutes, brushing occasionally with sauce.
Turn and cook for 3 to 4 minutes longer or until
scallops are opaque.   *Makes 6 servings*

Favorite recipe from **Florida Department of Agriculture & Consumer
Services, Bureau of Seafood and Aquaculture**

Chicken Shish-Kabobs

¼ cup CRISCO® Oil
¼ cup wine vinegar
¼ cup lemon juice
1 teaspoon dried oregano leaves
1 clove garlic, minced
¼ teaspoon black pepper
1½ pounds boneless, skinless chicken
   breasts, cut into 1- to 1½-inch cubes
12 bamboo or metal skewers (10 to
   12 inches long)
2 medium tomatoes, cut into wedges
2 medium onions, cut into wedges
1 medium green bell pepper, cut into
   1-inch squares
1 medium red bell pepper, cut into 1-inch
   squares
4 cups hot cooked brown rice
   (cooked without salt or fat)
   Salt (optional)

1. Combine Crisco Oil, vinegar, lemon juice, oregano, garlic and black pepper in shallow baking dish or glass bowl. Stir well. Add chicken. Stir to coat. Cover. Marinate in refrigerator 3 hours, turning chicken several times.

2. Soak bamboo skewers in water.

3. Prepare grill or heat broiler.

4. Thread chicken, tomatoes, onions and bell peppers alternately on skewers.

5. Place skewers on grill or broiler pan. Grill or broil
5 minutes. Turn. Grill or broil 5 to 7 minutes or until
chicken is no longer pink in center. Serve over hot
rice. Season with salt and garnish, if desired.

Makes 6 servings

Shrimp on the Barbie

1 **pound large raw shrimp, shelled and
    deveined**
1 **each red and yellow bell pepper, seeded
    and cut into 1-inch chunks**
4 **slices lime (optional)**
½ **cup prepared smoky-flavor barbecue
    sauce**
2 **tablespoons FRENCH'S®
    Worcestershire Sauce**
2 **tablespoons FRANK'S® Original
    REDHOT® Cayenne Pepper Sauce**
1 **clove garlic, minced**

Thread shrimp, peppers and lime, if desired, alternately
onto metal skewers. Combine barbecue sauce,
Worcestershire, RedHot® sauce and garlic in small
bowl; mix well. Brush on skewers.

Place skewers on grid, reserving sauce mixture. Grill
over hot coals 15 minutes or until shrimp turn pink,
turning and basting often with sauce mixture. (Do not
baste during last 5 minutes of cooking.) Serve warm.

Makes 4 servings

Buffalo Turkey Kabobs

⅔ cup HELLMANN'S® or BEST FOODS®
　　Real or Light Mayonnaise, divided
1 teaspoon hot pepper sauce
1½ pounds boneless turkey breast, cut into
　　1-inch cubes
2 red bell peppers or 1 red and 1 yellow
　　bell pepper, cut into 1-inch squares
2 medium onions, cut into wedges
¼ cup (1 ounce) crumbled blue cheese
2 tablespoons milk
1 medium stalk celery, minced
1 medium carrot, minced

1. In medium bowl combine ⅓ cup of the mayonnaise and hot pepper sauce. Stir in turkey. Let stand at room temperature 20 minutes.

2. On 6 skewers, alternately thread turkey, peppers and onions. Grill or broil 5 inches from heat, brushing with remaining mayonnaise mixture and turning frequently, 12 to 15 minutes.

3. Meanwhile, in small bowl blend remaining ⅓ cup mayonnaise with the blue cheese and milk. Stir in celery and carrot. Serve with kabobs.

Makes 6 servings

Satay Skewers with Sesame

1½ cups dry roasted peanuts
⅔ cup seasoned rice vinegar
½ cup light corn syrup
½ cup soy sauce
2 tablespoons sesame oil
2 tablespoons minced fresh ginger
2 tablespoons chopped fresh cilantro
½ teaspoon LAWRY'S® Garlic Powder with Parsley
½ teaspoon crushed red pepper flakes (optional)
1 pound beef sirloin steak or 1 pound boneless chicken, cut into strips
Skewers

In food processor, place peanuts, rice vinegar and corn syrup. Process until peanuts are puréed. Add soy sauce, sesame oil, ginger, cilantro, Garlic Powder with Parsley and red pepper flakes. Pulse until mixture is blended; cover. Refrigerate at least 1 hour. Thread meat onto skewers; brush with half of the sauce. Grill or broil to desired doneness, turning and brushing frequently with remaining sauce. In small saucepan, warm any remaining sauce for dipping. *Makes 4 servings*

Surf and Turf Brochettes

¾ cup orange juice
½ cup A.1. ORIGINAL® or A.1. BOLD®
   Steak Sauce
2 tablespoons white wine
1 clove garlic, minced
1½ teaspoons cornstarch
1 (12-ounce) beef top round steak, cut
   into ¾-inch cubes
24 small shrimp, peeled, deveined
1 green bell pepper, cut into 1-inch
   squares

Soak 12 (10-inch) wooden skewers in water at least
30 minutes.

In small saucepan, combine juice, steak sauce, wine
and garlic; reserve ½ cup mixture for basting
brochettes. Blend cornstarch into remaining steak
sauce mixture in saucepan. Over medium heat, cook
and stir until sauce thickens and begins to boil; keep
warm.

Alternately thread steak, shrimp and pepper onto
skewers. Grill brochettes over medium heat or broil
6 inches from heat source, 8 to 10 minutes or until
desired doneness and shrimp turn opaque, turning and
basting often with basting sauce. Serve brochettes with
warm sauce for dipping.

Makes 12 appetizers

Hot and Spicy Spareribs

1 **rack pork spareribs (3 pounds)**
2 **tablespoons butter or margarine**
1 **medium onion, finely chopped**
2 **cloves garlic, minced**
1 **can (15 ounces) tomato sauce**
⅔ **cup cider vinegar**
⅔ **cup firmly packed brown sugar**
2 **tablespoons chili powder**
1 **tablespoon prepared mustard**
½ **teaspoon black pepper**

Melt butter in large skillet over low heat. Add onion and garlic; cook and stir until tender. Add all remaining ingredients except ribs. Bring to a boil over high heat; reduce heat to low and simmer 20 minutes, stirring occasionally.

Prepare grill. Place large piece of heavy-duty foil over coals to catch drippings. Baste meaty sides of ribs with sauce. Place ribs on grid, meaty sides down; baste top side. Grill, on covered grill, about 6 inches from low coals 20 minutes; turn ribs and baste. Cook 45 minutes more or until ribs are tender, basting every 10 to 15 minutes with sauce. (Do not baste during last 5 minutes of grilling.)   *Makes 3 servings*

Favorite recipe from **National Pork Producers Council**

Micro-Grilled Pork Ribs

1 tablespoon firmly packed brown sugar
2 teaspoons ground cumin
1 teaspoon salt
½ teaspoon black pepper
  Dash ground red pepper (optional)
3 pounds pork back ribs
⅓ cup water
½ cup K.C. MASTERPIECE® Barbecue
  Sauce
  Grilled Sweet Potatoes (recipe follows)

Combine brown sugar, cumin, salt and peppers in
small bowl. Rub onto ribs. Arrange ribs in single layer
in 13X9-inch microwave-safe baking dish. Pour water
over ribs; cover loosely with plastic wrap. Microwave
on MEDIUM-HIGH (70% power) 15 minutes,
rearranging ribs and rotating dish halfway through
cooking time.

Arrange medium-hot KINGSFORD® Briquets on one
side of grill. Place ribs on grid area opposite briquets.
Barbecue ribs, on covered grill, 15 to 20 minutes,
turning every 5 minutes and basting with sauce the
last 10 minutes. Ribs should be browned and cooked
through. Serve with Grilled Sweet Potatoes.

Makes 4 servings

Grilled Sweet Potatoes or Baking Potatoes: Slice potatoes into ¼-inch-thick rounds, allowing about ⅓ pound potatoes per serving. Brush both sides of slices lightly with oil. Place on grid around edges of medium-hot KINGSFORD® Briquets. Cook potatoes, on covered grill, 10 to 12 minutes until golden brown and tender, turning once.

Baby Back Barbecued Ribs

2 to 3 teaspoons LAWRY'S® Seasoned
    Salt
4 pounds baby back ribs
1 cup vinegar
½ cup ketchup
3 tablespoons Worcestershire sauce
1 tablespoon sugar
1½ teaspoons hot pepper sauce
1½ teaspoons dry mustard
1 teaspoon LAWRY'S® Seasoned Salt
½ teaspoon LAWRY'S® Garlic Powder with
    Parsley

Sprinkle Seasoned Salt onto both sides of ribs. In
shallow glass baking dish, place ribs; cover dish.
Refrigerate 2 hours. In small saucepan, combine
remaining ingredients; simmer over medium heat
about 10 minutes. Heat grill for medium coals. Brush
ribs with sauce. Grill, 4 to 5 inches from heat, 45 to
60 minutes or until ribs are tender, turning and
basting with sauce every 10 minutes.

Makes 4 to 6 servings

Hint: Ribs may be baked in 375°F oven 45 to
60 minutes or until ribs are tender, turning and
basting with sauce every 10 minutes.

Charcoal Broiled Burgers
Cha Cha Cha

- **2 pounds lean ground beef**
- **½ cup *each* prepared salsa and finely crushed tortilla chips**
- **2 teaspoons chili powder**
- **½ teaspoon salt**
- **8 hamburger buns, split**
- **2 cups (8 ounces) SARGENTO® Classic Shredded Cheese For Tacos**
- **¾ cup chopped fresh tomatoes**
- **¾ cup shredded leaf lettuce or chopped pepperoncini (optional)**

Prepare grill. Combine ground beef, salsa, tortilla chips, chili powder and salt in large bowl; mix lightly but thoroughly. Shape into 8 (½-inch-thick) patties, about 4 inches in diameter. Place bun tops, cut sides up, in foil pan large enough to hold in one layer. Divide Taco cheese evenly over bun tops. Cover with foil. Place on one edge of grid and place patties in center of grid. Grill patties over medium-hot coals about 5 minutes on each side for medium or to desired doneness. Serve patties on bun bottoms; top with tomatoes and lettuce or pepperoncini, if desired. Cover with bun tops, cheese sides down. *Makes 8 servings*

Dijon Bacon Cheeseburgers

1 cup shredded Cheddar cheese
   (4 ounces)
5 tablespoons GREY POUPON Dijon
   Mustard,* divided
2 teaspoons dried minced onion
1 teaspoon prepared horseradish*
1 pound lean ground beef
4 onion sandwich rolls, split and toasted
1 cup shredded lettuce
4 slices tomato
4 slices bacon, cooked and halved

In small bowl, combine cheese, 3 tablespoons mustard,
onion and horseradish; set aside.

In medium bowl, combine ground beef and remaining
mustard; shape mixture into 4 patties. Grill or broil
burgers over medium heat for 5 minutes on each side
or until desired doneness; top with cheese mixture and
cook until cheese melts, about 2 minutes. Top each roll
bottom with ¼ cup shredded lettuce, 1 tomato slice,
burger, 2 bacon pieces and roll top. Serve immediately.

Makes 4 burgers

*5 tablespoons GREY POUPON® Horseradish Mustard may be
substituted for Dijon mustard; omit horseradish.

Cowboy Burgers

1   **pound ground beef**
½   **teaspoon LAWRY'S® Seasoned Salt**
½   **teaspoon LAWRY'S® Seasoned Pepper**
2   **tablespoons plus 2 teaspoons butter or margarine**
1   **large onion, thinly sliced and separated into rings**
1   **package (1.25 ounces) LAWRY'S® Taco Spices and Seasonings**
4   **slices Cheddar cheese**
4   **Kaiser rolls**
    Lettuce leaves
    Tomato slices

In medium bowl, combine ground beef, Seasoned Salt and Seasoned Pepper; shape into four patties. Grill or broil to desired doneness (about 4 minutes on each side for rare). Meanwhile, in medium skillet, melt butter. Add onion and Taco Spices & Seasonings; blend well. Sauté until onion is tender and translucent. Top each patty with cheese. Return to grill or broiler until cheese is melted. On bottom half of each roll, place lettuce, tomato and patty; cover with onion and top half of roll.   *Makes 4 servings*

Ranch Burgers

1¼ pounds lean ground beef
¾ cup prepared HIDDEN VALLEY
      RANCH® Original Ranch® Salad
      Dressing
¾ cup dry bread crumbs
¼ cup minced onions
1 teaspoon salt
¼ teaspoon black pepper
      Sesame seed buns
      Lettuce, tomato slices and red onion
        slices (optional)
      Additional Original Ranch® Salad
        Dressing

In large bowl, combine beef, salad dressing, bread
crumbs, onions, salt and pepper. Shape into 6 patties.
Grill over medium-hot coals 4 to 5 minutes for
medium doneness. Place on sesame seed buns with
lettuce, tomato and red onion slices, if desired. Serve
with a generous amount of additional salad dressing.

Makes 6 servings

The Other Burger

1   **pound ground pork (80% lean)**
1   **teaspoon black pepper**
¼   **teaspoon salt**
    Hamburger buns (optional)

Prepare grill. Gently mix together ground pork, pepper
and salt; shape into 4 burgers, each about ¾ inch thick.
Place burgers on grid. Grill, on covered grill, over
medium-hot coals 5 minutes on each side or until
barely pink in center. Serve on hamburger buns, if
desired.   *Makes 4 servings*

Eastern Burger: Add 2 teaspoons soy sauce,
2 tablespoons dry sherry and 1 tablespoon grated
ginger root to pork mixture; grill as directed.

Veggie Burger: Add 3 drops hot pepper sauce, 1 grated
carrot and 3 tablespoons chopped parsley to pork
mixture; grill as directed.

South-of-the-Border Burger: Add ¼ teaspoon *each*
ground cumin, dried oregano leaves, seasoned salt and
crushed red pepper to pork mixture; grill as directed.

Favorite recipe from **National Pork Producers Council**

Swiss Burgers

1   package (about 1¼ pounds) PERDUE®
    Fresh Ground Turkey, Ground Turkey
    Breast Meat or Ground Chicken
½   cup thinly sliced scallions
1   teaspoon Worcestershire sauce
4   ounces fresh, white mushrooms, thinly
    sliced
2   teaspoons olive oil
½   teaspoon salt
    Ground pepper to taste
4   to 5 pieces Swiss cheese
    Dijon mustard
4   to 5 Kaiser rolls
6   to 8 tablespoons sour cream

Prepare outdoor grill or preheat broiler. In large bowl,
combine ground turkey, scallions and Worcestershire
sauce. Shape mixture into 4 or 5 patties.

To grill: When coals are medium-hot, place burgers on
hottest area of cooking surface of grill; cook 1 to
2 minutes on each side to brown. Move burgers to edge
of grill; cook 4 to 6 minutes longer on each side until
thoroughly cooked, juices run clear and burgers spring
back to the touch.

To broil: Place burgers on rack in broiling pan 4 inches from heat source. Broil 4 to 6 minutes on each side until burgers are thoroughly cooked and spring back to the touch.

While burgers are cooking, toss mushrooms with oil and sprinkle lightly with salt and pepper. Place mushrooms on sheet of heavy-duty aluminum foil. Grill or broil along with burgers during last 1 to 2 minutes of cooking time.

When burgers are cooked through, place a piece of Swiss cheese on each; cook 1 minute longer or just enough to melt cheese. To serve, spread mustard on bottom halves of rolls; cover with burgers and equal portions of mushrooms. Top each with a generous dollop of sour cream and remaining roll half.

Makes 4 to 5 servings

Sizzling Chicken Sandwiches

4 boneless, skinless chicken breast halves
     (about 1 pound)
1 package (1.27 ounces) LAWRY'S®
     Spices & Seasonings for Fajitas
1 cup chunky salsa
¼ cup water
   Lettuce
4 large sandwich buns
4 slices Monterey Jack cheese
   Red onion slices
   Avocado slices
   Additional chunky salsa

In large resealable plastic bag, place chicken. In small
bowl, combine Spices & Seasonings for Fajitas, 1 cup
salsa and water; pour over chicken. Marinate in
refrigerator 2 hours. Heat grill for medium coals or
heat broiler. Remove chicken, reserving marinade.
Grill or broil, 4 to 5 inches from heat source, 5 to
7 minutes on each side or until chicken is no longer
pink in center, basting frequently with marinade. Place
on lettuce-lined sandwich buns. Top with cheese,
onion, avocado and salsa.   *Makes 4 servings*

Hint: Do not baste chicken with marinade during last 5
minutes of cooking.

Grilled Chicken Tortillas

3 whole broiler-fryer chicken breasts,
   halved, boned, skinned
Juice of 2 limes
3 tablespoons olive oil
1 clove garlic, crushed
½ teaspoon salt
¼ teaspoon bottled hot pepper sauce
12 flour tortillas
3 cups shredded lettuce
2 cups diced tomatoes
1½ cups shredded Monterey Jack cheese
1 jar (10 ounces) chunky salsa

In large, non-metallic container, mix lime juice, olive
oil, garlic, salt, and hot pepper sauce. Add chicken;
turn to coat with marinade. Marinate in refrigerator at
least 1 hour. Stack tortillas; wrap in foil and set aside.
Remove chicken from marinade; discard marinade.
Place chicken on prepared grill about 8 inches from
heat source. Grill, turning frequently, 16 to 20 minutes
or until chicken is fork-tender. While chicken is
cooking, heat tortillas by placing foil-wrapped package
on side of grill; grill until warmed, turning package
once or twice. Remove chicken to platter; cut into
¼-inch strips. To assemble, spread ¼ cup lettuce over
each tortilla. Top with chicken, tomatoes and cheese.
Drizzle with salsa; roll up.   *Makes 6 servings*

Favorite recipe from **Delmarva Poultry Industry, Inc.**

Barbecued Pork Tenderloin Sandwiches

½ cup ketchup
⅓ cup packed brown sugar
2 tablespoons bourbon or whiskey (optional)
1 tablespoon Worcestershire sauce
½ teaspoon dry mustard
¼ teaspoon ground red pepper
1 clove garlic, minced
2 whole pork tenderloins (about ¾ pound each), well trimmed
1 large red onion, sliced
6 hoagie rolls or Kaiser rolls, split

1. Prepare barbecue grill for direct cooking.

2. Combine ketchup, sugar, bourbon, Worcestershire sauce, mustard, ground red pepper and garlic in small, heavy saucepan with ovenproof handle; mix well. (If not ovenproof, wrap heavy-duty foil around handle.)

3. Set saucepan on one side of grid.* Place tenderloins on center of grid. Grill tenderloins, on uncovered grill, over medium-hot coals 8 minutes. Simmer sauce 5 minutes or until thickened, stirring occasionally.

4. Turn tenderloins with tongs; continue to grill, uncovered, 5 minutes. Add onion slices to grid. Set aside half of sauce; reserve. Brush tenderloins and onions with a portion of remaining sauce.

5. Continue to grill, uncovered, 7 to 10 minutes or until pork is juicy and barely pink in center, brushing with remaining sauce and turning onions and tenderloins halfway through grilling time. (If desired, insert instant-read thermometer** into center of thickest part of tenderloins. Thermometer should register 160°F.)

6. Carve tenderloins crosswise into thin slices; separate onion slices into rings. Divide meat and onion rings among rolls; drizzle with reserved sauce.

Makes 6 servings

*If desired, sauce may be prepared on rangetop. Combine ketchup, sugar, bourbon, Worcestershire sauce, mustard, ground red pepper and garlic in small saucepan. Bring to a boil over medium-high heat. Reduce heat to low and simmer, uncovered, 5 minutes or until thickened, stirring occasionally.

**Do not leave instant-read thermometer in tenderloins during grilling since the thermometer is not heatproof.

Open-Faced Mesquite Steak Sandwiches

1 pound flank steak
½ cup LAWRY'S® Mesquite Marinade with Lime Juice
8 slices sourdough bread or thin French bread
4 ounces refried beans
1 small red onion, thinly sliced
1 medium-sized green bell pepper, thinly sliced
½ cup chunky-style salsa
4 ounces Cheddar cheese, sliced

Pierce steak several times with fork; place in large resealable plastic bag or shallow glass baking dish. Pour Mesquite Marinade with Lime Juice over steak. Seal bag or cover dish. Refrigerate at least 30 minutes. Remove steak from marinade. Place on grill or rack of broiler pan. Grill or broil, 4 inches from heat source, 4 to 5 minutes on each side or to desired doneness. Thinly slice steak across the grain of meat; set aside. Spread bread slices with refried beans; cover with meat, onion and bell pepper. Top with salsa and cheese. Grill or broil 1 minute or just until cheese is melted.

Makes 4 servings

Ranch-Style Fajitas

2 **pounds flank or skirt steak**
½ **cup vegetable oil**
⅓ **cup lime juice**
2 **packages (1 ounce each) HIDDEN**
   VALLEY RANCH® Milk Recipe
   Original Ranch® Salad Dressing Mix
1 **teaspoon ground cumin**
½ **teaspoon black pepper**
6 **flour tortillas**
   Lettuce
   Guacamole, prepared HIDDEN VALLEY
   RANCH® Salad Dressing and picante
   sauce for toppings

Place steak in large baking dish. In small bowl, whisk together oil, lime juice, salad dressing mix, cumin and pepper. Pour mixture over steak. Cover and refrigerate several hours or overnight.

Remove steak; place marinade in small saucepan. Bring to a boil. Grill steak over medium-hot coals 8 to 10 minutes or to desired doneness, turning once and basting with heated marinade during last 5 minutes of grilling. Remove steak and slice diagonally across grain into thin slices. Heat tortillas following package directions. Divide steak strips among tortillas; roll up to enclose. Serve with lettuce and desired toppings.

Makes 6 servings

Simple

FIXINS'

Magically Moist Chicken

1 chicken (2½ to 3½ pounds), cut into
   pieces
½ cup HELLMANN'S® or BEST FOODS®
   Real or Light Mayonnaise or Low Fat
   Mayonnaise Dressing
1¼ cups Italian seasoned bread crumbs

1. Brush chicken on all sides with mayonnaise. Place bread crumbs in large plastic food storage bag. Add chicken 1 piece at a time; shake to coat well. Arrange on rack in broiler pan.

2. Bake in 425°F oven about 40 minutes or until golden brown and tender. *Makes 4 servings*

Greek-Style Baked Chicken

3 to 3½ pounds chicken pieces (Best of Fryer)
¼ cup lemon juice
1 tablespoon dried oregano, crushed
1 teaspoon LAWRY'S® Garlic Powder with Parsley
½ teaspoon LAWRY'S® Seasoned Salt
½ teaspoon LAWRY'S® Seasoned Pepper

Pierce chicken pieces several times with fork; place in large resealable plastic bag or shallow dish. In small bowl, combine all remaining ingredients; pour over chicken. Seal bag or cover dish. Refrigerate at least 30 minutes, turning often. Remove chicken from marinade, reserving marinade. In 13×9-inch baking dish, arrange chicken, skin side up. Brush with reserved marinade. Bake, uncovered, in 400°F oven 40 to 45 minutes or until chicken is no longer pink in center, basting frequently.   *Makes 4 to 6 servings*

Herb Batter Baked Chicken

⅔ cup prepared HIDDEN VALLEY
   RANCH® Original Ranch® Salad
   Dressing
1 egg, lightly beaten
1 broiler-fryer chicken (about 3 pounds),
   cut up
½ cup all-purpose flour
2 cups cornflake crumbs

Preheat oven to 350°F. On shallow plate, combine salad
dressing and egg; set aside. Rinse chicken; pat dry with
paper towels. Roll chicken pieces in flour; dip into
dressing mixture. Roll in cornflake crumbs. Place
chicken on large foil-lined baking pan. Bake until
tender, 45 to 50 minutes.   *Makes 4 servings*

Rolled Mexican Chicken

8 boneless, skinless chicken breast halves
    (2 pounds)
1 package (1.0 ounce) LAWRY'S® Taco
    Spices & Seasonings, divided
1 cup (4 ounces) shredded Monterey Jack
    cheese
1 can (4 ounces) diced green chiles,
    drained
¼ cup butter or margarine, melted, or 1 to
    2 egg whites, slightly beaten
1 bag (8 ounces) tortilla chips, crushed

Place chicken breasts between two sheets of waxed
paper; pound to ⅛-inch thickness. In medium bowl,
combine 1 tablespoon Taco Spices & Seasonings,
cheese and green chiles. Spread equal amounts of
cheese mixture onto chicken breasts. Roll up chicken
tightly; secure with toothpick. In shallow baking dish,
place butter. Roll each chicken bundle in melted
butter. In second shallow dish or on plate, combine
remaining Taco Spices & Seasonings and tortilla chips.
Roll each chicken bundle in seasoned chips to coat;
return to baking dish. Bake in 350°F oven 30 minutes
or until juices run clear when chicken is cut. Remove
from oven; let stand 5 minutes before slicing to serve.
Garnish, if desired.   *Makes 6 to 8 servings*

Lemon-Garlic Chicken

2 tablespoons parve margarine, melted
2 tablespoons soy sauce
2 tablespoons fresh lemon juice
3 cloves garlic, minced
1 package GALIL® Chicken Breast Cutlets
(1½ to 1¾ pounds)
Lemon slices (optional)

Preheat broiler. Combine margarine, soy sauce, lemon juice and garlic in small bowl; mix well. Place chicken on rack of broiler pan. Brush with half of margarine mixture. Broil 5 to 6 inches from heat 8 minutes. Turn chicken; brush with remaining margarine mixture. Broil 6 to 8 minutes or until chicken is no longer pink in center. Garnish with lemon slices, if desired.

Makes 4 servings

Italian Marinated Chicken

1 bottle (8 ounces) LAWRY'S® Classic
   Italian with Aged Parmesan Dressing
2 tablespoons finely chopped onion
2 tablespoons lemon juice
¾ teaspoon LAWRY'S® Seasoned Pepper
6 boneless, skinless chicken breast halves
   (about 1½ pounds)

In large resealable plastic bag or shallow glass dish,
combine all ingredients except chicken. Pierce chicken
several times with fork. Add to marinade. Seal bag or
cover dish. Refrigerate at least 1 hour, turning
occasionally. Broil or grill as desired.

Makes 6 to 8 servings

Hint: Chill leftover chicken and slice for use in salads
or sandwiches.

Chicken Picante

1 **medium lime**
½ **cup medium-hot chunky taco sauce**
¼ **cup Dijon-style mustard**
3 **whole chicken breasts, split, skinned and boned**
2 **tablespoons butter**
   Plain yogurt

1. Squeeze juice from lime; discard seeds. Combine lime juice, taco sauce and mustard in large bowl. Add chicken; turn to coat with marinade. Cover; marinate in refrigerator at least 30 minutes.

2. Melt butter in large skillet over medium heat until foamy.

3. Drain chicken, reserving marinade. Add chicken to skillet in single layer. Cook 5 minutes on each side or until chicken is lightly browned on both sides.

4. Add reserved marinade to skillet; cook 5 minutes or until chicken is tender and glazed with marinade. Remove chicken to serving platter; keep warm.

5. Boil marinade in skillet over high heat 1 minute; pour over chicken. Serve with yogurt.

Makes 6 servings

Chicken Cacciatore

8 ounces dry noodles
1 can (15 ounces) chunky Italian-style
  tomato sauce
1 cup chopped green bell pepper
1 cup sliced onion
1 cup sliced mushrooms
4 boneless skinless chicken breast halves
  (about 1 pound)

1. Cook noodles according to package directions; drain.

2. While noodles are cooking, combine tomato sauce, bell pepper, onion and mushrooms in microwavable dish. Cover loosely with plastic wrap or waxed paper; microwave on HIGH 6 to 8 minutes, stirring halfway through cooking time.

3. While sauce mixture is cooking, coat large skillet with nonstick cooking spray and heat over medium-high heat. Cook chicken breasts 3 to 4 minutes per side or until lightly browned.

4. Add sauce mixture to skillet with salt and pepper to taste. Reduce heat to medium and simmer 12 to 15 minutes. Serve over noodles.

Makes 4 servings

Grilled Italian Chicken

½ cup prepared HIDDEN VALLEY
   RANCH® Ranch Italian salad dressing
1 tablespoon Dijon-style mustard
4 boned chicken breast halves

In small bowl or measuring cup, whisk together salad dressing and mustard; reserve 3 tablespoons for final baste. Brush chicken generously with some of the remaining dressing mixture. Grill or broil, basting several times with dressing mixture, until chicken is golden and cooked through, about 5 minutes on each side. Brush generously with reserved dressing just before removing from grill.   *Makes 4 servings*

Rosemary's Chicken

4 **large boneless skinless chicken breast**
   halves (about 1½ pounds)
¼ **cup FRENCH'S® CLASSIC YELLOW®**
   Mustard
¼ **cup frozen orange juice concentrate,**
   undiluted
2 **tablespoons cider vinegar**
2 **teaspoons dried rosemary leaves,**
   crushed
4 **strips thick sliced bacon**

Place chicken in large resealable plastic food storage
bag or glass bowl. To prepare marinade, combine
mustard, orange juice concentrate, vinegar and
rosemary in small bowl. Pour over chicken. Seal bag or
cover bowl and marinate in refrigerator 30 minutes.
Wrap 1 strip bacon around each piece of chicken;
secure with toothpicks.*

Place chicken on grid, reserving marinade. Grill over
medium coals 25 minutes or until chicken is no longer
pink in center, turning and basting often with
marinade. (Do not baste during last 10 minutes of
cooking.) Remove toothpicks before serving.

Makes 4 servings

*Soak toothpicks in water 20 minutes to prevent burning.

Micro-Grilled Chicken

¼ **cup soy sauce**
2 **tablespoons firmly packed brown sugar**
2 **cloves garlic, pressed**
½ **teaspoon dry mustard**
½ **teaspoon paprika**
1 **chicken (about 3 pounds), cut up**

Combine first 5 ingredients in a small bowl. Arrange chicken in a single layer in 13×9-inch microwave-safe baking dish; place meatiest portions to outside edge. Pour soy mixture over chicken; turn to coat. Cover loosely with plastic wrap. Microwave on HIGH (100% power) 15 to 18 minutes, rearranging pieces halfway through cooking.* Chicken is done when juices run clear.

Oil hot grid to help prevent sticking. Grill chicken, on a covered grill, over medium KINGSFORD® Briquets, 10 minutes until skin is crisp and browned, turning once. *Makes 4 to 6 servings*

*This recipe was tested in a 700-watt microwave oven. If your oven's wattage is different, the cooking time will need to be adjusted.

Hot & Spicy Buffalo Chicken Wings

> 1 **can (15 ounces) DEL MONTE®**
>   **Original Sloppy Joe Sauce**
> ¼ **cup DEL MONTE® Thick & Chunky**
>   **Salsa, Medium**
> 1 **tablespoon red wine or cider vinegar**
> 20 **chicken wings (about 4 pounds)**

1. Preheat oven to 400°F.

2. Combine sloppy joe sauce, salsa and vinegar in small bowl. Remove ¼ cup sauce mixture to serve with cooked chicken wings; cover and refrigerate. Set aside remaining sauce mixture.

3. Arrange wings in single layer in large, shallow baking pan; brush wings with sauce mixture.

4. Bake chicken, uncovered, on middle rack in oven, 35 minutes or until chicken is no longer pink in center, turning and brushing with remaining sauce mixture after 15 minutes. Serve with reserved ¼ cup sauce. Garnish, if desired.   *Makes 4 servings*

Grilled Game Hens

½ cup K.C. MASTERPIECE® Barbecue
    Sauce

¼ cup dry sherry

3 tablespoons frozen orange juice
    concentrate, thawed

4 Cornish game hens (each about 1 to
    1½ pounds)

Combine barbecue sauce, sherry and orange juice
concentrate in a small saucepan. Bring to a boil.
Simmer 10 minutes; cool. Rinse hens; pat dry with
paper towels. Brush sauce onto hens. Oil hot grid to
help prevent sticking. Grill hens, on a covered grill,
over medium-hot KINGSFORD® Briquets, 40 to
50 minutes or until thigh moves easily and juices run
clear when pierced with fork, turning once. Baste with
sauce during last 10 minutes of grilling. Remove hens
from grill; baste with sauce.

Makes 4 to 6 servings

Quick Grilled Turkey
-----

1 **(12-pound) turkey, thawed**
¼ **cup olive oil**
   LAWRY'S® Seasoned Salt
   LAWRY'S® Seasoned Pepper
   LAWRY'S® Garlic Powder with Parsley

Preheat grill. Place turkey, breast side down, in large
shallow microwave-safe dish. Brush with olive oil;
sprinkle generously with Seasoned Salt and Seasoned
Pepper. Microwave on HIGH 12 minutes. Turn dish;
baste turkey with drippings in dish. Microwave on
MEDIUM-HIGH (75%) 20 to 25 minutes or until
internal temperature reaches 135°F, turning dish after
13 minutes. Sprinkle with Seasoned Salt and Garlic
Powder with Parsley. Place turkey on large sheet of
heavy-duty aluminum foil. Insert meat thermometer
into thickest part of turkey breast, making sure
thermometer does not touch any bones. Wrap in foil,
crimping foil around thermometer, making sure foil
does not touch rod of thermometer. (Or, if using a
turkey with a pop-up thermometer, make sure you can
easily open foil to check for presence of thermometer
during grilling.) Place turkey, breast side up, on grill.
Grill 13 to 15 minutes per pound (2½ to 3 hours) or
until internal temperature is 185°F and juices run
clear.   *Makes 8 to 10 servings*

Cajun Turkey Cutlets

⅓ cup KIKKOMAN® Teriyaki Baste &
   Glaze
2 tablespoons prepared spicy brown
   mustard
1 tablespoon prepared horseradish
1 teaspoon dried thyme leaves, crumbled
¾ teaspoon garlic powder
4 turkey breast cutlets*

Blend teriyaki baste & glaze, mustard and horseradish;
set aside. Combine thyme and garlic powder. Rub herb
mixture thoroughly onto both sides of cutlets; brush
lightly with teriyaki baste & glaze mixture. Let stand
30 minutes. Meanwhile, prepare coals for grilling.
Place cutlets on grill 5 to 7 inches from hot coals;
brush thoroughly with baste & glaze mixture. Cook
5 minutes; turn over. Brush with remaining baste &
glaze mixture. Cook 5 minutes longer, or until turkey
is no longer pink in center. (Or, place seasoned turkey
cutlets on rack of broiler pan; brush thoroughly with
baste & glaze mixture. Broil 4 to 5 inches from heat
7 minutes; turn over. Brush with remaining baste &
glaze mixture. Broil 7 minutes longer or until turkey is
no longer pink in center.)   *Makes 4 servings*

*Or, use a 2½- to 3-pound turkey half breast, skinned, boned and cut
lengthwise into 4 to 5 equal parts.

Prime Rib of Beef a la LAWRY'S®

1 (8-pound) prime rib roast
LAWRY'S® Seasoned Salt
Rock salt

Preheat oven to 500°F. Score fat on meat and rub
generously with Seasoned Salt. Cover bottom of
roasting pan with rock salt 1 inch thick. Place roast
directly on rock salt and roast, uncovered, 8 minutes
per pound for rare. *Makes 8 servings*

Christmas Two-Rib Beef Roast

1 (3-pound) 2-rib beef roast, well
   trimmed
1 teaspoon each dried sage, thyme and
   kosher or sea salt

Preheat oven to 325°F. Place roast, bone side down, on rack in open roasting pan. Rub surface with herbs and salt. Do not add water. Do not cover. Insert meat thermometer in thickest part not touching fat or bone. Roast to desired doneness, 27 to 30 minutes per pound for medium. Remove roast when meat thermometer registers 155°F. Allow roast to stand tented with foil 10 to 20 minutes before carving. (Roast temperature will continue to rise about 5°F.)

Makes 4 to 6 servings

Favorite recipe from **California Beef Council**

Rolled Mexican-Style Flank Steak

1 (2-pound) beef flank steak, butterflied
¾ cup A.1. ORIGINAL® or A.1. BOLD®
   Steak Sauce, divided
1 medium tomato, chopped
1 (4-ounce) can diced green chiles,
   undrained
1½ cups shredded Cheddar cheese
   (6 ounces)

Open butterflied steak like a book on smooth surface
and flatten slightly. Spread steak with ¼ cup steak
sauce. Layer with tomato, chiles and cheese. Roll up
steak from short edge; secure with wooden toothpicks
or tie with string if necessary. Place, seam side down,
in 13×9×2-inch baking pan. Top with remaining
½ cup steak sauce. Bake at 375°F 40 to 45 minutes or
to desired doneness. Remove toothpicks; let steak rest
10 minutes. Slice steak across grain. Serve
immediately. *Makes 6 servings*

Red Vinaigrette Marinated Beef

- 1 bottle (8 ounces) LAWRY'S® Classic Red Wine Vinaigrette with Cabernet Sauvignon Dressing
- ¾ teaspoon LAWRY'S® Garlic Salt
- ½ teaspoon dried rosemary, crushed
- ½ teaspoon dried oregano, crushed
- 1½ pounds sirloin, round or flank steak

In large resealable plastic bag or shallow glass dish, combine Classic Red Wine Vinaigrette, Garlic Salt, rosemary and oregano. Pierce steak several times with fork. Add steak to marinade; seal bag or cover dish. Refrigerate at least 1 hour, turning occasionally. Remove steak from marinade. Broil or grill, 4 to 5 inches from heat source, to desired doneness. Thinly slice steak.   *Makes 4 servings*

Hint: Toss any leftover cooked meat with greens, tomatoes, red onion and extra Classic Red Wine Vinaigrette for a hearty salad.

Marinated Flank Steak with Pineapple

1 can (15¼ ounces) DEL MONTE®
      Pineapple Slices In Its Own Juice,
      undrained
¼ cup teriyaki sauce
2 tablespoons honey
1 pound flank steak

1. Drain pineapple, reserving 2 tablespoons juice. Set aside pineapple for later use.

2. Combine reserved juice, teriyaki sauce and honey in shallow 2-quart dish, mix well. Add meat; turn to coat. Cover and refrigerate at least 30 minutes or overnight.

3. Remove meat from marinade, reserving marinade. Grill meat over hot coals (or broil), brushing occasionally with reserved marinade. Cook about 4 minutes on each side for rare; about 5 minutes on each side for medium; or about 6 minutes on each side for well done. During last 4 minutes of cooking, brush pineapple slices with marinade; grill until heated through.

4. Slice meat across grain; serve with pineapple. Garnish, if desired.   *Makes 4 servings*

Tip: Marinade that has come into contact with raw meat must be discarded or boiled for several minutes before serving with cooked food.

Garlic-Pepper Steak

1¼ teaspoons LAWRY'S® Garlic Powder
   with Parsley
1¼ teaspoons LAWRY'S® Seasoned Pepper
½ teaspoon LAWRY'S® Seasoned Salt
1 pound sirloin steak

Combine Garlic Powder with Parsley, Seasoned Pepper
and Seasoned Salt. Press seasoning mixture into both
sides of steak with back of spoon. Let stand 30 minutes.
Grill or broil as desired. *Makes 4 servings*

Tenderloins with Roasted Garlic Sauce

 2 whole garlic bulbs, separated into
 cloves but not peeled
 (about 5 ounces)
 ⅔ cup A.1. ORIGINAL® or A.1. BOLD®
 Steak Sauce, divided
 ¼ cup dry red wine
 ¼ cup finely chopped onion
 4 (4- to 6-ounce) beef tenderloin steaks,
 about 1 inch thick

Place unpeeled garlic cloves on baking sheet. Bake at
500°F 15 to 20 minutes or until garlic is soft; cool.

Squeeze garlic pulp from skins; coarsely chop pulp. In
small saucepan, over high heat, heat garlic pulp, ½ cup
steak sauce, wine and onion to a boil; reduce heat.
Simmer 5 minutes; keep warm.

Grill steaks over medium heat or broil 6 inches from
heat source 5 minutes on each side or to desired
doneness, basting occasionally with remaining steak
sauce. Serve steaks with warm sauce. Garnish as
desired. *Makes 4 servings*

Pork Medallions with Marsala

1   **pound pork tenderloin, cut into
    ½-inch-thick slices**
    All-purpose flour
2   **tablespoons olive oil**
1   **clove garlic, minced**
½   **cup sweet Marsala wine**
2   **tablespoons chopped fresh parsley**

1. Lightly dust pork with flour. Heat oil in large skillet over medium-high heat until hot. Add pork slices; cook 3 minutes per side or until browned. Remove from pan. Reduce heat to medium.

2. Add garlic to skillet; cook and stir 1 minute. Add pork and wine; cook 3 minutes or until pork is barely pink in center. Remove pork from skillet. Stir in parsley. Simmer wine mixture until slightly thickened, 2 to 3 minutes. Serve over pork.

Makes 4 servings

Oriental Glazed Tenderloins

⅓ cup KIKKOMAN® Teriyaki Baste &
   Glaze
1 tablespoon dry sherry
½ teaspoon ginger juice*
¼ teaspoon grated orange peel
2 pork tenderloins (¾ pound each)

Combine teriyaki baste & glaze, sherry, ginger juice
and orange peel; set aside. Place tenderloins on grill
4 to 5 inches from hot coals. Cook 25 minutes, turning
over occasionally. Brush both sides of tenderloins with
baste & glaze mixture. Cook 10 minutes longer, or
until meat thermometer inserted into thickest part of
meat registers 160°F, turning over and brushing
frequently with remaining baste & glaze mixture. Let
stand 10 minutes. To serve, cut meat across grain into
thin slices. *Makes 4 to 6 servings*

*Press enough fresh ginger root pieces through garlic press to
measure ½ teaspoon juice.

Stuffed Pork Chops

4 rib pork chops, cut 1¼ inches thick, slit
for stuffing
1½ cups prepared stuffing
1 tablespoon vegetable oil
Salt and pepper
1 bottle (12 ounces) HEINZ® Chili Sauce

Trim excess fat from chops. Place stuffing in pockets of
chops; secure with toothpicks. Brown chops in oil;
season with salt and pepper. Place chops in 2-quart
oblong baking dish. Pour chili sauce over chops. Cover
dish with foil; bake in 350°F oven 30 minutes. Stir
sauce to blend; turn and baste chops. Cover; bake
additional 30 to 40 minutes or until chops are tender.
Remove toothpicks from chops. Skim excess fat from
sauce. *Makes 4 servings*

Smothered Mexican Pork Chops

- 1 tablespoon vegetable oil
- 4 boneless thin-cut pork chops (about ¾ pound)
- 1 can (14½ ounces) chunky tomatoes, salsa- or Cajun-style
- 1 can (16 ounces) black beans
- 2 cups BIRDS EYE® frozen Farm Fresh Mixtures Broccoli, Corn and Red Peppers*

• Heat oil in large skillet over high heat. Add pork; cook until browned, about 4 minutes per side.

• Add tomatoes; reduce heat to medium. Cover and cook 5 minutes. Uncover and push pork to side of skillet.

• Add beans and vegetables. Place pork on top of vegetables. Increase heat to medium-high; cover and cook 5 minutes or until heated through.

Makes about 4 servings

*Or, substitute 2 cups BIRDS EYE® frozen Corn.

Spicy Glazed Short Ribs

1½ teaspoons dry mustard
½ teaspoon water
3 pounds beef short ribs, about 2½ inches long
½ cup KIKKOMAN® Teriyaki Baste & Glaze
2 cloves garlic, pressed
¼ teaspoon ground red pepper (cayenne)

Combine mustard with water to make a smooth paste; cover. Let stand 10 minutes. Meanwhile, score meaty side of ribs, opposite bone, ½ inch apart, ½ inch deep, both lengthwise and crosswise. Combine teriyaki baste & glaze, garlic, red pepper and mustard mixture. Place ribs on grill 5 to 7 inches from hot coals; brush thoroughly with baste & glaze mixture. Cook 15 minutes, or until ribs are brown and crispy, turning over and brushing frequently with remaining baste & glaze mixture. (Or, place ribs, scored side up, on rack of broiler pan; brush thoroughly with baste & glaze mixture. Broil 4 to 5 inches from heat 13 minutes, or until ribs are brown and crispy, turning over and brushing frequently with remaining baste & glaze mixture.)   *Makes 4 servings*

Grilled Ham Steaks with Apricot Glaze

> 1 **pound boneless fully cooked ham, cut into 4 (½-inch-thick) slices**
> ¼ **cup apricot jam**
> 2 **teaspoons Dijon mustard**
> 2 **teaspoons cider vinegar**

Prepare grill. Combine jam, mustard and vinegar in small bowl; blend well. Grill ham slices over hot coals 8 to 10 minutes or until lightly browned, brushing with apricot sauce occasionally and turning once. Serve immediately.   *Makes 4 servings*

Favorite recipe from **National Pork Producers Council**

The Original Baked Spam®

1 (12-ounce) can SPAM® Luncheon Meat
  Whole cloves
⅓ cup packed brown sugar
1 teaspoon water
1 teaspoon prepared mustard
½ teaspoon vinegar

Heat oven to 375°F. Place Spam® on rack in shallow baking pan. Score surface; stud with cloves. In small bowl, combine brown sugar, water, mustard and vinegar, stirring until smooth. Brush glaze over Spam®. Bake 20 minutes, basting often. Cut into slices to serve.   *Makes 6 servings*

Roast Leg of Lamb

3 tablespoons coarse-grained mustard
2 cloves garlic, minced*
1½ teaspoons rosemary leaves, crushed
½ teaspoon freshly ground black pepper
1 leg of lamb, well-trimmed, boned, rolled
    and tied (about 4 pounds)
  Mint jelly (optional)

Preheat oven to 400°F. Combine mustard, garlic, rosemary and pepper. Rub mustard mixture over surface of lamb. At this point lamb may be covered and refrigerated up to 24 hours before roasting.

Place roast on meat rack in shallow foil-lined roasting pan. Insert meat thermometer in thickest part of roast. Roast 15 minutes. *Reduce oven temperature to 325°F;* roast 20 minutes per pound until roast registers 150°F for medium.

Transfer roast to cutting board; tent with foil. Let stand 10 minutes before carving. Temperature will continue to rise 5° to 10°F during stand time.

Cut strings; discard. Carve roast into thin slices; serve with mint jelly, if desired.   *Makes 6 to 8 servings*

*For more intense garlic flavor inside the meat, cut garlic into slivers. Cut small pockets at random intervals throughout roast with tip of sharp knife; insert garlic slivers.

Bone-in Roast Leg of Lamb: Prepare as directed above, except roast a 5- to 6-pound bone-in leg of lamb 25 minutes per pound. After stand time, carve roast into thin slices with carving knife.

Lemony Lamb Chops

⅓ cup KIKKOMAN® Soy Sauce
½ lemon, thinly sliced
¼ teaspoon dried oregano leaves,
    crumbled
4 to 6 lamb rib or shoulder chops

Combine soy sauce, lemon and oregano; pour over
lamb chops in shallow pan. Turn chops over to coat
both sides well. Let stand 30 minutes, turning chops
over occasionally. Reserving marinade, remove chops.
Place on grill 4 to 5 inches from hot coals. Cook
4 minutes on each side (for rare), or to desired
doneness, turning over and brushing occasionally with
reserved marinade. (Or, place lamb chops on rack of
broiler pan. Broil 4 to 5 inches from heat 5 minutes;
turn over. Brush with reserved marinade. Broil
5 minutes longer [for rare], or to desired doneness.)

Makes 4 to 6 servings

Grilled Fresh Fish

3 to 3½ pounds fresh tuna or catfish
¾ cup prepared HIDDEN VALLEY Ranch®
Original Ranch® salad dressing
Chopped fresh dill
Lemon wedges (optional)

Place fish on heavy duty foil. Cover with salad dressing. Grill over medium-hot coals until fish turns opaque and flakes easily when tested with fork, 20 to 30 minutes. Or broil fish 15 to 20 minutes. Sprinkle with dill; garnish with lemon wedges, if desired.

Makes 6 servings

Grilled Lemon-Teriyaki Fish Steaks

⅓ cup KIKKOMAN® Teriyaki Baste & Glaze
¾ teaspoon grated lemon peel
2 tablespoons lemon juice
¾ teaspoon dried basil leaves, crumbled
2 pounds fish steaks (halibut, bass, swordfish or salmon), 1 inch thick

Combine teriyaki baste & glaze, lemon peel, lemon juice and basil. Place fish on oiled grill 4 to 6 inches from hot coals; brush generously with baste & glaze mixture. Cook 4 minutes; turn over. Brush with baste & glaze mixture. Cook 4 minutes longer, or until fish flakes easily with fork, brushing occasionally with remaining baste & glaze mixture. (Or, place fish on rack of broiler pan; brush with baste & glaze mixture. Broil 4 to 5 inches from heat 4 minutes; turn over. Brush with remaining baste & glaze mixture. Broil 4 to 5 minutes longer, or until fish flakes easily with fork.)

Makes 4 servings

Baked Cod with Tomatoes and Olives

- 1 pound cod fillets (about 4 fillets), cut into 2-inch-wide pieces
- 1 can (14½ ounces) diced Italian-style tomatoes, drained
- 2 tablespoons chopped pitted ripe olives
- 1 teaspoon bottled minced garlic
- 2 tablespoons chopped fresh parsley

1. Preheat oven to 400°F. Spray 13×9-inch baking dish with nonstick olive oil cooking spray. Arrange cod fillets in dish; season to taste with salt and pepper.

2. Combine tomatoes, olives and garlic in medium bowl. Spoon over fish.

3. Bake 20 minutes or until fish flakes when tested with fork. Sprinkle with parsley.

Makes 4 servings

Seafood Dijonnaise

1   **pound salmon or halibut fillets**
¾ **cup LAWRY'S® Chicken Sauté Country Dijon**
½ **medium onion, sliced**
¼ **cup toasted slivered almonds**
   Chopped fresh parsley or watercress (garnish)
   Lemon slices (garnish)

Place fish in shallow glass baking dish; cover with Chicken Sauté Country Dijon. Top with onion slices and almonds; cover with aluminum foil. Bake in 350°F oven 20 minutes. Uncover; bake 5 minutes longer or until fish flakes easily with fork.

Makes 4 servings

Presentation: Garnish with chopped parsley and lemon slices.

Chicken Dijonnaise: Substitute 1 pound boneless chicken breast halves for fish. Bake 25 to 30 minutes or until chicken is no longer pink in center.

Savory Salmon

6 **small salmon steaks (6 ounces each)**
¾ **cup prepared HIDDEN VALLEY**
   RANCH® Original Ranch® Salad
   Dressing
2 **teaspoons chopped fresh dill *or***
   ¼ teaspoon dried dill weed
1 **teaspoon chopped parsley**
   Lemon wedges
   Fresh dill sprigs (optional)

Preheat oven to 375°F. Arrange salmon in 13×9×2-inch
buttered baking dish; spread 2 tablespoons salad
dressing over each steak. Sprinkle with dill and parsley.
Bake until fish flakes easily when tested with fork,
10 to 15 minutes. Place under broiler 45 to 60 seconds
to brown. Serve with lemon wedges and garnish with
dill sprigs, if desired. *Makes 6 servings*

Teriyaki Trout

4   whole trout (about 2 pounds)
¾   cup LAWRY'S® Teriyaki Marinade with
     Pineapple Juice
½   cup sliced green onion
2   medium lemons, sliced
     Chopped fresh parsley (optional)

Pierce skin of trout several times with fork. Brush the inside and outside of each trout with Teriyaki Marinade with Pineapple Juice; stuff with green onion and lemon slices. Place in shallow glass baking dish. Pour all but ¼ cup Teriyaki Marinade with Pineapple Juice over trout; cover. Refrigerate at least 30 minutes. Meanwhile, heat grill. Remove trout from marinade. Place trout in oiled grill basket; brush with reserved marinade. Grill, 4 to 5 inches from heat source, 10 minutes or until trout flakes easily with fork, turning and brushing occasionally with reserved ¼ cup Teriyaki Marinade with Pineapple Juice. Sprinkle with parsley, if desired.   *Makes 4 servings*

Shrimp Miami

- **2 pounds shrimp, fresh or frozen**
- **¼ cup olive or vegetable oil**
- **2 teaspoons salt**
- **½ teaspoon white pepper**
- **¼ cup extra dry vermouth**
- **2 tablespoons lemon juice**

Thaw frozen shrimp. Peel shrimp, leaving last section of shell on. Remove sand veins and wash. Preheat electric frying pan to 320°F. Add oil, salt, pepper and shrimp. Cook 8 to 10 minutes or until shrimp are pink and tender, stirring constantly. Increase temperature to 420°F. Add vermouth and lemon juice. Cook 1 minute longer, stirring constantly. Drain. Serve hot or cold as an appetizer or entrée.

Makes 6 servings

Favorite recipe from **Florida Department of Agriculture and Consumer Services, Bureau of Seafood and Aquaculture**

Grilled Chicken Skewers

2 **boneless, skinless chicken breast halves
     (about ½ pound), cut into thin strips**
½ **pound bacon slices**
⅓ **cup lemon juice**
⅓ **cup honey**
1½ **teaspoons LAWRY'S® Lemon Pepper**
½ **teaspoon LAWRY'S® Seasoned Salt**

Thread chicken strips and bacon slices onto wooden
skewers. In shallow glass dish, combine remaining
ingredients. Add prepared skewers; cover dish and
marinate in refrigerator 1 hour or overnight. Heat grill
for medium coals or heat broiler. Remove skewers,
reserving marinade. Grill or broil skewers, 4 to
5 inches from heat source, 10 to 15 minutes or until
chicken is no longer pink in center and bacon is crisp,
basting with reserved marinade.

Makes 2 servings

Hint: Soak wooden skewers in water before adding
chicken and bacon to prevent skewers from burning.

Teriyaki Glazed Beef Kabobs

1¼ to 1½ pounds beef top or bottom
    sirloin, cut into 1-inch cubes
½ cup bottled teriyaki baste & glaze
1 teaspoon Oriental sesame oil (optional)
1 clove garlic, minced
8 to 12 green onions
1 or 2 plum tomatoes, cut into slices
    (optional)

Thread beef cubes on metal or bamboo skewers. (Soak bamboo skewers in water for at least 20 minutes to keep them from burning.) Combine teriyaki glaze, sesame oil and garlic in a small bowl. Brush beef and onions with part of the glaze, saving some for grilling; let stand 15 to 30 minutes.

Oil hot grid to help prevent sticking. Grill beef, on a covered grill, over medium KINGSFORD® Briquets, 6 to 9 minutes for medium doneness, turning several times and brushing with glaze. Add onions and tomatoes, if desired, to the grid 3 or 4 minutes after the beef; grill until onions and tomatoes are tender. Remove from grill; brush skewers, onions and tomatoes with remaining glaze.

Makes 4 servings

Island Surf & Turf Kabobs

1   **pound boneless tender beef, 1 inch
      thick**
¼   **cup KIKKOMAN® Lite Teriyaki
      Marinade & Sauce**
1   **clove garlic, pressed**
½   **pound medium-size raw shrimp**
1   **teaspoon sesame seed, toasted
      (optional)**

Trim beef and cut into 1-inch cubes; combine with lite
teriyaki sauce and garlic in medium bowl. Marinate
30 minutes. Meanwhile, leaving tails on, shell and
devein shrimp. Add shrimp to beef and teriyaki sauce
mixture; cover and refrigerate 30 minutes. Reserving
marinade, remove beef and shrimp. Thread each of
8 (10-inch) metal or bamboo* skewers alternately with
beef and shrimp. Place on grill 5 inches from hot coals.
Cook about 4 minutes; brush with reserved marinade.
Cook 4 minutes longer, or until shrimp turn pink. (Or,
place skewers on rack of broiler pan. Broil 3 minutes;
turn over. Brush with reserved marinade. Broil
3 minutes longer, or until shrimp turn pink.) Sprinkle
sesame seed evenly over beef and shrimp before
serving, if desired.   *Makes 4 to 6 servings*

*Soak bamboo skewers in water 30 minutes to prevent burning.

Grilled Prawns with Salsa Vera Cruz

1½ cups DEL MONTE® Thick & Chunky
     Salsa, Mild
1 orange, peeled and chopped
¼ cup sliced green onions
¼ cup chopped cilantro or parsley
1 small clove garlic, crushed
1 pound medium shrimp, peeled and
    deveined

1. Combine salsa, orange, green onions, cilantro and garlic in medium bowl.

2. Thread shrimp onto skewers; season with salt and pepper, if desired.

3. Brush grill with oil. Cook shrimp over hot coals about 3 minutes on each side or until shrimp turn pink. Top with salsa. Serve over rice and garnish, if desired. *Makes 4 servings*

Helpful Hint: Thoroughly rinse shrimp in cold water before cooking.

Glazed Lamb and Nectarines en Brochette

½ cup KIKKOMAN® Teriyaki Baste & Glaze
2 cloves garlic, pressed
½ teaspoon dried oregano leaves, crumbled
⅛ teaspoon pepper
1½ pounds boneless tender lamb or beef, 1 inch thick
4 to 6 medium-size ripe nectarines

Combine teriyaki baste & glaze, garlic, oregano and pepper; set aside. Cut lamb into 1½-inch pieces. Cut nectarines in half lengthwise; carefully remove pits. Cut enough halves to make 24 wedges. Thread each of 6 (12-inch) metal or bamboo* skewers alternately with lamb and nectarines; brush thoroughly with baste & glaze mixture. Place kabobs on grill 5 to 7 inches from hot coals. Cook 5 minutes on each side (for rare), or to desired doneness, brushing occasionally with remaining baste & glaze mixture. (Or, place kabobs on rack of broiler pan. Broil 4 to 5 inches from heat 3 to 5 minutes on each side [for rare], turning over and brushing occasionally with remaining baste & glaze mixture.)   *Makes 4 to 6 servings*

*Soak bamboo skewers in water 30 minutes to prevent burning.

Sloppy Joes

8   ounces lean ground beef or turkey
½   cup finely chopped onion
½   cup CONTADINA® Dalla Casa Buitoni
     Pizza Sauce
2   sandwich-size English muffins, split,
     toasted
½   cup (2 ounces) shredded cheddar
     cheese

CRUMBLE beef into medium skillet. Add onion; cook over medium-high heat for 4 to 5 minutes or until no longer pink. Drain. Stir in pizza sauce; cook, stirring occasionally, for 5 to 6 minutes or until heated through. Spoon mixture onto muffin halves; sprinkle with cheese.

BROIL 6 to 8 inches from heat for 1 to 2 minutes or until cheese is melted.   *Makes 4 servings*

French Dip Sandwiches

½ cup A.1. ORIGINAL® or A.1. BOLD®
  Steak Sauce, divided
1 tablespoon GREY POUPON® Dijon
  Mustard
4 steak rolls, split horizontally
8 ounces sliced cooked roast beef
1 (13¾-fluid-ounce) can COLLEGE INN®
  Beef Broth

In small bowl, blend ¼ cup steak sauce and mustard;
spread mixture evenly on cut sides of roll tops. Arrange
2 ounces beef on each roll bottom; replace roll tops
over beef. Slice sandwiches in half crosswise if desired.
In small saucepan, heat broth and remaining ¼ cup
steak sauce, stirring occasionally. Serve as a dipping
sauce with sandwiches. Garnish as desired.

Makes 4 servings

Mustard-Glazed Chicken Sandwiches

½ cup honey-mustard barbecue sauce,
    divided
4 Kaiser rolls, split
4 boneless skinless chicken breast halves
    (1 pound)
4 slices Swiss cheese
4 leaves leaf lettuce
8 slices tomato

1. Spread about 1 teaspoon barbecue sauce on cut sides of each roll.

2. Pound chicken breast halves between 2 pieces of plastic wrap to ½-inch thickness with flat side of meat mallet or rolling pin. Spread remaining barbecue sauce over chicken.

3. Cook chicken in large nonstick skillet over medium-low heat 5 minutes per side or until no longer pink in center. Remove skillet from heat. Place cheese slices on chicken; let stand 3 minutes to melt.

4. Place lettuce leaves and tomato slices on roll bottoms; top with chicken and roll tops.

Makes 4 servings

Hot Diggity Dogs

   2   **tablespoons butter or margarine**
   2   **large (1 pound) sweet onions, thinly
        sliced**
   ½   **cup FRENCH'S® CLASSIC YELLOW®
        Mustard**
   ½   **cup ketchup**
  10   **frankfurters**
  10   **frankfurter buns**

Melt butter in medium skillet over medium heat. Add
onion; cook 10 minutes or until very tender, stirring
often. Stir in mustard and ketchup. Cook over low heat
2 minutes, stirring often.

Place frankfurters and buns on grid. Grill over medium
coals 5 minutes or until frankfurters are browned and
buns are toasted, turning once. To serve, spoon onion
mixture into buns; top each with 1 frankfurter.

Makes 10 servings (about 2½ cups onion topping)

Tip: Onion topping is also great on hamburgers or
smoked sausage heros.

French Onion Burgers

2 pounds lean ground beef
1 package (1 ounce) HIDDEN VALLEY
   RANCH® French Onion Dip Mix
1 can (4 ounces) mushroom pieces,
   undrained

Combine beef, dip mix and mushrooms in a medium bowl. Shape beef mixture into 8 patties.

Oil hot grid to help prevent sticking. Grill patties, on a covered grill, over medium Kingsford briquets, 7 to 12 minutes for medium doneness, turning once.

Makes 8 servings

New-Age Reuben

½ medium head red cabbage, shredded
½ cup LAWRY'S® Herb & Garlic Marinade
    with Lemon Juice
8 slices rye bread
¾ pound thinly sliced cooked turkey
¾ pound thinly sliced Swiss cheese

In large resealable plastic bag or bowl, combine
cabbage and Herb & Garlic Marinade with Lemon
Juice. Refrigerate at least 1 hour or overnight; drain.
Layer ¼ of the cabbage mixture on top of each of four
bread slices; top with turkey, cheese and remaining
bread slices.   *Makes 4 servings*

Presentation: To serve warm, wrap sandwiches in
aluminum foil. Place in 300°F oven 20 minutes. Or,
spread outside surfaces of bread with softened butter.
Grill in nonstick skillet until browned on both sides.

Hint: Use turkey from the delicatessen.

🍓 **Make It** 🍓

HEALTHY

Crispy Oven-Baked Chicken

4 boneless skinless chicken breast halves
(about 4 ounces each)
¾ cup GUILTLESS GOURMET® Salsa
(mild, medium or hot)
Nonstick cooking spray
1 cup (3.5 ounces) crushed* GUILTLESS
GOURMET® Baked Tortilla Chips
(yellow corn, white corn or chili
& lime)

Wash chicken; pat dry with paper towels. Place chicken in shallow nonmetal pan or place in large resealable plastic food storage bag. Pour salsa over chicken. Cover with foil or seal bag; marinate in refrigerator 8 hours or overnight.

Preheat oven to 350°F. Coat baking sheet with cooking spray. Place crushed chips on waxed paper. Remove chicken from salsa, discarding salsa; roll chicken in crushed chips. Place on prepared baking sheet; bake 45 minutes or until chicken is no longer pink in center and chips are crisp. Serve hot.   *Makes 4 servings*

*Crush tortilla chips in the original bag or between two pieces of waxed paper with a rolling pin.

Nutrients per Serving:

Total Fat	4 g	Sodium	272 mg
Calories	237	Cholesterol	69 mg

Chicken Cordon Bleu

6   boneless skinless chicken breast halves
      (1¼ pounds)
1   tablespoon Dijon-style mustard
3   slices (1 ounce each) lean ham, cut into
      halves
3   slices (1 ounce each) reduced-fat Swiss
      cheese, cut into halves
      Nonstick cooking spray
¼   cup unseasoned dry bread crumbs
2   tablespoons minced fresh parsley
3   cups hot cooked rice

1. Preheat oven to 350°F. Pound chicken breasts between 2 pieces of plastic wrap to ¼-inch thickness using flat side of meat mallet or rolling pin. Brush mustard on 1 side of each chicken breast; layer 1 slice each of ham and cheese over mustard. Roll up each chicken breast from short end; secure with wooden picks. Spray tops of chicken rolls with cooking spray; sprinkle with bread crumbs.

2. Arrange chicken rolls in 11×7-inch baking pan. Cover; bake 10 minutes. Uncover; bake about 20 minutes or until chicken is no longer pink in center.

3. Stir parsley into rice; serve with chicken. Serve with vegetables, if desired.   *Makes 6 servings*

Nutrients per Serving:

Total Fat	6 g	Sodium	294 mg
Calories	297	Cholesterol	55 mg

Crispy Baked Chicken

8 ounces (1 cup) nonfat French onion dip
   Skim milk
1 cup corn flake crumbs
½ cup wheat germ
6 skinless chicken breast halves or thighs
   (about 1½ pounds)

1. Preheat oven to 350°F. Spray baking pan with nonstick cooking spray.

2. Place dip in shallow bowl; stir until smooth. Add milk, 1 tablespoon at a time, until pourable consistency is reached.

3. Combine cornflake crumbs and wheat germ on plate.

4. Dip chicken pieces in milk mixture; then roll in corn flake mixture. Place chicken in prepared pan. Bake 45 to 50 minutes or until juices run clear when pierced with fork and chicken is no longer pink near the bone.   *Makes 6 servings*

Nutrients per Serving:

Total Fat	4 g	Sodium	373 mg
Calories	267	Cholesterol	69 mg

Tex-Mex Chicken

1   teaspoon ground red pepper
¾   teaspoon onion powder
¾   teaspoon garlic powder
½   teaspoon dried basil leaves
½   teaspoon salt, divided
⅛   teaspoon dried oregano leaves
⅛   teaspoon dried thyme leaves
⅛   teaspoon gumbo file powder*
6   boneless skinless chicken breast halves
      (1½ pounds)
¾   pound potatoes, cut into 1-inch wedges
      Nonstick cooking spray
¼   teaspoon black pepper

*Gumbo file powder is a seasoning widely used in Creole cooking. It
is available in the spice or gourmet section of most large
supermarkets.

1. Combine ground red pepper, onion powder, garlic
powder, basil, ¼ teaspoon salt, oregano, thyme and
gumbo file powder in small bowl. Rub mixture on all
surfaces of chicken. Place chicken in single layer in
13×9-inch baking pan. Refrigerate, covered, 4 to 8
hours.

2. Preheat oven to 350°F. Place potatoes in medium
bowl. Spray potatoes lightly with cooking spray; toss to
coat. Sprinkle with remaining ¼ teaspoon salt and
black pepper; toss to combine. Add to chicken in pan.

3. Bake, uncovered, 40 to 45 minutes or until potatoes are tender and chicken is no longer pink in center. Or, grill chicken and potatoes, in aluminum foil pan, on covered grill over medium-hot coals, 20 to 30 minutes or until potatoes are tender and chicken is no longer pink in center. Serve with additional vegetables, if desired.   *Makes 6 servings*

Nutrients per Serving:

Total Fat	3 g	Sodium	237 mg
Calories	262	Cholesterol	55 mg

Stuffed Chicken Breasts à la Française

6   boneless, skinless chicken breast
    halves, with pockets (6 ounces each)
6   ounces (1 carton) ALPINE LACE® Fat
    Free Cream Cheese with Garlic
    & Herbs
½   cup finely chopped green onions
    (tops only)
2   teaspoons snipped fresh rosemary
    leaves *or* ¾ teaspoon dried rosemary
½   cup all-purpose flour
1   teaspoon freshly ground black pepper
⅛   cup low sodium chicken broth
⅓   cup dry white wine or low sodium
    chicken broth
8   sprigs fresh rosemary, about 8 inches
    long (optional)

1. Preheat the oven to 350°F. Spray a 13×9×2-inch baking dish with nonstick cooking spray. Rinse the chicken and pat dry with paper towels. In a medium-size bowl, mix the cream cheese with the green onions and rosemary until well blended. Stuff the pockets of the chicken breasts with this mixture.

2. On a piece of wax paper, blend the flour and pepper. Roll each chicken breast in the seasoned flour, then arrange in the baking dish. Pour over the broth and the wine.

3. Cover the dish tightly with foil and bake for 30 minutes. Uncover and bake 10 minutes more or until the juices run clear when the thickest piece of chicken is pierced with a fork.

4. Transfer the chicken to a serving platter and garnish each with a sprig of rosemary, if you wish.

Makes 6 servings

Nutrients per Serving (½ chicken breast):

Total Fat	3 g	Carbohydrate	21 g
Calories	274	Cholesterol	107 mg

Chicken Breasts with Crabmeat Stuffing

    4   boneless skinless chicken breast halves
        (about 1 pound)
    ¾   cup whole wheat cracker crumbs,
        divided
    3   ounces canned crabmeat, drained and
        rinsed twice
    ¼   cup fat-free mayonnaise
    2   tablespoons grated Parmesan cheese
    2   tablespoons finely chopped green
        onions
    2   tablespoons fresh lemon juice
    ¼   teaspoon hot pepper sauce
    1   tablespoon dried parsley flakes
    1   teaspoon ground black pepper
    1   teaspoon paprika
    ½   cup 1% low fat milk

1. Pound chicken breasts between two pieces of plastic wrap to ¼-inch thickness, using flat side of meat mallet or rolling pin.

2. Combine ¼ cup cracker crumbs, crabmeat, mayonnaise, cheese, onions, lemon juice and pepper sauce in medium bowl. Divide filling evenly among chicken breasts. Roll up each chicken breast from short side, tucking in ends; secure with wooden pick.

3. Combine remaining ½ cup cracker crumbs, parsley flakes, black pepper and paprika in shallow bowl. Dip chicken in milk; roll in cracker crumb mixture.

4. Place chicken in microwavable round or square baking dish. Cover with waxed paper. Microwave at HIGH 10 minutes or until chicken is no longer pink in center. Remove chicken from dish. Remove wooden picks. Add remaining milk to pan juices; microwave at HIGH 1 minute or until sauce comes to a boil. Serve chicken with sauce. *Makes 4 servings*

Nutrients per Serving:

Total Fat	5 g	Sodium	424 mg
Calories	246	Cholesterol	83 mg

Southwestern Pineapple and Chicken

1   can (20 ounces) DOLE® Pineapple
    Slices
1   tablespoon lime juice
1   tablespoon vegetable oil
½   teaspoon chili powder
½   teaspoon dried oregano leaves, crushed
1   garlic clove, finely chopped
6   boneless, skinless chicken breast
    halves, crushed

• Drain pineapple; reserve ½ cup juice.

• Combine reserved pineapple juice, lime juice, oil, chili powder, oregano and garlic in shallow, non-metallic dish. Add chicken and pineapple; turn to coat both sides with marinade. Cover and marinate 15 minutes in refrigerator.

• Grill or broil chicken and pineapple, brushing occasionally with reserved marinade, 10 to 15 minutes on each side or until chicken is no longer pink in center and pineapple is lightly browned. Discard any remaining marinade.   *Makes 6 servings*

Nutrients per Serving:

Total Fat	6 g	Sodium	83 mg
Calories	252	Cholesterol	92 mg

Southwestern Pineapple and Fish: Substitute 2 pounds fish steaks such as halibut or sea bass for chicken. Prepare recipe as directed except grill fish 8 to 10 minutes on each side or until fish flakes easily with fork.

Balsamic Chicken

6   boneless skinless chicken breast halves
1½ teaspoons fresh rosemary leaves,
       minced, *or* ½ teaspoon dried
       rosemary
2   cloves garlic, minced
¾   teaspoon pepper
½   teaspoon salt
1   tablespoon olive oil
¼   cup good-quality balsamic vinegar

1. Rinse chicken and pat dry. Combine rosemary,
garlic, pepper and salt in small bowl; mix well. Place
chicken in large bowl; drizzle chicken with oil and rub
with spice mixture. Cover and refrigerate overnight.

2. Preheat oven to 450°F. Spray heavy roasting pan or
iron skillet with nonstick cooking spray. Place chicken
in pan; bake 10 minutes. Turn chicken over, stirring in
3 to 4 tablespoons water if drippings are beginning to
stick to pan.

3. Bake about 10 minutes or until chicken is golden
brown and no longer pink in center. If pan is dry, stir
in another 1 to 2 tablespoons water to loosen
drippings.

4. Drizzle balsamic vinegar over chicken in pan.
Transfer chicken to plates. Stir liquid in pan; drizzle
over chicken.   *Makes 6 servings*

Roasted Rosemary-Lemon Chicken

- 1 whole chicken (3¼ pounds)
- ½ teaspoon ground black pepper
- 1 lemon, cut into eighths
- ¼ cup fresh parsley
- 4 sprigs fresh rosemary
- 3 fresh sage leaves
- 2 sprigs fresh thyme
- 1 can (14 ounces) ⅓-less-sodium chicken broth
- 1 cup sliced onions
- 4 cloves garlic
- 1 cup thinly sliced carrots
- 1 cup thinly sliced zucchini

1. Preheat oven to 350°F. Trim fat from chicken, leaving skin on. Rinse chicken and pat dry with paper towels. Fill cavity of chicken with black pepper, lemon, parsley, rosemary, sage and thyme. Close cavity with skewers.

2. Combine broth, onions and garlic in heavy roasting pan. Place chicken over broth. Bake 1½ hours or until juices run clear when pierced with fork. Remove chicken to serving plate.

3. Combine carrots and zucchini in small saucepan with tight-fitting lid. Add ¼ cup water; bring to a boil over high heat. Reduce heat to medium. Cover and steam 4 minutes or until vegetables are crisp-tender. Transfer vegetables to colander; drain.

4. Remove skewers. Discard lemon and herbs from cavity of chicken. Remove skin from chicken. Cut chicken into pieces. Remove onions and garlic from pan with slotted spoon to medium serving bowl or plate. Add carrots and zucchini; mix well. Arrange vegetable mixture around chicken.

Makes 6 servings

Nutrients per Serving:

Total Fat	10 g	Sodium	133 mg
Calories	282	Cholesterol	120 mg

Light-Style Lemon Chicken

2 egg whites, slightly beaten
¾ cup fresh bread crumbs
2 tablespoons sesame seeds (optional)
¾ teaspoon salt
¼ teaspoon black pepper
4 boneless skinless chicken breast halves
    (about 1¼ pounds)
2 tablespoons all-purpose flour
¾ cup ⅓-less-salt chicken broth
4 teaspoons cornstarch
¼ cup fresh lemon juice
2 tablespoons brown sugar
1 tablespoon honey
2 tablespoons vegetable oil
4 cups thinly sliced napa cabbage or
    romaine lettuce

1. Place egg whites in shallow dish. Combine bread crumbs, sesame seeds, salt and pepper in another shallow dish.

2. Dust chicken with flour; dip into egg whites. Roll in crumb mixture.

3. Blend broth into cornstarch in small bowl until smooth. Stir in lemon juice, brown sugar and honey.

4. Heat oil in large nonstick skillet over medium heat. Add chicken; cook 5 minutes. Turn chicken over; cook 5 to 6 minutes until browned and no longer pink in center. Transfer to cutting board; keep warm.

5. Wipe skillet clean with paper towel. Stir broth mixture and add to skillet. Cook and stir 3 to 4 minutes until sauce boils and thickens.

6. Place cabbage on serving dish. Cut chicken crosswise into ½-inch slices; place over cabbage. Pour sauce over chicken. *Makes 4 servings*

Nutrients per Serving:

Total Fat	10 g	Sodium	541 mg
Calories	292	Cholesterol	57 mg

Curried Chicken Cutlets

4 boneless skinless chicken breast halves
½ cup all-purpose flour
1 teaspoon salt
1 teaspoon ground red pepper
1 tablespoon curry powder
2 red bell peppers, cut lengthwise into
   ¼-inch-thick slices
1 teaspoon olive oil
¼ cup lemon juice
¼ cup finely chopped fresh cilantro

1. Pound chicken breasts to ¼-inch thickness between 2 pieces of plastic wrap with flat side of meat mallet or rolling pin.

2. Combine flour, salt, ground red pepper and curry powder in shallow bowl. Dip chicken cutlets in flour mixture to coat both sides well; shake off excess flour.

3. Generously spray nonstick skillet with nonstick cooking spray; heat over medium heat. Add 2 chicken cutlets; cook 3 to 4 minutes per side. Transfer to warm plate; cover and set aside. Repeat with remaining chicken.

4. Add bell peppers and olive oil to skillet; cook and stir 5 minutes or until peppers are tender. Stir in lemon juice and cilantro; heat through. Pour sauce over chicken cutlets. *Makes 4 servings*

Nutrients per Serving:

Total Fat	5 g	Cholesterol	73 mg
Calories	230	Sodium	599 mg

Broiled Chicken Breast with Cilantro Salsa

4   small boneless skinless chicken breast
     halves (4 ounces each)
4   tablespoons lime juice, divided
     Black pepper
2   tablespoons pine nuts (optional)
½   cup lightly packed fresh cilantro,
     chopped
⅓   cup thinly sliced or minced green
     onions
¼   to ½ jalapeño pepper, seeded, minced

1. Spray broiler pan or baking sheet with nonstick cooking spray.

2. Brush chicken with 2 tablespoons lime juice. Place on prepared pan. Sprinkle generously with pepper; set aside.

3. To make Cilantro Salsa, heat large nonstick skillet over medium heat. Add pine nuts. Cook and stir 6 to 8 minutes or until golden. Combine remaining 2 tablespoons lime juice, pine nuts, cilantro, onions and jalapeño in small bowl; stir to combine. Set aside.

4. Broil chicken 1 to 2 inches from heat 8 to 10 minutes or until chicken is no longer pink in center. Serve with Cilantro Salsa.   *Makes 4 servings*

Nutrients per Serving:

Total Fat	3 g	Sodium	80 mg
Calories	122	Cholesterol	58 mg

Chicken and Mozzarella Melts

2   cloves garlic, crushed
4   boneless skinless chicken breast halves
      (¾ pound)
    Nonstick cooking spray
⅛   teaspoon salt
⅛   teaspoon pepper
1   tablespoon prepared pesto sauce
4   small hard rolls, split
12 fresh spinach leaves
8   fresh basil leaves* (optional)
3   plum tomatoes, sliced
½   cup (2 ounces) shredded part-skim
      mozzarella cheese

*Omit basil leaves if fresh are unavailable. Do not substitute dried basil leaves.

1. Preheat oven to 350°F. Rub garlic on all surfaces of chicken. Spray medium nonstick skillet with cooking spray; heat over medium heat until hot. Add chicken; cook 5 to 6 minutes on each side or until no longer pink in center. Sprinkle with salt and pepper.

2. Brush pesto sauce on bottom halves of rolls; layer with spinach, basil, if desired, and tomatoes. Place chicken in rolls; sprinkle cheese evenly over chicken. (If desired, sandwiches may be prepared up to this point and wrapped in aluminum foil. Refrigerate until ready to bake. Bake in preheated 350°F oven until chicken is warm, about 20 minutes.)

3. Wrap sandwiches in aluminum foil; bake about 10 minutes or until cheese is melted.

Makes 4 servings

Nutrients per Serving:

Total Fat	5 g	Sodium	498 mg
Calories	299	Cholesterol	47 mg

Barbecued Cheese Burgers

BARBECUE SPREAD
- ¼ cup reduced calorie mayonnaise
- ¼ cup bottled barbecue sauce
- ¼ cup red or green pepper hamburger relish

BURGERS
- 1½ pounds ground lean turkey or ground beef round
- ⅓ cup bottled barbecue sauce
- ⅓ cup minced red onion
- 1 teaspoon hot red pepper sauce
- ½ teaspoon garlic salt
- 6 sesame seed hamburger buns, split
- 6 slices (1 ounce each) ALPINE LACE® Fat Free Pasteurized Process Skim Milk Cheese Product—For Cheddar Lovers

1. To make the Barbecue Spread: In a small bowl, stir all of the spread ingredients together until well blended. Cover and refrigerate.

2. To make the Burgers: In a medium-size bowl, mix the turkey, barbecue sauce, onion, hot pepper sauce and garlic salt. Form into 6 patties (5 inches each), about 1¼ inches thick. Cover with plastic wrap and refrigerate for at least 30 minutes or overnight.

3. To cook the Burgers: Preheat the grill (or broiler). Grill over medium-hot coals (or broil) 4 inches from the heat for 4 minutes on each side for medium or until cooked the way you like them. Place the buns alongside the burgers for the last 5 minutes to heat, if you wish. Top each burger with a slice of cheese.

4. To serve, spread the insides of the buns with the Barbecue Spread and stuff each bun with a burger.

Makes 6 burgers

Nutrients per Serving:

Total Fat	10 g	Cholesterol	63 mg
Calories	351		

Vegetable-Stuffed Turkey Breast

¾ cup chopped onion
2 tablespoons margarine, divided
1 cup cooked regular long-grain rice
1 cup shredded carrots
1 cup sliced mushrooms
½ cup chopped fresh parsley
¼ cup EGG BEATERS® Healthy Real Egg
   Product
½ teaspoon poultry seasoning
1 whole turkey breast (about 5 pounds)

In small skillet, over medium heat, sauté onion in
1 tablespoon margarine until tender; set aside.

In large bowl, combine rice, carrots, mushrooms,
parsley, Egg Beaters® and poultry seasoning; stir in
onion. Remove skin from turkey breast. Place rice
mixture into cavity of turkey; cover cavity with foil.
Place turkey, breast-side up, on rack in roasting pan.
Melt remaining margarine; brush over turkey. Roast at
350°F according to package directions or until meat
thermometer registers 170°F. If necessary, tent breast
with foil after 30 minutes to prevent overbrowning. Let
turkey stand 15 minutes before carving. Portion 3
ounces sliced turkey and ½ cup stuffing per serving.
(Freeze remaining turkey for another use.)

Makes 8 servings

Nutrients per Serving:

Total Fat	5 g	Sodium	99 mg
Calories	207	Cholesterol	59 mg

Broiled Turkey Burgers

- 1 **pound ground turkey**
- ¼ **cup finely chopped green onions**
- ¼ **cup finely chopped fresh parsley**
- 2 **tablespoons dry red wine**
- 1 **teaspoon Italian seasoning**
- ¼ **teaspoon salt**
- ¼ **teaspoon ground black pepper**
- 4 **whole wheat hamburger buns**

1. Preheat broiler.

2. Combine turkey, onions, parsley, wine, Italian seasoning, salt and pepper in large bowl; mix well. Shape turkey mixture into 4 (¾-inch-thick) burgers.

3. Spray rack of broiler pan with nonstick cooking spray; place burgers on rack. Broil burgers, 4 inches from heat source, 5 to 6 minutes per side or until burgers are no longer pink in centers. Serve on whole wheat buns with lettuce, grilled pineapple slice and bell pepper strips, if desired.   *Makes 4 servings*

Nutrients per Serving:

Total Fat	3 g	Sodium	585 mg
Calories	291	Cholesterol	50 mg

Beef Pot Roast

3 pounds beef eye of round roast
1 can (14 ounces) fat-free reduced-
   sodium beef broth
2 cloves garlic
1 teaspoon herbs de Provence *or*
   ¼ teaspoon *each* rosemary, thyme,
   sage and savory
4 small turnips, peeled and cut into
   wedges
10 ounces fresh brussels sprouts, trimmed
20 baby carrots
4 ounces pearl onions, outer skins
   removed
2 teaspoons cornstarch mixed with
   1 tablespoon water

1. Heat large nonstick skillet over medium-high heat.
Place roast, fat side down, in skillet. Cook until evenly
browned. Remove roast from skillet; place in Dutch
oven.

2. Pour broth into Dutch oven; bring to a boil over
high heat. Add garlic and herbs de Provence. Cover
tightly. Reduce heat; cook 1½ hours.

3. Add turnips, brussels sprouts, carrots and onions to
Dutch oven. Cover; cook 25 to 30 minutes or until
vegetables are tender. Remove meat and vegetables
from Dutch oven. Arrange on serving platter; cover
with foil to keep warm.

4. Strain broth; return to Dutch oven. Stir blended cornstarch mixture into broth. Bring to a boil over medium-high heat; cook and stir 1 minute or until thick and bubbly. Serve immediately with pot roast and vegetables. *Makes 6 servings*

Nutrients per Serving:			
Total Fat	7 g	Sodium	287 mg
Calories	299	Cholesterol	79 mg

Meat Loaf with Parmesan Crust

1   tablespoon vegetable oil
1   cup chopped yellow onion
1   cup chopped green bell pepper
2   teaspoons minced garlic
2   pounds ground lean turkey or ground
     beef round
¼   cup egg substitute *or* 1 large egg,
     beaten
⅓   cup bottled chili sauce
2   cups seasoned bread crumbs, divided
½   teaspoon freshly ground black pepper
¾   cup (3 ounces) shredded ALPINE
     LACE® Fat Free Pasteurized Process
     Skim Milk Cheese Product—For
     Parmesan Lovers
½   cup firmly packed parsley leaves
3   strips turkey bacon (optional)

1. Preheat the oven to 350°F. Spray a 9×5×3-inch loaf pan with nonstick cooking spray. In a large skillet, heat the oil over medium-high heat. Add the onion, bell pepper and garlic and sauté for 5 minutes or until tender. Transfer to a large bowl.

2. Add the turkey, egg substitute (or the egg), chili sauce, 1½ cups of the bread crumbs and the black pepper to the onion mixture. Mix with your hands until well blended.

3. In a food processor or blender, process the Parmesan, parsley and the remaining ½ cup of bread crumbs for 30 seconds or until fine crumbs form. Mix into the turkey mixture.

4. Transfer the turkey mixture to the pan and pat into a loaf, mounding it slightly in the center. Place the bacon strips diagonally across the top of the loaf, if you wish.

5. Bake for 1 hour or until an instant-read thermometer inserted into the center registers 165°F. Loosely cover meat loaf with foil during the last 15 minutes. Transfer to a warm platter, let stand for 10 minutes, then slice and serve.   *Makes 12 servings*

Nutrients per Serving (¾-inch slice):

Total Fat	8 g	Cholesterol	61 mg
Calories	212		

Mexican Meatloaf

1½ pounds lean ground turkey or beef
1 cup GUILTLESS GOURMET® Salsa
   (mild, medium or hot), divided
1 cup (3.5 ounces) crushed GUILTLESS
   GOURMET® Baked Tortilla Chips
   (yellow or white corn)
½ medium onion, chopped
3 egg whites, slightly beaten
½ teaspoon coarsely ground black pepper

Preheat oven to 350°F. Mix turkey, ½ cup salsa, crushed chips, onion, egg whites and pepper in large bowl until lightly blended. Shape into loaf and place in 9×5-inch loaf pan.

Bake 1 hour or until firm. Pour remaining ½ cup salsa over top; bake 10 minutes more. Let stand 10 minutes before slicing and serving.   *Makes 4 servings*

Nutrients per Serving:

Total Fat	3 g	Sodium	357 mg
Calories	209	Cholesterol	50 mg

Veal in Gingered Sweet Bell Pepper Sauce

1   teaspoon olive oil
¾   pound veal cutlets, thinly sliced
½   cup skim milk
1   tablespoon finely chopped fresh
    tarragon
2   teaspoons crushed capers
1   jar (7 ounces) roasted red peppers,
    drained
1   tablespoon lemon juice
½   teaspoon freshly grated ginger
½   teaspoon ground black pepper

1. Heat oil in medium saucepan over high heat. Add veal; lightly brown both sides. Reduce heat to medium. Add milk, chopped tarragon and capers. Cook, uncovered, 5 minutes or until veal is fork-tender and milk evaporates.

2. Place roasted peppers, lemon juice, ginger and black pepper in food processor or blender; process until smooth. Set aside.

3. Remove veal from pan with slotted spoon; place in serving dish. Spoon roasted pepper sauce over veal. Sprinkle with cooked capers and fresh tarragon, if desired.   *Makes 4 servings*

Nutrients per Serving:

Total Fat	4 g	Sodium	89 mg
Calories	120	Cholesterol	54 mg

Stuffed Pork Tenderloin

2 teaspoons minced garlic
2 teaspoons snipped fresh rosemary
  leaves *or* ½ teaspoon dried rosemary
2 teaspoons snipped fresh thyme leaves
  or ½ teaspoon dried thyme
1 teaspoon salt
½ teaspoon freshly ground black pepper
1 boneless endcut rolled pork loin with
  tenderloin attached (4 pounds), tied
1 tablespoon unsalted butter substitute
1 cup thin strips yellow onion
2 large tart apples, peeled, cored and
  thinly sliced (2 cups)
10 thin slices (½ ounce each) ALPINE
   LACE® Reduced Fat Swiss Cheese
1 cup apple cider or apple juice

1. Preheat the oven to 325°F. Fit a 13×9×3-inch baking pan with a rack. In a small bowl, combine the garlic, rosemary, thyme, salt and pepper. Untie and unroll the pork loin, laying it flat. Rub half of the spice mixture onto the pork.

2. In a medium-size skillet, melt the butter over medium-high heat. Add the onion and apples and sauté for 5 minutes or until soft. Spread this mixture evenly on the pork and cover with the cheese slices.

3. Starting from one of the widest ends, re-roll the pork, jelly-roll style. Tie the roast with cotton string at 1-inch intervals and rub the outside with the remaining spice mixture. Place the roast on the rack in the pan and pour the apple cider over it.

4. Roast, uncovered, basting frequently with the pan drippings, for 2 to 2½ hours or until an instant-read thermometer inserted in the thickest part registers 160°F. Let the roast stand for 15 minutes before slicing.   *Makes 16 servings*

Nutrients per Serving (½-inch slice):

Total Fat	10 g	Cholesterol	57 mg
Calories	190		

Moo Shu Pork

1 cup DOLE® Tropical Fruit Juice or Pineapple Juice
1 tablespoon low-sodium soy sauce
2 teaspoons sesame seed oil
2 teaspoons cornstarch
8 ounces pork tenderloin, cut into thin strips
1 package (10 oz.) DOLE® Oriental Style Vegetables
¼ cup hoisin sauce (optional)
8 (8-inch) flour tortillas, warmed
2 DOLE® Green Onions, cut into thin strips

• **Stir** juice, soy sauce, sesame seed oil and cornstarch in shallow, non-metallic dish until blended; remove ½ cup mixture for sauce.

• **Add** pork to remaining juice mixture in shallow dish. Cover and marinate 15 minutes in refrigerator. Drain pork; discard marinade.

• **Cook** and stir pork in large, nonstick skillet over medium-high heat 2 minutes or until pork is lightly browned. Add vegetables, cutting broccoli into smaller pieces, if desired. Cook and stir 3 to 4 minutes or until vegetables are tender-crisp. Stir in reserved ½ cup juice mixture; cook 1 minute or until sauce thickens.

• **Spread** hoisin sauce onto center of each tortilla, if desired; top with moo shu pork. Sprinkle with green onions. Fold opposite sides of tortilla over filling; fold remaining sides of tortilla over filling.

Makes 4 servings

Nutrients per Serving:

Total Fat	6 g	Sodium	374 mg
Calories	256	Cholesterol	27 mg

Grilled Pork Tenderloin with Apple Salsa

  1 tablespoon chili powder
½ teaspoon garlic powder
  1 pound pork tenderloin
  2 Granny Smith apples, peeled, cored and finely chopped
  1 can (4 ounces) chopped green chilies, undrained
¼ cup lemon juice
  3 tablespoons finely chopped fresh cilantro
  1 clove garlic, minced
  1 teaspoon dried oregano leaves, crushed
½ teaspoon salt

1. Spray grid well with nonstick cooking spray. Preheat grill to medium-high heat.

2. Combine chili powder and garlic powder in small bowl; mix well. Coat pork with spice mixture.

3. Grill pork 30 minutes, turning occasionally, until internal temperature reaches 155°F when tested with meat thermometer in thickest part of tenderloin. Cover with foil and let rest 10 minutes before slicing.

4. To make apple salsa, combine apples, chilies, lemon juice, cilantro, garlic, oregano and salt in medium bowl; mix well.

5. Slice pork across grain; serve with salsa.

Makes 4 servings

Nutrients per Serving:

Total Fat	5 g	Sodium	678 mg
Calories	201	Cholesterol	81 mg

Pork Chops in Creamy Garlic Sauce

1 **cup fat-free reduced-sodium chicken broth**

¼ **cup garlic cloves, peeled and crushed (about 12 to 15)**

½ **teaspoon olive oil**

4 **boneless pork loin chops, each about ¼ inch thick**

1 **tablespoon minced fresh parsley**

½ **teaspoon tarragon**

¼ **teaspoon salt**

¼ **teaspoon pepper**

1 **tablespoon all-purpose flour**

2 **tablespoons water**

1 **tablespoon dry sherry**

2 **cups cooked white rice**

1. Place chicken broth and garlic in small saucepan. Bring to a boil over high heat. Cover; reduce heat to low. Simmer 25 to 30 minutes or until garlic mashes easily with fork. Set aside to cool. Purée until smooth in blender or food processor.

2. Heat olive oil in large nonstick skillet over medium-high heat. Add pork; cook 1 to 1½ minutes on each side or until browned. Pour garlic purée into skillet. Sprinkle with parsley, tarragon, salt and pepper. Bring to a boil; cover. Reduce heat to low; simmer 10 to 15 minutes or until pork is juicy and barely pink in center. Remove pork from skillet; keep warm.

3. Combine flour and water in small cup. Slowly pour flour mixture into skillet; bring to a boil. Cook and stir until mixture thickens. Stir in sherry. Serve sauce over pork and rice. Garnish as desired.

Makes 4 servings

Nutrients per Serving:

Total Fat	9 g	Sodium	260 mg
Calories	188	Cholesterol	40 mg

Ham Rolls with Fresh Asparagus

1   **pound trimmed fresh asparagus spears
    or frozen asparagus spears, thawed
    and drained**
8   **slices (1 ounce each) ALPINE LACE®
    Boneless Cooked Ham**
½   **cup thin strips red bell pepper**
2   **cups (8 ounces) shredded ALPINE
    LACE® Reduced Sodium Muenster
    Cheese, divided**
1½ **cups 2% low fat milk**
2   **tablespoons all-purpose flour**
2   **teaspoons snipped fresh dill *or***
    ½ teaspoon dill weed
¼   **teaspoon white pepper
    Paprika**

1. Preheat the oven to 375°F. Spray an 8-inch square baking dish with nonstick cooking spray.

2. To assemble the ham rolls: In a large saucepan, bring 1 inch of water to a boil. Add the asparagus and steam just until crisp-tender; drain well. Lay out the slices of ham. Place 1 or 2 asparagus spears and a few strips of bell pepper in the center of each and sprinkle with 1 tablespoon of the cheese, reserving 1½ cups of cheese. Roll up and place, seam side down, in the dish.

3. To make the Havarti-dill sauce: In a medium-size saucepan, combine the milk, flour, dill and white pepper. Stir over medium-high heat until mixture boils. Reduce the heat and stir until thickened. Stir in the reserved 1½ cups cheese until melted. Pour over the ham rolls and sprinkle with the paprika.

4. Cover with foil and bake for 15 minutes. Remove the foil and bake 15 minutes more or until the sauce is bubbly. Turn the oven to broil and broil 4 inches from the heat for 3 minutes or just until golden brown. Serve hot.   *Makes 8 servings*

Nutrients per Serving:

Total Fat	10 g	Cholesterol	41 mg
Calories	167		

Grilled Swordfish Polynesian

1 tablespoon lime juice
2 cloves garlic, minced
4 swordfish steaks (5 ounces each)
½ teaspoon chili powder *or* black pepper
Pineapple Salsa (recipe follows)

Combine lime juice and garlic on plate. Dip swordfish
in juice; sprinkle with chili powder. Spray cold grid
with nonstick cooking spray. Adjust grid 4 to 6 inches
above heat. Preheat grill to medium-high heat. Grill
fish, covered, 3 minutes. Turn over; grill 1 to 2 minutes
more or until just opaque in center and still very
moist. Top each serving with about 3 tablespoons
Pineapple Salsa. *Makes 4 servings*

Pineapple Salsa

½ cup finely chopped fresh pineapple
¼ cup finely chopped red bell pepper
1 green onion, thinly sliced
2 tablespoons lime juice
½ jalapeño pepper, seeded, minced
1 tablespoon chopped fresh cilantro *or*
 fresh basil

Combine all ingredients in small nonmetallic bowl.
Serve at room temperature. *Makes 4 servings*

Nutrients per Serving:			
Total Fat	6 g	Sodium	183 mg
Calories	194	Cholesterol	56 mg

Salmon with Dill-Mustard Sauce

2 tablespoons fresh lemon juice
2 tablespoons fresh lime juice
4 salmon fillets (8 ounces each)
¼ cup fat free mayonnaise
1 tablespoon Dijon mustard
1 tablespoon chopped fresh dill

1. Combine lemon juice and lime juice in glass baking dish. Rinse salmon; pat dry. Place salmon in juices; marinate 10 minutes, turning once.

2. Combine mayonnaise, mustard and dill in small bowl.

3. Preheat broiler. Spray rack of broiler pan with nonstick cooking spray. Remove salmon from juices; discard juices. Pat dry. Place salmon on rack. Broil, 4 inches from heat, 3 to 4 minutes on each side or until salmon flakes in center. Serve salmon with sauce. Garnish with fresh dill, if desired.

Makes 4 servings

Nutrients per Serving:

Total Fat	4 g	Sodium	253 mg
Calories	146	Cholesterol	59 mg

Sole Florentine

1¼ pounds washed fresh spinach or
    2 packages (10 ounces each) frozen
    spinach, thawed
¼ teaspoon salt or to taste
¼ teaspoon white pepper or to taste
½ cup dry white wine or low sodium
    chicken broth
1½ pounds boneless sole fillets (about 6)
6 ounces (1 carton) ALPINE LACE® Fat
    Free Cream Cheese with Garlic &
    Herbs
½ cup fat free sour cream
3 tablespoons unsalted butter substitute
¼ cup (1 ounce) shredded ALPINE LACE®
    Fat Free Pasteurized Process Skim
    Milk Cheese Product—For Parmesan
    Lovers
    Paprika

1. Preheat the oven to 350°F. Spray an 8-inch square baking dish with nonstick cooking spray.

2. In a large saucepan, bring 1 inch of water to a boil. Add the spinach and steam just until wilted; drain well. Line the bottom of the baking dish with the cooked spinach, then sprinkle with the salt and pepper.

3. In a large nonstick skillet, bring the wine to a simmer over medium-high heat. Slide in the sole fillets, cover and poach for 4 minutes or until opaque and springy to the touch. Using a slotted spatula, carefully remove the fillets and arrange on top of the spinach.

4. In a small bowl, blend the cream cheese with the sour cream, then spread on top of the fillets.

5. Dot with the butter and sprinkle with the Parmesan and paprika. Bake, uncovered, for 20 minutes or until the cheese mixture is bubbly. Serve immediately.

Makes 6 servings

Nutrients per Serving:			
Total Fat	9 g	Cholesterol	8 mg
Calories	232		

Snapper Veracruz

Nonstick cooking spray
1 teaspoon olive oil
¼ large onion, thinly sliced
⅓ cup low sodium fish or vegetable broth, defatted and divided
2 cloves garlic, minced
1 cup GUILTLESS GOURMET® Salsa (mild, medium or hot)
20 ounces fresh red snapper, tilapia, sea bass or halibut fillets

Preheat oven to 400°F. Coat baking dish with cooking spray. (Dish needs to be large enough for fish to fit snugly together.) Heat oil in large nonstick skillet over medium heat until hot. Add onion; cook and stir until onion is translucent. Stir in 3 tablespoons broth. Add garlic; cook and stir 1 minute more. Stir in remaining broth and salsa. Bring mixture to a boil. Reduce heat to low; simmer about 2 minutes or until heated through.

Wash fish thoroughly; pat dry with paper towels. Place in prepared baking dish, overlapping thin edges to obtain an overall equal thickness. Pour and spread salsa mixture over fish.

Bake 15 minutes or until fish turns opaque and flakes easily when tested with fork. Serve hot.

Makes 4 servings

Nutrients per Serving:

Total Fat	3 g	Sodium	353 mg
Calories	184	Cholesterol	52 mg

Southern Breaded Catfish

⅓ cup pecan halves
¼ cup cornmeal
2 tablespoons all-purpose flour
1 teaspoon paprika
¼ teaspoon ground red pepper
2 egg whites
4 catfish fillets (about 1 pound)
4 cups cooked rice

1. Place pecans in food processor or blender; process until finely chopped. Combine pecans, cornmeal, flour, paprika and ground red pepper in shallow bowl.

2. Beat egg whites in small bowl with wire whisk until foamy. Dip catfish fillets in pecan mixture, then in egg whites, then again in pecan mixture. Place fillets on plate; cover and refrigerate at least 15 minutes.

3. Spray large nonstick skillet with nonstick cooking spray; heat over medium-high heat. Place catfish fillets in single layer in skillet.

4. Cook fillets 2 minutes per side or until golden brown. Serve over rice.   *Makes 4 servings*

Nutrients per Serving:

Total Fat	8 g	Sodium	76 mg
Calories	297	Cholesterol	65 mg

Mustard-Grilled Red Snapper

½ cup Dijon mustard
1 tablespoon red wine vinegar
1 teaspoon ground red pepper
4 red snapper fillets (about 1½ pounds)

1. Spray cold grid or broiling rack with nonstick cooking spray. Prepare grill or preheat broiler.

2. Combine mustard, vinegar and ground red pepper in small bowl; mix well. Coat fish fillets thoroughly with mustard mixture.

3. Grill fish over medium-high heat or broil about 4 minutes per side or until fish flakes easily when tested with fork. Serve immediately.   *Makes 4 servings*

Nutrients per Serving (1 fillet of sole):

Total Fat	4 g	Sodium	477 mg
Calories	200	Cholesterol	62 mg

Herbed Scallops and Shrimp

¼ cup chopped fresh parsley
¼ cup lime juice
2 tablespoons chopped fresh mint
2 tablespoons chopped fresh rosemary
1 tablespoon honey
1 tablespoon olive oil
2 cloves garlic, minced
¼ teaspoon ground black pepper
½ pound raw jumbo shrimp, peeled and
    deveined
½ pound bay or halved sea scallops

1. Preheat broiler. Combine parsley, lime juice, mint, rosemary, honey, oil, garlic and black pepper in medium bowl; blend well. Add shrimp and scallops. Cover; refrigerate 1 hour.

2. Arrange shrimp and scallops on skewers. Place on broiler pan. Brush with marinade. Broil 5 to 6 minutes or until shrimp are opaque and scallops are lightly browned. Serve immediately.   *Makes 4 servings*

Nutrients per Serving:

Total Fat	5 g	Sodium	223 mg
Calories	152	Cholesterol	111 mg

Butterflied Shrimp Parmesan

1½ pounds large shrimp
1 cup (4 ounces) shredded ALPINE
  LACE® Fat Free Pasteurized Process
  Skim Milk Cheese Product—For
  Parmesan Lovers
¼ cup Italian seasoned dry bread crumbs
2 tablespoons unsalted butter substitute
¾ cup chopped red bell pepper
½ cup thinly sliced green onions
1 tablespoon minced garlic
⅛ teaspoon crushed red pepper flakes
  or to taste
⅓ cup minced fresh parsley
6 tablespoons 2% low fat milk

1. Peel the shrimp, leaving the tails on. Then butterfly each shrimp by cutting it along the outer curved edge almost all the way through. Open the shrimp up like a book and remove the dark vein. In a small bowl, toss the cheese with the bread crumbs and set aside.

2. In a large nonstick skillet, melt the butter over medium-high heat. Add the bell pepper, green onions, garlic and red pepper flakes and cook for 5 minutes or until soft. Add the shrimp and sauté for 5 minutes or just until the shrimp turn pink and opaque. Stir in the parsley.

3. In a small saucepan, bring the milk just to a boil, then stir into the shrimp mixture. Stir in the cheese mixture and cook until the cheese is melted. Serve immediately.   *Makes 4 servings*

Nutrients per Serving:			
Total Fat	9 g	Sodium	281 mg
Calories	312		

Maryland Crab Cakes

1¼ pounds lump crab meat, picked over
    and flaked
¾ cup plain dry bread crumbs, divided
1 cup (4 ounces) shredded ALPINE
    LACE® Reduced Fat Swiss Cheese
¼ cup plain low fat yogurt
⅓ cup finely chopped green onions
¼ cup minced fresh parsley
2 tablespoons fresh lemon juice
1 teaspoon minced garlic
½ teaspoon hot red pepper sauce
¼ cup egg substitute *or* 1 large egg,
    beaten
   Butter-flavor nonstick cooking spray
2 large lemons, thinly sliced

1. In a large bowl, lightly toss the crab with ¼ cup of
the bread crumbs, the cheese, yogurt, green onions,
parsley, lemon juice, garlic and hot pepper sauce.
Gently stir in the egg substitute (or the whole egg).

2. Form the mixture into twelve 3-inch patties, using
about ⅓ cup of crab mixture for each. Spray both sides
of the patties with the cooking spray.

3. On wax paper, spread out the remaining ½ cup of
bread crumbs. Coat each patty with the crumbs,
pressing lightly, then refrigerate for 1 hour.

4. Preheat the oven to 400°F. Spray a baking sheet with the cooking spray. Place the crab cakes on the baking sheet and bake for 20 minutes or until golden brown and crispy, turning once halfway through. Serve immediately with the lemon slices.

Makes 6 servings (2 crab cakes each)

Nutrients per Serving:

Total Fat	6 g	Sodium	54 mg
Calories	215		

The publishers would like to thank the companies and organizations listed below for the use of their recipes in this publication.

Alpine Lace Brands, Inc.
Best Foods, a Division of CPC International Inc.
Birds Eye
Bob Evans Farms®
California Beef Council
Chef Paul Prudhomme's® Magic Seasoning Blends®
Dean Foods Vegetable Company
Delmarva Poultry Industry, Inc.
Del Monte Corporation
Dole Food Company, Inc.
Filippo Berio Olive Oil
Florida Department of Agriculture and Consumer Services, Bureau of Seafood and Aquaculture
Guiltless Gourmet, Incorporated
Heinz U.S.A.

Hormel Foods Corporation
The HVR Company
Kellogg Company
Kikkoman International Inc.
Kraft Foods, Inc.
Lawry's® Foods, Inc.
McIlhenny Company
Nabisco, Inc.
National Foods, Inc.
National Honey Board
National Pork Producers Council
Nestlé Food Company
Norseland, Inc.
Perdue Farms Incorporated
The Procter & Gamble Company
Reckett & Colman Inc.
Sargento® Foods Inc.
StarKist® Seafood Company
USA Rice Council
Wisconsin Milk Marketing Board

VOLUME MEASUREMENTS (dry)

⅛ teaspoon = 0.5 mL
¼ teaspoon = 1 mL
½ teaspoon = 2 mL
¾ teaspoon = 4 mL
1 teaspoon = 5 mL
1 tablespoon = 15 mL
2 tablespoons = 30 mL
¼ cup = 60 mL
⅓ cup = 75 mL
½ cup = 125 mL
⅔ cup = 150 mL
¾ cup = 175 mL
1 cup = 250 mL
2 cups = 1 pint = 500 mL
3 cups = 750 mL
4 cups = 1 quart = 1 L

VOLUME MEASUREMENTS (fluid)

1 fluid ounce (2 tablespoons) = 30 mL
4 fluid ounces (½ cup) = 125 mL
8 fluid ounces (1 cup) = 250 mL
12 fluid ounces (1½ cups) = 375 mL
16 fluid ounces (2 cups) = 500 mL

WEIGHTS (mass)

½ ounce = 15 g
1 ounce = 30 g
3 ounces = 90 g
4 ounces = 120 g
8 ounces = 225 g
10 ounces = 285 g
12 ounces = 360 g
16 ounces = 1 pound = 450 g

DIMENSIONS

1/16 inch = 2 mm
⅛ inch = 3 mm
¼ inch = 6 mm
½ inch = 1.5 cm
¾ inch = 2 cm
1 inch = 2.5 cm

OVEN TEMPERATURES

250°F = 120°C
275°F = 140°C
300°F = 150°C
325°F = 160°C
350°F = 180°C
375°F = 190°C
400°F = 200°C
425°F = 220°C
450°F = 230°C

BAKING PAN SIZES

Utensil	Size in Inches/ Quarts	Metric Volume	Size in Centimeters
Baking or Cake Pan (square or rectangular)	8×8×2	2 L	20×20×5
	9×9×2	2.5 L	23×23×5
	12×8×2	3 L	30×20×5
	13×9×2	3.5 L	33×23×5
Loaf Pan	8×4×3	1.5 L	20×10×7
	9×5×3	2 L	23×13×7
Round Layer Cake Pan	8×1½	1.2 L	20×4
	9×1½	1.5 L	23×4
Pie Plate	8×1¼	750 mL	20×3
	9×1¼	1 L	23×3
Baking Dish or Casserole	1 quart	1 L	—
	1½ quart	1.5 L	—
	2 quart	2 L	—